Advanced General Studies
for OCR – student book

Heinemann Educational Publishers
Halley Court, Jordan Hill, Oxford, OX2 8EJ
Part of Harcourt Education

Heinemann is the registered trademark of
Harcourt Education Limited

Text © Trevor Green, John Hancock and Pat Turton, 2001
First published in 2001

05 04
10 9 8 7 6 5 4 3

British Library Cataloguing in Publication Data
A catalogue record for this book is available from the British Library

ISBN 0 435 79522 8

Typeset by Techset
Picture research by Virginia Stroud Lewis
Printed and bound in Great Britain by The Bath Press Ltd, Bath

Acknowledgements
The publishers would like to thank the following for permission to reproduce copyright
material: David Austin, p. 161; *The Big Issue* and Nicole Hanke, p. 92; *The Carmarthen Journal*,
p. 72; *The Daily Mail*, pp. 98 and 161; *The Guardian*, pp. 73, 75, 78, 79, 81, 83, 85, 88, 89, 91, 92, 93,
94, 95, 96, 100, 101, 104, 162, 163, 164, 167, 168, 169, 174, 175, 176, 177 and 178; Headline, p. 189;
The Independent/ Syndication, pp. 26, 31, 149–50, 157, 161 and 178; Andrzej Krauze, p. 159;
Mirror Syndication International, p. 84; News International Limited, pp. 25 and 180, © Times
Newspapers Limited (2000 and 1998); News International Limited, pp. 26, 161 and 166,
© News International Limited (2000); Chris Riddell, pp. 99, 101 and 103; *The South Wales
Guardian*, p. 79; *The Times Educational Supplement*, p. 58, © Times Supplements Limited.

The publishers would like to thank the following for permission to use photographs: AKG,
pp. 141, 142, 148, 153, 154; Elizabeth Allen, pp. 84; Martin Argles and *The Guardian*, p. 168;
Corbis pp. 10, 13, 19, 114, 140, 143, 145, 149, 153, 155, 156, 185; Environmental Images, p. 179;
ISDN Steve George: *The Sutton Coldfield Observer*, p. 181; Roy Kilcullen, *The Bournemouth
News*, p. 181; The National Portrait Gallery, London and DACS, London, 2001, p. 156;
Popperfoto, pp. 25, 171, 175, 186; Popperfoto/Environmental Images, p. 179; The Press
Association, p. 164; Rex/Andrew Testa, p. 163; Philip Wolmuth, p. 171.

Cover photograph by Corbis

Tel: 01865 888058 www.heinemann.co.uk

Contents

Unit 2964: The social domain 1

A2 units

Unit 2965 (A): The scientific domain

Unit 2965 (B): The cultural domain

Unit 2966: The social domain 2 ✓

Unit 2967: The social domain 2: Coursework

Unit 2968: Culture, science and society: Making connections

Appendices

Introduction

Why General Studies?

A course in General Studies offers the opportunity to develop and assess knowledge, understanding and a wide range of important and relevant skills. It is the study of the world in which you live. General Studies crosses the boundaries between subjects and challenges you to make links and appreciate overlaps. When studied in a robust manner, General Studies forces you to make decisions, formulate opinions and communicate fluently.

Skills for life and for life-long learning

Following a General Studies course gives you the opportunity to develop important skills that can be transferred into other areas of study, the world of work and the rest of your life.

In General Studies you develop the skills for:

- research
- communication
- application of number
- thinking and analysis
- problem solving
- working with others
- information technology.

Thinking and analytical skills

These skills help in problem solving and in making sense of, and learning from, experience. For example, you will be required to think about what you believe. Is this belief the same as knowledge? You will be asked to analyse situations to decide the truth behind an argument and to distinguish between belief, truth and knowledge. Can you recognize a false argument? How do you support your opinion in order to strengthen your case?

Exercises and examples of these skills are provided throughout this book.

Key Skills

General Studies can also create opportunities to prepare for the Key Skills tests and to generate portfolio evidence for the Key Skills qualification. This can be an important consideration for students following a narrow range of A level subjects when evidence generation can prove difficult. Key Skills focus on your ability to collect, process and present information.

UCAS and employers

Many students find the UCAS points gained from a General Studies grade help to secure a place in Higher Education. Increasingly, universities and colleges are including General Studies in the offers they make to applicants. For those of you entering directly into the world of work you will have developed skills that are in demand by employers.

... and finally

Studying General Studies puts you in touch with the world in which you live. It will give you an insight into:

- spiritual, moral, ethical, social and cultural debates
- environmental and health problems
- scientific and mathematical problems.

It offers a European dimension, which is so vital for the future. Issues that are raised by the course are those about which all of us should have awareness and opinions based on sound judgement, if we are to play a part in our democratic society.

How to use this book

This book has been written specifically to support the OCR General Studies specification 3831 (AS) and 7831 (A2), but it will provide content for any Advanced level General Studies course as the subject criteria for all specifications has a core of content as defined by the Qualifications and Curriculum Authority (QCA).

Syllabus coverage

This book has been structured in three subject domains:

- the **cultural domain**: culture, morality, arts and humanities
- the **scientific domain**: science, mathematics and technology
- the **social domain**: society, politics and the economy.

Each domain is covered in a separate section. All the AS requirements are dealt with in the first half of the book and A2 in the second. Finding your way around the topics is, therefore, straightforward.

Each of the three domain areas are sub-divided into sections that deal with the six topics outlined in the OCR specification – three for AS and a further three for A2. Each of these sections begins with an introduction to the topic, and the important points identified within the topic are then covered in one-, two- or three-page sub-sections.

Content

The content outlined in this book is by no means exhaustive. The nature of General Studies makes it impossible to produce a book that provides comprehensive coverage of all the possibilities. However, the book does look at a wide range of contemporary issues and provides more than a basic core. In addition, you will need to look for yourself at the issues raised in order to be fully prepared for the examination. This book provides the basics needed and acts as a springboard for research and investigation. In order to help you to do this, each topic is structured as follows.

1 Introduction

This contains:

- **Definitions** – This list of key words and definitions has been included to aid understanding and establish a focus.
- **Getting started** – These will give you food for thought: a range of issues raised by the topic, presented as a series of statements or questions. They are intended to get you thinking and provide topics for debate.
- **Outline** – This section gives an outline of the content, knowledge and concepts that are part of the topic on the OCR specification.

2 Content detail

Each important point identified in the OCR specification is then considered in terms of knowledge content: the content that underpins understanding. The content may be technical information, expert opinion, empirical knowledge or research findings. It provides a basic insight into each point in the specification.

Within the content pages you will also find:

- **Key Skills** – AS sections provide an opportunity for both the development of a specific Key Skill and an example of evidence that could be produced using an activity that covers the content and develops the skill.
- **Thinking and analytical skills** – Each section will cover the skill that is possible for you to practise and develop.

3 Examination preparation

At the end of each content unit you will find suggestions for further study and examples of examination questions for you to consider.

4 Coursework

General Studies AS and Advanced level specifications offer coursework options. Through coursework it is possible to cover all of the Key Skills and to generate portfolio evidence. Two coursework sections are included to help you structure coursework tasks and a checklist is provided so that you can monitor your collection of evidence.

5 Synoptic unit

All A level courses involve synoptic assessment. In the OCR specification this is the final unit of the course.

In the synoptic unit you need to make links between the three domains: science, culture and society. The links are in terms of the knowledge content of the domains and also in your understanding of the nature of knowledge itself. Three case studies have been included to help you with this. These case studies explore ways in which you can develop your synoptic view.

Not just knowledge!

General Studies is about 'joined-up thinking' and the more successful you are at this, the better your final grade is likely to be. Questions you are challenged with in an examination paper will require you to show that you can do more than just reproduce acquired knowledge. You will be required to develop Thinking and Analytical Skills.

So, what are they and how do you develop them?

Thinking and Analytical Skills 1–2

- Think critically, logically and constructively about significant problems.
- Evaluate information against available observations and data.

Take any topic from the scientific domain – for example, the area dealing with moral responsibility – and you will readily see that technical knowledge will not be enough to tackle an examination question. Simply considering, for example, how nuclear power is generated and how the process differs from that of generating power from fossil fuels will not be enough. You will need to consider all the implications and issues that are linked with providing power. You will be required to weigh up advantages, disadvantages, offer logical arguments and evaluation.

Thinking and Analytical Skills 3–5

- Solve problems which may be both qualitative and quantitative.
- Make predictions and propose hypotheses.
- Present reasoned explanations for phenomena, patterns and relationships.

Should you decide to undertake the coursework option, these three skills will be vital. The majority of coursework tasks will pose a problem for you to attempt. You may need to decide on an effective way forward (qualitative) and produce evidence in justification (quantitative). Presenting reasoned arguments requires you to go beyond the obvious.

Thinking and Analytical Skills 6–8

- Interpret and evaluate opinions.
- Distinguish between knowledge and belief.
- Recognize common fallacies.

Have a brief look at page 11 in order to prepare yourself for the intellectual activity required by these three skills.

Thinking and Analytical Skill 9

- Use deductive and inductive arguments.

Consider these:

1 Education should prepare young people for life. Do you agree? How successful has your school or college been in preparing you for the next stage?
   (This question requires you to use deductive arguments: from the general to the particular.)
2 Outline the problems that have affected the nuclear reprocessing plant at Sellafield in recent years. How typical are they of the problems that affect the nuclear power industry? Are there implications here that need addressing globally? Is there an inevitability that these problems will arise again?
   (This question requires you to use inductive arguments: from the particular to the general.)

1 Beliefs, values and moral reasoning

Definitions

Belief	Persuasion of the truth. Faith or conviction.
Conscience	Moral sense. 'Stern daughter of the voice of God.' The 'still small voice' that guides.
Ethics	A set of principles, ideals or standards by which one lives.
Faith	That which is believed. A system of religious belief or the religion one considers true.
Indoctrination	To convince. To make someone believe something.
Instinct	Intuition. The natural impulse by which a person is guided, apparently independently of reason or experience.
Knowledge	Assured belief. That which is known.
Morality	That which makes an action right or wrong.
Reason	Justification of a belief. To think out. To set forth logically.
Revelation	An enlightening experience.
Tolerance	The ability to endure or put up with something. A willingness to allow.

Getting started

1 'Live and let live.' Is this an ideal?
2 'Give me a child until he is seven and I'll show you the man' (Jesuit saying). Are the first seven years as formative as this suggests?
3 'We are slaves to our upbringing.' Is this the case?
4 The Ten Commandments sum up Christian morals, and it is never acceptable to break any of them.
5 Natural justice usually prevails!
6 It's every man for himself when the chips are down.
7 We are all motivated by self-interest.
8 Does travel broaden the mind?
9 'You never really understand a man until you consider things from his point of view – until you climb into his skin and walk around in it' (Atticus Finch in *To Kill a Mockingbird* by Harper Lee).
10 Is it true that we are judged by the company we keep?
11 Each of us is the sum total of our experiences. Is this a fair comment?
12 I don't believe in God: there is no evidence that he exists.
13 It's not a crime if you don't get caught.
14 'Honour thy father and thy mother.' Is this always possible?
15 Do most religions indoctrinate?

Outline

This topic requires you to make informed judgements in a number of areas.

You will need to understand and give examples of the difference between knowledge, belief and unbelief. This unit requires a personal interpretation of these concepts rather than one linked to religious faith.

Instruction, indoctrination, personal experience, reason, faith and revelation play a part in determining how we act at certain times in our lives. Some of these are more influential than others. You will need to consider which of them play a significant role in shaping your behaviour, that of society, the behaviour of people in other countries, and public morality.

There are a number of formative influences in our lives. You will need to explore these influences and evaluate how and when each is reflected in your personality, judgement, morality and behaviour, and in that of others. A consideration of the importance of conscience, (indeed whether everyone has one) is also required in this unit, along with a consideration of how prepared individuals are to tolerate the beliefs and actions of others.

Knowledge, belief and unbelief

Rodin's The Thinker

What does it mean when we say we 'know' something? How accurately do you use the word?

Consider these five sentences:

- I know that John Lennon is the greatest songwriter in the twentieth century.
- I know that dogs have four legs.
- I know that Arsenal will win their next home game.
- I know my way to college.
- I know that there is no God.

In each of these sentences 'know' means something different. Which of the assertions are based on fact, which on opinion or impression and which on belief?

There are many theories about the nature of knowledge and how it differs from belief and unbelief. What follows is a brief summary of some of these theories. Read the quotations carefully then go back to the sentences above and decide if the 'knowledge' in them can be ascribed in part, or wholly, to any of these theories.

> Knowledge is recollecting what is in your head. I believe that the visible world of the sense gives rise to opinion and that the intelligible world, one beyond the sense, is the world of true knowledge.
>
> Plato (427–348 BC)

> Knowledge is perception. The natural world is the real world. I believe that perception and sense-experience are the foundations of scientific knowledge, that knowledge is in matter.
>
> Aristotle (384–322 BC)

I believe that knowledge comes through experience. There are three kinds of knowledge:
- intuitive knowledge – knowledge that comes through knowledge of self
- demonstrative knowledge – rather like mathematical proof
- sensitive knowledge – an informed guess.

Locke (1632–1704)

I am concerned, as a religious man, that the philosophies that only accept knowledge as that which can be perceived through the sense are encouraging atheism. I believe that mind is more important than matter.

Bishop Berkeley (1685–1753)

Consider the following:

There was a young man, who said, God,
I find it exceedingly odd,
That this tree that I see
Should continue to be
When there's no one about in the Quad.

Reply
Dear Sir: your astonishment's odd.
I am always about in the Quad;
And that's why the tree
Will continue to be
Since observed by
Yours faithfully,
God!

TASKS

1 a Write five sentences that begin 'I know', but which use different interpretations of knowing. Now analyse your own assertions in terms of knowledge, opinion and belief. Have you used 'know' in different ways?

b Compare your list with that of another student. Do you agree about what you can know and what you cannot know? If you find it difficult don't worry! You are in very good company.

2 Where does belief (or unbelief) come from? Can you differentiate between knowledge and belief?

3 a Write down five statements that you know to be true, for example, rain is wet.

b Write down five statements that you believe to be true, for example, God loves me.

c Write down five opinions that you hold, for example, London is an unattractive city.

4 Where does your knowledge come from? How did you gain your beliefs? How have you formed your opinions?
(If you can write the answers to these questions in a well-constructed paragraph you have arrived at your own philosophy or understanding of the nature of knowledge and how it is distinct from belief.)

5 Consider the arguments both for and against a belief in the existence of a Supreme Being.

The roles of instinct, indoctrination, personal experience, reason, faith and revelation

This section contains a lot of questions and does not offer many answers. It will be up to you to consider the concepts and formulate your own answers and judgements. You will find that much of what is here is linked with concepts in other parts of this AS unit on culture.

Instinct

How would you define 'instinct'? Some people would argue that instinct is the same as conscience. Do we instinctively know what is right or wrong because our conscience tells us, or because we have been told by others or have been given a moral code? Is instinct a behaviour that is automatic – like getting food, escaping from enemies, reproducing, protecting the young, surviving at all cost, winning? Is it possible to train someone to act in a way that is not instinctive? Are there occasions when our instincts are replaced by something more powerful?

Indoctrination

Indoctrination is when we are made to believe something or are convinced of something by others.

Make a list of all the individuals or organizations that are likely to indoctrinate other human beings. Consider occasions when indoctrination could be acceptable and occasions when it is not. Does the word have sinister connotations?

Personal experience

Values and beliefs are tested by personal experience. Interaction with family, friends, local people, teachers and employers as well as the information and experiences provided by the media are all influential on what we believe and how we act. The following sayings reinforce this point of view:

> 'Once bitten: twice shy.'
> 'The burnt child fears the flame.'
> 'We are the sum total of all our experiences.'
> 'You live and learn.'
> 'You learn by your mistakes.'
> 'Some people never learn!'

Reason and faith

Faith is believing that something is true when we cannot be absolutely certain that it is true. Perhaps that is why religions are often referred to as 'faiths'. All religions contain a measure of faith, since religious faith isn't something that can readily be proved in the way that a scientific experiment can prove something. However, we can give reasons to back up our faith. Take a simple example:

You buy a pair of walking boots and go out onto the wet moorlands. You probably have faith in the boots' ability to keep your feet dry. You can back up this faith with reasons.

1. They were expensive.
2. You have bought this make before and they didn't leak.
3. A friend recommended them.
4. They are particularly strong, well-fitting boots.
5. The Ramblers' Association endorses them.

Faith and reason go hand in hand, in everyday life and in terms of religious faith. What have you got faith in? Do you have faith that a friend won't let you down? What reasons can you give? Similarly, do you have faith in your doctor, your teacher and your God? How often do you perform an 'act of faith' in your everyday life?

Revelation

Revelation is the act or experience of revealing an enlightening experience through divine or supernatural communication. Revelation is often associated with a special experience, particularly when considering religious or spiritual revelation. Sometimes revelation appears to be the opposite of reason as an individual takes on beliefs that are difficult to support or substantiate.

Many religions record events of revelation that are of the utmost significance to the followers of that religion. But as the above suggests, revelation can be a very personal experience. It can be an experience that cuts across all religions, and both religious and non-religious people claim to have had 'religious' experiences.

> 'I am not an educated man – not a lama or scholar who can speak of matters of theology. But I feel that there is room on earth for many faiths, as for many races and nations. It is with God Himself as it is with a great mountain. The important thing is to come to Him not with fear, but with love.'
>
> From *Man of Everest – The Autobiography of Tensing*, Janus, Ramsey, Ullman

'It is with God Himself as it is with a great mountain. The important thing is to come to Him not with fear, but with love.'

TASKS

1 Consider the following:
- The soldier who stands his ground when all his instincts tell him to run.
- The mother who gives the remaining food to her child while she starves.
- The honest man who steals bread to feed his family.
- The martyr who is prepared to die for what he or she believes.

In what ways is 'instinct' at work here? Can instinct be limited or modified by indoctrination or personal experience?

2 Experiences are formative. This means they can have a significant effect on future behaviour and attitudes.
a Describe an occasion when an event or experience has caused you to act differently the second time around.
b It is said that few learn from their experiences. What is the evidence for this?

c Consider five pieces of evidence that suggest that personal (or collective) experience is always formative. Why is the behaviour or thinking of some human beings not modified by their experience?

3 How many spiritual revelations can you list from your own religion (if you have one) or any of the other major religions?

4 If religion is simply a question of feeling, belief and emotional experience what intellectual issues does this raise? Is it possible to have religion without feeling or emotion or revelation?

In preparing your answer distinguish between knowledge and belief. Consider the assumptions you make and the ways you evaluate opinions.

Formative influences

Where do your beliefs, values and moral code come from? As soon as you were born, a number of influences began to mould your personality. Sociologists believe that the major part of human behaviour is learned. This isn't consistent with the views of some philosophers and psychologists, who believe that much of our reasoning is instinctive or intuitive (see pages 12 and 140–4). However, most sociologists would argue that the influences with which you come into contact will have an effect on the way you arrive at your own set of values.

Think about yourself:

1   from birth to five years of age
2   between the ages of six and eleven
3   between the ages of eleven and sixteen
4   currently
5   at the next stage of your life.

For each of steps 1–5 think about the most important influences in your life. Put your thoughts into a ranking order and decide which is the most significant influence.

Were you able to predict the likely influences in the next stage of your life?

What follows is a brief summary of all the accepted formative influences on human beings.

The influence of family

Most people would say that this is where fundamental values and moral codes are formed. Children identify with their parents and copy them. The theory is that most children want to please their parents and so they behave in a way that meets with approval. Consider your own situation. What values or morals have you taken from your family and why these ones? At what age did other influences begin to take over?

The influence of friends

We all like to belong, and acceptance by our peer group is very important. This may mean accepting the values and moral codes of the group in order to be accepted. None of us likes to be an outsider.

The influence of school or college

Parent: What did you learn in school today?
Child: Oh nothing much!

Do you recognize this conversation? It is said that there are two curricula, the National Curriculum and the hidden curriculum. In what ways is each of these an influence?

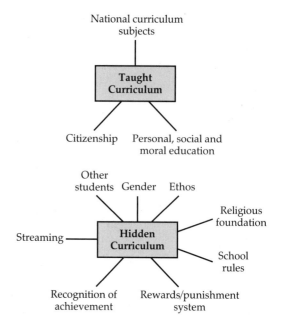

Figure 1   *The two curricula*

Each of the spider's legs in Figure 1 shows a different influence. It shows the range of influences that can be at work in terms of your beliefs, values and moral reasoning.

The influence of the workplace

A workplace also has what is known as its ethos. This means it has its own character. Some workplaces and professions are considered to be institutionally racist, sexist, ageist or elitist. Experience in the workplace influences beliefs, values and moral reasoning. In some workplaces the drive for profit is placed ahead of working conditions. In others success is rewarded, individuals are recognized for the contributions they make and staff development has a high priority.

Think of examples from your own experience or knowledge. Share them with others in order to increase the set of examples you could use in an examination answer. How can the ethos of a workplace influence an individual's moral reasoning?

The influence of the neighbourhood

Neighbourhoods have an ethos, in the same way as schools and workplaces. This means that where you live can be instrumental in the development of your values and moral reasoning?

There are many types of neighbourhood and each will provide its own unique atmosphere and ethos. Consider the following types of neighbourhood – there are, of course, many others.

- Small rural hamlet
- Large rural village
- Private housing estate on the edge of a large city
- Council estate in an inner-city area
- Bed-sit land

Each may be significant in forming the values of the individuals living there. For example, in a small rural village there could be families who have lived there for generations. Newcomers to the hamlet might include the retired looking for a quieter life and a house with a garden. There could be an established small village school with a headteacher who has taught there for many years. The public house has its own teams for darts, skittles, crib and football. The village hall hosts the WI and the Art Club. Each morning the school bus takes local children to the secondary school some five miles away. The influence of this neighbourhood will be dramatically different from the changing population of acquaintances in the inner city.

However, there is a danger of stereotyping. People's reactions to their environment are unique. Some will find inspiration and freedom in the cosmopolitan life of the big city, whilst others feel loneliness. The influence of the neighbourhood on the individual links to the social domain is discussed on pages 161–72, particularly the sections dealing with the explanation and evaluation of human behaviour (pages 166–72).

Media, leisure and travel

Agents of the media offer us information and experiences throughout the day. These impinge upon our beliefs and values and can challenge our accepted position. Newspapers, television and radio keep us up to date with the news; they entertain and inform us and bring us expert and celebrity opinions. They provide a valuable source of ideas for us to think about and share with others. In the course of this exchange we shape our beliefs and values.

What do we learn from leisure? It is said that travel broadens the mind. Leisure and travel widen the range of experiences we have. They take us beyond our family, friends, school, workplace and neighbourhood. We meet a greater diversity of people in terms of class, culture and financial status. As we view the lives of others we are influenced in our beliefs and values. Empathy for the poor in a shanty town, revulsion at the drunken behaviour of holiday-makers, and wonder at a beautiful site – all help us to shape our beliefs and values.

TASKS

1 Make a list of the most important influences upon you to date. Compare your list with someone else's. Try to explain both the similarities and differences.

2 Are families or friends the most important influence on you at the present time? Discuss your thoughts with a group of friends. Are you beginning to reject some of the values from your parents and replacing them with others?

3 How did your study of history, literature, science and physical education influence your beliefs and values? How can the qualities that your school or college values, rewards or celebrates influence your set of values?

4 It has been suggested that the family is the most significant of all the formative influences in giving you a moral code, beliefs and values. Do you agree? What other influences are involved?

5 Use the topic for group discussion leading to group work. Form groups of four or five, with each member of the group taking one of the influences described in this section. They should research the influence thoroughly and present their findings. Each group member has to argue for his or her particular concept as being of *significant* influence. This may require some students to play 'Devil's Advocate', which is a useful skill to practice.

6 Find the meanings of the words 'contradiction' and 'fallacy'. Now, during a conversation, try to detect a contradiction and a fallacy in your colleague's comments.

Matters of conscience and public morality; the limits of tolerance

What, as an individual, are you not prepared to tolerate? What is society not prepared to tolerate? Consider Figure 2, which shows some of the limits to tolerance.

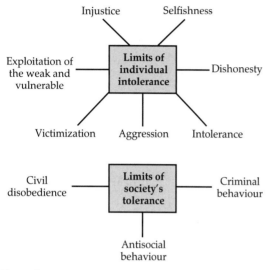

Figure 2 *Limits of tolerance*

Individuals' limits of tolerance vary. It's worth looking back over pages 9–15. These dealt with beliefs, values and moral reasoning. What an individual is prepared to tolerate will be linked to these concepts, and will be affected by the formative influences considered on pages 14 and 15.

Society punishes those who overstep the bounds of society's tolerance. Definitions of criminal behaviour are enshrined in law and punished by our justice system. They are beyond our stated limits of tolerance. Antisocial behaviour and civil disobedience are also covered by law. Those challenging these limits may be taking a criminal risk by protesting about the limit that has been set.

It is not easy to set legal limits to our tolerance. Some dishonest behaviour is a criminal offence but some is not. If you lie under oath you commit an offence, but if you lie about your whereabouts to a parent you have probably not committed a criminal offence. Find other examples like this.

Society is not unanimous in its view on certain tolerances. There are some issues on which individuals and those who guard public morality are divided. They include:

- the legalization of some drugs
- Clause 28 and the age of consent
- pressure groups and activities at the limit of the law
- sentencing and miscarriages of justice
- the private lives of public figures
- standards of behaviour of people in public office
- the application of public decency laws.

This list is not exhaustive and you could add others. Daily newspapers often have examples of this sort of tension, when individual conscience comes into conflict with the law of the land.

TASKS

Over the next week build a list of issues and conflicts concerning tolerance. Use both newspapers and news broadcasts. At the time of writing this question a list would have included:

- the use of cannabis in medicine
- euthanasia
- civil disobedience in relation to GM crops.

KEY SKILLS: *Communication*

1 Produce an information leaflet on any issue that brings individuals and their conscience into conflict with public morality. Include a justification of your position and use the leaflet to promote your views. You can include an element of intra-domain synopticity by linking your leaflet to the area of media and communication (pages 22–9). The words you choose – the way you use language to persuade – can influence, just as the language of the journalist is used to influence. (*Level 3*)

2 Organize a debate on the motion: 'It is always wrong to break the law'. You may speak for or against the motion. Be sure to make careful notes for your speech, which will be enhanced if you include at least one image. A report on this debate can form part of your Key Skills portfolio. (*Level 3*)

2 Aspects of culture

Definitions

Background   The kind of socialization you are exposed to in childhood.

Culture   A type of civilization. The ethos of a group. The character or disposition of a particular group.

Lifestyle   A way of life. A way of life that reflects an individual's standards or values.

Nationalism   The favouring of one's own nation to the extent of excluding the interests or needs of other nations or nationalities. Striving for domination by one's own nation.

Patriotism   A love of one's own country.

Social class   A group you are placed in by the society you live in. It is usually a hierarchical position that may be based on birth.

Sub-culture   A group within a particular culture. A group from a particular class whose behaviour is different in some distinct way.

Getting started

1 'We are slaves to our upbringing.'
2 'The moment we start to speak we betray our social class.'
3 Is there a difference in effect between nationalism and patriotism?
4 'Britain is an island and for that reason the British have an island mentality that verges on the xenophobic.'
5 How far have we got towards the goal of being a classless society?
6 'A multicultural society is a rich society.'
7 'When in Rome ...' Is this an acceptable maxim in a multicultural society?
8 What's the difference between multi-cultural and multi-ethnic?
9 Should we allow minority culture schools?
10 Why is it necessary to pass legislation to protect minority groups?
11 'Most wars are wars of religion.'
12 How sensible is it to preserve the Welsh language?
13 How important are 'old boys' networks' and the regimental tie today?
14 'All animals are equal but some are more equal than others' (Orwell).
15 'Give me a child until he is seven and I'll show you the man' (Jesuit saying).
16 How unacceptable is tokenism?

Outline

In this topic you need to show an understanding and knowledge of various cultures, what they have in common and what their distinctive characteristics are. You may be asked to comment on contemporary Western society, the way it is structured, its fundamental values, and its multicultural dimensions.

You will need to consider how cultures:
■ are determined
■ evolve
■ conflict
■ are sustained or survive
■ merge
■ interact.

You will also need to consider the cultures of minority groups such as those determined by:
■ class
■ race
■ age
■ religion
■ special interests.

The culture of minority groups and evolving or conflicting cultures

It is difficult to consider the cultures of minority groups separately from their evolution and the conflict they can cause. In the following pages, therefore, the issues will be studied together. This part of the specification requires you to explore all aspects of various cultures and to discover what they have in common and what makes each distinct.

What is culture?

Culture is the whole of the knowledge, ideas and habits of a society.

A **subculture** is a distinct way of life within a wider social culture.

A **contra-culture** is where a set of values arises in opposition to a wider culture.

It must also be remembered that cultures are dynamic, ever changing and developing.

Is there a difference between 'multi-racial' and 'multi-cultural'? Are the terms interchangeable? They are both used loosely, particularly in General Studies essays! Minority communities might not be distinct because members share the same ethnic background and so 'multi-cultural' has to be a wider term than 'multi-racial'.

What do various cultures have in common?

Sociologist suggest that cultures have the following in common:
- beliefs – shared understanding
- values – an acceptance of what is right
- expected and accepted patterns of behaviour or lifestyle
- an acceptance of roles within the group.

Other specialists might add:
- wealth
- age-range
- education
- location.

Cultures of various minority groups

There are many ways in which minority groups can be defined. In this section we look at a sample of five, which includes age, race and ethnicity, religion, social class and special interest groups.

Minority groups based upon age

Figure 3 shows some of the groups that can be identified within youth culture. Each of these groups can be defined using the eight criteria listed above.

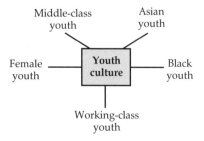

Figure 3   *Youth subcultures*

Another group that can be identified in terms of its age are the elderly. The number of retired people in Western society is growing and life expectancy is increasing. Many of these people have high purchasing power after a lifetime at work and (in some cases thanks to advances in medicine) they have the energy to enjoy their lives. They claim more than their proportionate share of health services and make heavy demands upon leisure and recreation facilities. They are an important part of purchasing power for many industries including food, cars, houses and holidays.

The elderly can be articulate and pressure their representatives through their votes. They are a growing group for whom new provision has to be made.

Race and ethnicity

Race is the term used to indicate a group who are assumed to share particular biological traits. It's not an easy concept to define. Ethnic groups share a common culture that is often different from that of the majority. However, minority race or ethnic groups are usually only noticeable when their culture, form of dress or skin colour is different from that of the majority. Sometimes they become noticeable because they form a distinctive community, partially separate from the rest – for example, the Jewish community in England in the Middle Ages and areas of western Europe today.

Religion

The religion followed by an individual is often (but not always) linked with their race. For example, many Hindus are Asians. Shared identity in terms of belief, values and patterns of behaviour are much easier to observe and recognize within different religions.

Social class

There are various ways of dividing any society into classes. In the UK we use the Registrar General's Classification. This uses types of occupation. This is not the place to discuss the difficulties in measuring social class, and there is always a danger of stereotyping. However, further study into the ways in which social class is measured and described would be useful.

People in the UK are divided by occupation into five social classes. However, the range of attitudes, values and interests that an individual holds can also identify social class. In the past, people from the upper, middle and working classes were believed to have different views, tastes and lifestyles. Today the divisions have become blurred, though certain cultural traits – such as an enjoyment of classical music, ballet and opera – are presumed, by some, to be signs of a higher class.

Social class will also be considered in other contexts on pages 71–104 and 159–82. This is a good opportunity for you to make links between the cultural domain and the social domain, identifying how social class affects culture and how it is linked with wealth, leisure and the relationship between law and culture. This is another example of the way synopticity works.

Special interest groups: the new tribalism?

A list of special interest groups would include:
- theatre goers
- football fans
- New-Age travellers
- vegetarians
- fitness fanatics
- feminists
- homosexuals
- 'northerners'
- Scottish and Welsh nationalists
- monarchists
- 'anoraks'
- punks
- environmentalists
- students.

This list is not exhaustive and new cultural groups are constantly emerging and evolving. A list in 2005 will be different from the one drawn up in 2001. Does each of the above (and any you have added yourself) have a distinct culture? Can you identify aspects of that distinctive culture?

Cultural conflicts

Most Western societies are both multi-racial and multi-cultural and it would be surprising if conflicts did not arise. Conflicts arise within families because members have different beliefs, values and patterns of behaviour; so to expect that a community, nation or continent will not have problems is unrealistic.

For example, consider the different social sets or cliques within your own sixth form, youth club, sports club or student common room. They will have arisen through issues related to:
- gender
- age (for example, Year 12 v. Year 13!)
- the choice of music played at socials and during breaks from study
- the apparent ability of some to get away with breaking the rules
- differences in values, beliefs and patterns of behaviour.

Global examples of cultural conflict

At any one time there are a number of cultural conflicts taking place in the world. For example, at the turn of the millennium the following conflicts were in the news:
1. Australian Aborigine culture and that of the immigrant community
2. New Zealand Maori culture and that of the immigrant community
3. Muslims and Christians in Kosovo
4. Native Americans in the USA and their dispute with other cultural groups
5. white farmers in Zimbabwe and the native Zimbabweans
6. Northern Ireland and clashes between Catholics and Protestants
7. devolution and the challenges of Nationalists and Unionists
8. the North–South divide, with differences in comparative wealth
9. all the 'isms' – for example, socialism, materialism and individualism.

The Peace Agreement: is it a possibility?

Conflicts between age groups: ageism and the generation gap

'The generation gap' isn't just a count of the number of years between young people and the old. It's a term used to express or explain differences in beliefs, values and behaviour patterns between one age group and another. There is a perceived gap between teenagers and their parents, between 30 year olds and retired people. However, it doesn't necessarily mean that there will be conflict. The conflict often arises between particular age groups and the rest of society.

Figures 4 and 5 show how conflicts can occur within and between two age groups. What would you add to these spider diagrams.

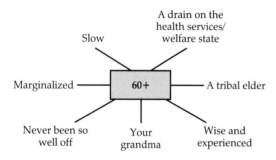

Figure 4   *How are the elderly perceived?*

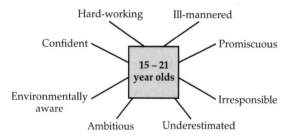

Figure 5   *How are 15–21 year olds perceived?*

Conflicts, gender and sexism

The following terms are worth investigating in terms of sexist practice:

- a glass ceiling
- pulling up the drawbridge
- jobs for the boys
- the statutory woman
- an honorary man
- the old-boy network
- laddism
- feminism.

What do these terms suggest?

Gender is still an issue that causes conflict. It's arguable that this particular culture (that of male and female) is evolving more obviously than any other. Despite equal opportunity legislation in the UK there are still marked inequalities between men and women, and not just those that disadvantage women. Further research in the following areas would be useful:

- work and pay
- benefits
- the hidden curriculum in schools (see page 14)
- stereotypical roles.

Conflicts, racism and sectarianism

Included under this heading will be the conflicting culture of both race and religion, as they often go together. Current events or issues at a local, national and global scale often reflect racial or sectarian interests. The different views of racial groups and intolerant attitudes can cause conflicts, especially if a resource is in short supply. This is a very big topic and you will need to take it further yourself.

To counter-balance intolerant attitudes, the law and many community projects attempt to reduce racial and sectarian conflict. Recent reports into the behaviour of the police and sports supporters have shown the way forward.

Tribalism

For all the special interest groups listed on page 19 under the heading 'Special interest groups: the new tribalism?' consider the way each (and any you have added yourself) can be a source of conflict within contemporary Western society. Make sure you support your opinion with fact. Here's an easy one to start you off.

Environmentalists: Often cause chaos through their policy of civil disobedience. For example, the problems associated with the Newbury bypass, their damage to GM crops and the extensions to Manchester Airport.

TASKS

1 Take each of the youth groups and, using the eight bullet points listed on page 18, describe their distinct characteristics. Does working-class youth culture have a different understanding of Western society from middle-class youth culture? Is it possible to apply all the bullet points to each?

2 Consider the distinct characteristics of the elderly group, the 'grey population'. What issues and conflicts arise when they are compared with members of the youth culture?

3 Identify the distinct characteristics of one or two racial or ethnic minority cultures in the UK?

4 Consider the following minority religious groups: (a) Jehovah's witnesses (b) Mormons. To what extent do they have a distinct culture within Christianity? (See pages 140–4 for further information on world religions.)

5 Identify two social classes or groups. Apply the criteria given in the bulleted list on page 18 and brainstorm your thoughts. Compare the results of each brainstorming. Are these two groups significantly different? Analyse any differences.

6 Explore a cultural conflict that is in the news. Identify its main causes and the ways in which the conflict manifests itself in terms of culture.

7 Draw two spider diagrams for two age groups to show how each might view the other. Comment on the contrasts.

8 Note the main contributory factors to a racial or sectarian conflict that has been in the news. Suggest actions that the community could take to reduce the tensions listed in the report.

9 Select a special interest group and identify the cultural conflicts with which they are associated. What types of action do they take to draw attention to their beliefs?

❸ Media and communication

Definitions

Communicate	To give a share of. To impart information. To convey an idea. To broadcast. To connect.
Communication	An act of sharing. Correspondence/message.
Influence (*noun*)	Power to produce an effect.
Influential	Capable of bringing about an effect. Capable of causing something to happen.
Medium	That through which communication is maintained. An instrument or agency.
Propaganda	A plan or strategy to communicate or spread opinions or principles to bring about a desired response.

Getting started

1 'There is never a case for any form of censorship in a democratic society.'
2 'There should be legislation to prevent intrusive journalism.'
3 Are people in the public domain allowed a private life?
4 'Tabloid newspapers are comics for grown-ups!'
5 'The Internet will eventually replace the national daily newspaper.'
6 Email provides the opportunity for an increase in communication. However, does 'more' equal 'better'?
7 'How are we to protect the vulnerable from the pornography and violence of TV, Internet, film and video?'
8 'Soap operas reflect real life. That is why they are so popular.'
9 'Why advertise? It is a form of propaganda.'
10 Can you explain why some radio audiences are increasing in number?
11 'Bad news is more interesting than good news.'
12 Is it 'your BBC'?
13 Communication is a two-way thing!

Outline

A wide range of media is available for communication. For this topic you need to consider the use you make of the following:

- newspapers
- magazines
- periodicals
- film
- video
- television
- the Internet.

The nature and function of many of these are constantly evolving and yet they all have an influence on public opinion and individual behaviour. You will need to consider how this influence is achieved and make comparisons between the roles and methods of the different media. Many moral issues arise from the activity of the media. These too, will need to be given some thought.

You will also need to be aware of current developments within media and communication. These include:

- mobile phones with their many functions
- text messages
- the web
- email
- CD/DVD/digital broadcasting.

Some of these have been criticized for dehumanizing communication and being a social menace. Indeed mobile phones are considered by some a health risk. They are certainly here to stay and further developments are inevitable. Do you have a view on these changes? Do the advantages outweigh the changes caused and the possible risks?

Current developments within media and communications

We are in an age of faster, more efficient and versatile communication. Development is almost daily.

The media has always responded to developments within communication. The role of national newspapers changed when a television became standard equipment in almost every home. How did the newspapers change with this innovation?

Local radio arrived on the scene in the 1960s and local newspapers also had to respond to this threat by changing their focus. Find out how.

New technology, such as digital television and the WAP mobile phone, is providing the various parts of the media with different challenges and opportunities.

Developments within TV and radio broadcasting

The introduction of cable and satellite TV more than doubled the number of available channels. It also made it possible to receive stations from other European countries. Do you think that having more channels means better television?

Satellite companies have purchased the rights to major sporting events in order to boost their viewing figures. They are introducing 'pay per view' for popular events. Should national sport only be available to satellite viewers?

Digital broadcasting

What is digital radio? Why do we need to convert to digital TV? Why is it seen as the way forward for television and radio broadcasting?

Digital broadcasts use computer technology. Instead of converting sounds and pictures into waves that are sent from a transmitter and received by aerials, the sounds and pictures are converted into a series of digits which are transmitted using modified transmitters and are received by digital dish aerials.

Some advantages of digital broadcasting:

- It is more efficient and capable of broadcasting more channels than analogue systems.
- It gives an improved sound and picture quality with interference-free reception.
- It offers more choice, wide-screen programmes and the possibility of interactive facilities.
- It provides online services, such as email.
- It allows access to Internet websites.

Of course it has the disadvantage that you need a digital radio and a digital decoder for your TV – or a new digital TV set!

This rapid development is expected to increase the range of services that we can access through our TV, PC and radio. Future developments suggest that it may be possible to store programmes in the set-top box or digital TV.

Newspapers and magazines

Is there a future for newspapers and magazines? In the past, when communication became faster, newspapers responded. They were threatened by the broadcasting companies' use of fax and satellite links. Now in this digital age the threat is renewed. The newspapers have to adapt once again. They will need to consider what advantages a newspaper has to offer to its readers and how to respond to the digital challenge.

The Internet: the information superhighway

The information technology industry and the government expect the future to bring a PC into every home. Is the PC an expensive toy or a necessary part of life in the 21st century? What does being online offer? Do you see a future where going to work at the office is a thing of the past and we simply log-on and work from home with a link to the main office? We can work from anywhere – plug in your laptop computer and you're off!

There are dangers to this view of the future. We may be moving into a time of information overload or become increasingly vulnerable to the messages of the hidden persuaders. In addition there are problems of censoring and monitoring material from the Internet. Some people have suggested that too much time spent in front of a screen is physically damaging, whilst others suggest that Internet Service Providers (ISPs) are able to penetrate our privacy.

TASKS

1 A year or two ago the list of the latest communications technology would have contained mobile phones, fax machines, scanned images and text messages. Today these are no longer considered the 'latest', as technology moves so quickly. By the time the ink is dry on this page further innovation or development may well have taken place. Much of this is as a direct result of computer technology.

A list of some of the latest developments within communication includes:

- DVD
- Internet – with email, online services, instant news updates, interactive viewing
- cable/satellite/aerial TV channels
- digital broadcasting
- WAP.

a Can you add to this list?

b In what ways and to whom are these developments challenges or opportunities?

2 a Since fewer newspapers are being sold, are the days of the national daily numbered?

b Newsagents' shelves display an increasing number of specialist magazines. Suggest reasons for this development. What is the role of the specialist magazine?

3 a When did you last write a letter by hand?

b When did you last sit for 30 minutes reading a newspaper?

c Explain the reasons for the general decrease in these activities over recent years.

4 An argument requires a person to offer a statement and then put forward reasons for believing the statement to be true. Some reasons are better than others! Consider this statement: 'Digital technology will revolutionize communication.'

a Can you list reasons for holding this belief? Which reasons are good? Which are not good?

b Which reasons are based on technical knowledge? Which are based on a personal belief?

c How do you recognize a good reason?

KEY SKILLS: *Communication*

Compare a web page that covers news updates with a national newspaper. They could be analysed in terms of content, style and layout. If you then present your findings you will produce evidence for C3.1b and C3.2. (*Level 3*)

Ways in which the media influence public opinion

YOUR COUNTRY NEEDS YOU!

We all know about this recruitment campaign in newspapers, magazines and posters in 1914 and 1915 and how it persuaded young men to volunteer for the army. Today a wider range of media continues to influence attitudes and behaviour, though perhaps with a little more subtlety.

You need to be aware of the variety of ways in which the media influence public opinion and behaviour. What follows is a selection. Some of the methods are to be found in written media, others more are from TV, film or video.

- Language and style chosen
- Images chosen, such as cartoons, beautiful women, children or red cars
- Headlines used
- Editorial comments
- News item selection, scheduling and positioning
- Ownership or stake holder interference and political bias

Language and style chosen

Gotcha!

This was the headline in *The Sun* in 1982 when the Argentinean warship *Belgrano* was sunk off the Falkland Islands. News coverage of war always produces emotive language chosen for effect. Allied forces in the Gulf War of 1990 were reported as being responsible for 'collateral damage' and causing death through 'friendly' fire. These and similar euphemisms were common in newspapers at the time.

How close were these headlines to being propaganda? Have a look at similar techniques currently being used by analysing news reports of similar events taking place today.

What do you make of the following headline?

Now Hollywood scorns tawdry Hewitt's kiss and tell tale

Why 'scorns'? Why 'tawdry' and why 'now'? What effect does the choice of words have? How is opinion being managed here?

Images chosen

Photographs, cartoons and film footage are chosen with great care. What messages are intended by the images shown below?

Pinochet must face trial or be found insane

The Times, 7 March 2000

Watch a piece of footage that accompanies a news story. What effect does the 'live' action have on the way the audience might focus on the story? Are *you* being manipulated to respond in a particular way?

Headlines used

Consider the following headlines. They actually refer to the same news story. In what ways is the reader being led into an opinion? The story being covered is concerned with benefit cheats.

FLEECED

The Sun, 9 March 2000

Dole cheats banned from benefit

The Independent, 9 March 2000

Editorial comments

Below is an editorial from a tabloid newspaper. Note the language, headline and style of the article. How has each of these been used to attempt to influence the reader?

It's all spin for this coin

SEVEN out of 10 people in Britain don't want to scrap the pound.

So why is the Government spending millions to persuade us the euro is good for us?

Gordon Brown's second National Changeover Plan – which has a ring of the old Soviet Union about it – shows one thing:

You can't believe what Labour says about the single currency.

It's all just spin.

Brown and Tony Blair try to convince everyone that joining is not on the agenda unless the economic conditions are right.

They insist we can trust them because the people will have the final say in a referendum.

And yet they spend millions and millions on propaganda – like the travelling road show that will bombard us with euro nonsense.

More sinister are the euro education games for children.

Do parents want young minds influenced this way?

Even the DSS computers are to be adapted to print cheques in euros. What's that for – to make it easier for all the foreign scroungers to get at our money?

Labour has got its mind set on joining the euro, whether you like it or not.

Don't let them get away with it.

The Sun, 10 March 2000

Should Blair delay the election?

EVER since he became Prime Minister, Tony Blair has known when the next general election will be.

He has been determined to go on May 3, 2001, even though it is a year before he has to.

A month ago, with Labour so far ahead in the polls, that date looked a certainty.

Then came foot and mouth. And "going to the country" took on a new meaning.

Mr Blair is now under pressure to delay the election.

So today The Mirror gives you the chance to say what you think.

Every reader can cast a vote by phoning the hotline below. Your call will cost no more than 10p.

The election debate is dividing the nation. Polls are split 50/50, families, friends and workmates cannot agree. Before you vote, turn to Page 4 & 5 and read the arguments for and against.

Tony Blair must decide this week if there is to be a delay.

The verdict you give may help him make up his mind.

Front page of *The Mirror*, 26 March 2001

Blair may play for time with 7 June election

Troops dig pits for 500,000 animals as farm crisis grows

BY ANDREW GRICE
Political Editor

TONY BLAIR is drawing up contingency plans to delay the general election until June to buy the Government more time to bring the foot-and-mouth epidemic under control.

Ministers will launch a drive today to convince the public that the government has "got a grip" on the crisis and that it would be in the nation's interest for the local and general elections to go ahead on 3 May, the date long favoured by the Prime Minister.

But cabinet ministers admitted privately last night that the foot-and-mouth crisis could force Mr Blair to postpone both elections and announce a "month-long pause" to 7 June, the most likely alternative date.

Mr Blair and Gordon Brown, the Chancellor, do not want to delay the general election until October, seen as the earliest possible date after June because of the summer holidays. With America heading towards a recession, they fear that Britain's economic posi-

tion might look very different by the autumn, and delaying the poll until then could upset Labour's entire re-election strategy.

Cabinet sources conceded that there could be "genuine problems" in holding county council elections in May in areas worst hit by foot-and-mouth, such as Cumbria and Devon. They wanted local people to feel "comfortable" before the elections went ahead.

Mr Blair has a week to resolve his most difficult dilemma since becoming Prime Minister. One option is to go "to the wire" by delaying his decision until a week from today in the hope that the foot-and-mouth crisis eases and he can stick to the 3 May poll date.

A minister said yesterday: "In the next few days we will be able to tell whether we can get on top of it – and be seen to get on top of it. But we are going to have to provide evidence of real progress."

Front page of *The Independent*, (abridged) 7 March 2001

News item selection, scheduling and positioning

Newspapers have editorial policies. For example, *The Independent* does not cover gossip stories about the royal family. Articles, issues and events will find themselves front-page news in some papers and not in others. Similarly the order of news stories in TV news coverage changes from channel to channel and according to the time of day. What is dealt with first on the early evening news on one channel will not always be so prioritized by another channel later in the evening. If we accept that the events that are covered first are more important or significant, what effect can the decisions made about priority have on audiences or readers?

For example, what message is being given in these front pages? How are they influencing us?

Ownership or stakeholder interference/political bias

Owners of newspapers and television networks have great power to influence events and public opinion. The owners have their particular political views on events and government policy. They believe they can shape events towards their own view of society. Who are these powerful owners of the media? It would be worth finding out who owns the following:

The Times	*Sun*	the various ITV regional stations
Telegraph	*Mail*	BBC
Guardian	*Mirror*	Sky TV
Independent		

Have a look at some newspaper editorials and note how they make their influence clear? Does the coverage and treatment of events, national and international, seek to manipulate opinion?

Imagine a breaking story that involved a scandal within the royal family or a person in high public office with a high political profile. How would each of the newspapers and broadcasting companies present the event? What might be their motives?

A word about advertising

Advertising is not a medium in itself. The medium (for example, TV) is the agent for the advertisement. However, the sole purpose of the advertisement is to influence choice or opinion. Here is a list of some of the ways in which advertising works. Look out for examples of advertisements that use these strategies:

- preying on the need to belong, to be accepted
- creating a need and raising expectations
- presenting an image to strive to achieve
- using peer pressure
- allowing association with role models and ideals.

TASKS

1 Use the six criteria listed on page 25 to compare and analyse the same news story in two newspapers and one television news programme.

2 Thinking and analytical skills include interpreting and evaluating opinions and recognizing common fallacies. Analyse the editorials in a variety of newspapers.

Consider the assertions made. Can you separate opinions from fact? Can you recognize any opinions that are judgements of others that may not be based on sound premises or demonstrated facts?

3 How do advertisements disguise themselves as news stories or reports?

KEY SKILLS: *Communication*

Compare editorials from different types of newspapers in terms of style and analyse their likely or intended influence. You could develop and generate evidence for Key Skill C3.2. (*Level 3*)

Moral issues arising from the activity of the media

Moral issues arising from media activity are complex and not easy to separate as one issue often impinges on another. Brainstorming is often a useful way of ensuring you get an overall picture.

Consider Figure 6. How do the issues identified relate to one another? It's an interesting exercise to draw further lines connecting these issues. For example, how do we balance the obvious advantages of a free press with the need for responsible journalism? Are there any other issues you would wish to add to this diagram?

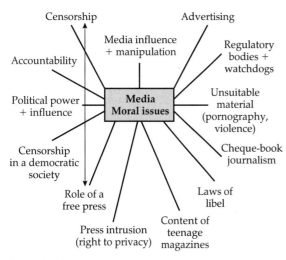

Figure 6 *Moral issues arising from media activity*

Regulation and control

The UK is a democracy with a free press. However there are a number of bodies to which the press and other media are accountable. Some of these bodies have considerable power. All forms of media are of course subject to the law, for example:

- the Obscene Publications Act 1959
- the Official Secrets Act 1989
- the Defamation Act 1952
- the Broadcasting Act 1990.

The following list shows some of the bodies whose role it is to monitor standards, handle complaints from the public, make recommendations following enquiries and ensure all types of media operate within the law:

- the Broadcasting Complaints Commission
- the Press Complaints Commission
- the Broadcasting Standards Council
- the Advertising Standards Authority
- the British Board of Film Classification
- the Independent Television Commission.

So how much of a role does the public have? We can always exert pressure by not buying a particular publication or by pressing the OFF button on the radio or television. However, is this enough to protect the vulnerable from unsuitable or damaging material? This brings us to a consideration of perhaps the biggest moral issue …

Censorship

Question: Does censoring a television play today lead to book-burning tomorrow, or does it make sense to have some control or regulation about what is published or broadcast? Where should the line be drawn and who draws it?

Question: Who censors the censors?

Most regulatory bodies are made up of expert members of the public who are appointed by government departments. The public they are working to protect does not elect them. Can you see any problems arising from this? The members of such bodies need to be representative of our society and without any financial or political interest. Who ensures that they are?

Intrusive journalism

Do we have a right to privacy? This issue is not only concerned with the intrusion into the private lives of public figures but also the privacy of ordinary individuals who, for whatever reason, find themselves thrown into a media spotlight. There is currently very little legislation to protect an individual's privacy.

Question: Should people in public life have a right to a private life away from media intrusion?

Question: Is there a case for stronger legislation to protect an individual's right to privacy or would this be a form of censorship, unacceptable in a democracy? Would a voluntary code of conduct for the media have any effect?

Question: How moral is the growing phenomenon of cheque-book journalism? Are the 'kiss and tell' stories that are published from time to time simply in bad taste rather than unethical or criminal?

Influence

This has been dealt with earlier (pages 25–6), but it does play a part in the debate about moral issues and therefore needs reinforcing here.

Question: How moral is it for the various types of media to use their considerable power to influence public opinion and behaviour?

Thinking and analytical skills

Consider the two skills of 'interpreting and evaluating opinions' and 'distinguishing between knowledge and belief'.

Topics such as 'Moral issues arising from the activity of the media' give you the opportunity to distinguish between knowledge and belief. When the rights and wrongs of a situation or action are questioned you are involved in using moral knowledge that requires an understanding of yourself and others. You are distinguishing between what you know (that it is against the law to publish obscene material) and what you believe (pornography is damaging). The former is based on the intellectual perception of fact, the latter on the acceptance of evidence.

KEY SKILLS: *Communication*

Issues that involve an individual's perception or interpretation of morality lend themselves to debate and discussion. Moral issues arising from the activity of the media is a complex subject. Class discussion, group work or a debate on a motion based on the contents of this section would generate evidence for Key Skill C3.1a. Make sure that any contributions you make are relevant to the topic, that you show you can listen to others and ask them appropriate questions, and that you show you know how to invite others to contribute. (*Level 3*)

Further study suggestions and example questions

Further reading

Banton, M. (1997) *The Idea of Race*, Tavistock Publications, London.
Barret, D. (1986) *Media Sociology*, Routledge, London.
Cole, W. O. (ed.) (1991) *Moral Issues in Six Religions*, Heinemann Educational, Oxford.
Moore, S. (1999) *Sociology*, Letts Educational, London.
Shepherd, C. A. R. and White, C. (1996) *Essential Articles*, Carel Press, Carlisle.
Sperber, D. (1996) *Explaining Culture*, Blackwell, Oxford.

Guidance on answering questions

A written answer that scores high marks is one that gives up-to-date examples to illustrate ideas or assertions. So to answer questions effectively you need to keep yourself informed and be aware of when and how issues are raised or become high profile. (See page 191 for help on how to write a successful essay.)

It will be to your advantage in your A level General Studies course to make connections and links between the three sections covered in this unit. How much have you been required to use your own experience or that of others to answer the questions raised? Some of the issues raised in this unit require moral knowledge, which involves an understanding of yourself and others. Can you make the connections when the media is described as a formative influence in one section of this unit, and the moral issues that arise from its activities are described in another section?

It's possible to make links between this unit and other domains. How much of your understanding of the cultural domain has relied on scientific knowledge? For example, propaganda articles can often justify scientific discoveries. Some environmentalists suggest that the literature published by the visitors' centre at the Sellafield nuclear reprocessing plant is a form of propaganda. The scientific domain asks you to consider the moral responsibility of the scientist. When you look at issues in the social domain you are required to consider the nature of objectivity in social sciences. How much of party political literature is in fact a form of propaganda?

This question on propaganda may help you to see the connections.

a What do you understand by the term 'propaganda', and how does it work? [10]

b Consider the suggestion that there is never a case for the use of propaganda. How far do you agree with the suggestion? [40]

For part (a) a good answer will start with a sound definition of 'propaganda', with some consideration of examples to show how it works.

In part (b) the question suggests that there is never a case for propaganda. An answer could begin with a description of propaganda used in wartime. This would suggest that there is a case when the circumstances demand it. This would lead to consideration of a range of circumstances such as:

- that it is possible to justify persuading people of something when it is in the interest of public safety, morale or the country's security
- that to block propaganda is not acceptable in a democratic society as it is a form of censorship
- that rules should be made so that the public is aware of propaganda, for example, in advertisements.

The essay could conclude with a discussion of whether, and in what circumstances, the end justifies the means.

Questions

1 a What do you understand by the term 'Religious Education'? [10 marks]

b To what extent might it be argued that it is the role of the family rather than schools to provide RE for young people? [40 marks]

2 a Compare the following terms: nationalism, patriotism and xenophobia. [10 marks]

b How much of the movement for devolution within the United Kingdom is motivated by nationalism? [40 marks]

3 Section A
Answer all of the questions in this section.

Read the following extract from an article by Jade Garratt from *The Independent*, 18 April 2000.

Storm in a Typhoo teacup

Advertising has never been a social science. Agreed. But is it OK to show the workers on an Indian tea plantation behaving like a bunch of 'mental retards' in order to flog a few boxes of Typhoo tea?

A new Typhoo TV campaign from Mother – the agency behind the Super Noodles and Lilt ads – has just aired on national TV and is re-igniting the racism-in-advertising debate. The ads, which are part of a £15m integrated campaign, introduce the character of Tommy Singh, the owner of a southern India tea plantation where Typhoo is grown. Tommy talks viewers around his plantation explaining the freshness of the air, soil and water – nothing harmful there.

But it's the way the plantation workers are depicted that has raised eyebrows. They clap inanely, offer cheesy grins to camera, have subtitles appear on screen when they talk and are shown offering exaggerated demonstrations of plantation equipment.

'There's something a bit sinister about these ads,' says Alfredo Marcantonio, European creative director at rival agency D'Arcy. 'It's not affectionate and I don't like the idea of doing people down. Tommy, who is surrounded by dim-witted workers, sets out to convince us that Typhoo tea is "two-thumbs fresh". Quite frankly I don't believe him and I'm worried that people will find these ads offensive.'

Marcantonio is a fan of the agency's work for Lilt – where two large Caribbean women are shown encouraging punters to find their rhythm – he describes those ads as 'charming, positive and light-hearted as an interpretation of the Caribbean culture'. The gentle lampooning of a culture is fine, he says, when it is handled sensitively.

Jim Thorton, who created the Typhoo campaign for Mother, is keen to defend his latest work. While he admits that he can't be completely confident that no one will complain ('because some people may interpret it wrongly') he is confident that the agency has done its homework.

The agency worked with Meera Syal, one of the stars of the Anglo-Asian sitcom 'Goodness Gracious Me', as well as conducting their own research within the Asian community. This involved reading scripts to members of the Asian community. And as the ad has its champions, even among Asians, Ms Syal, who helped write the script, defends it, saying: 'Well, I thought it was funny.' It is also defended by Abba Pomar from the Asian *Trader* magazine: 'The ads are very Asian-friendly and good humoured.'

a What does the writer object to in the advertisement?   [5]

b What do you understand by 'gentle lampooning of a culture'?   [5]

c In what ways is the advertisement using stereotypes? Do you find the use acceptable?   [10]

d Alfredo Marcantonio finds the advert sinister and offensive. In what ways could it be so considered?   [10]

e Can it be argued that in a multi-cultural society, like that of the United Kingdom, such an advertising campaign is harmful to race relations? Put *either* the case for *or* against this notion.   [20]

1 Characteristics of the sciences (physical, life and earth)

Definitions

Conservation   Protection of the environment and buildings from harm.

Energy   Power from electricity, gas, coal, wind and so on, that allows machines to work.

Fertility   May refer to population change, female fertility or the ability of the land to produce crops.

Greenhouse gases   Carbon dioxide, methane, nitrous oxide and CFCs.

Pollution   Chemical particles and gases in the air, water and on land as well as from noise and visual intrusion.

Getting started

1   Some everyday sayings that include an element of science:
'As light as a feather.'
'As blind as a bat.'
'As clear as crystal.'
'Getting long in the tooth.'
'Having one's hair stand on end.'
'Red sky at night, shepherds delight.'
'Red sky at morn, shepherds mourn.'
2   What is the difference between physical and social science?
3   Why is science so unpopular and scientists not liked?
4   Is it true that students studying pure mathematics, applied mathematics and physics at A level are doing the same subject three times? Do you know the differences between biology, botany, zoology, organic chemistry, inorganic chemistry, biochemistry and physics?

Greenhouse gases and global warming

1   With threats of global warming, is the future of the earth in balance?
2   Can we be sure global warming is real, or is it just another cycle of climate?

Energy

1   Why are we using more and more energy?
2   Whatever happened to nuclear energy?

3   When do those alternative energy sources really start to play a part?

Transport

1   Will your children fly to the moon for their holiday of a lifetime?
2   What will be the next form of air transport? Will passenger jets get bigger and faster?
3   Will the next set of space travel developments be sub-orbital and similar to the space shuttle? What timescale is being considered?
4   Will babies born today live in a petroleum-free world?
5   In what ways can we get rid of the journey to work?
6   If Heathrow airport is up to flight capacity, should it be expanded to meet demand?

Space exploration

1   Astronomy, space, cosmology and the origins of the universe are all topics people find interesting in science. Science becomes interesting when it is about frontiers, both intellectual and real.
2   How did the universe begin and to where does it reach?
3   What should be the priority for the competing American and British landers when they arrive on Mars?

4   Which space film impressed you most for its depiction of the science of the future?

Population dynamics and fertility control

1   Why do birth rates vary between countries?
2   What new problems arise from increasing life expectancy?
3   Why are some countries trying to increase their population when others are trying to reduce it?

Genetic engineering and biotechnology

1   Why do we study genetics?
2   Is the deliberate creation of a human embryo for use in therapy permissible?
3   Can any benefits outweigh the dangers posed by the manipulation of the human species?

Health and fitness

1   Should the recorded times of sports people be allowed to stand if they are later caught using drugs?
2   Why are so many people buying bottled water at the supermarket?
3   When we are all living longer why are we joining health clubs?
4   How old would you like to be when you die?

Organ transplantation

1   What is being alive and what is being dead? Anaesthetists are calling for the use of anaesthetics when organs, such as the liver, heart and lungs, are removed from a dead body. Researchers are also questioning at what point a baby or foetus can feel pain. Both groups fear that pain may be present in the pre-birth and post-death worlds. The normal upper limit for abortions is 24 weeks but research suggests that the foetus may feel pain as early as 18 weeks. Certainly babies born prematurely, 23 weeks after conception, have survived through the use of intensive care.
2   The first heart surgery was performed in 1938. Heart transplants have now become common but shortage of donor and immune system problems have turned the focus on artificial pumps. Why was 2000 an important year in this respect?
3   Will donor organ transplantation be replaced by organs grown from stem cells?

Conservation

1   What is the difference between conservation and preservation?
2   Are National Parks museums, sanctuaries, or playgrounds?
3   Should we conserve fossil fuels? Coal, oil and natural gas are fossil fuels, the remains of plants and animals living millions of years ago. Fossil fuels:
    - contain carbon and give out heat energy when burned
    - produce carbon dioxide and water vapour when burned
    - are non-renewable, and known reserves of some will run out in about 50 years' time.

Environmental pollution

1   There are 30 car-manufacturing plants in the UK plus eight truck and bus building companies. This is the largest number of any country in Europe. Are we putting jobs before the environment?
2   We all breathe the same air and we all cherish our children's future, so what are our obligations?
3   Since environmental problems are interconnected, where should we start?
4   What are the main pollutants and who are the polluters in urban areas?
5   'If the environment does not work nothing else – not schools, not health, not care, not the economy – can work.' Do you agree with this presidential candidate?

Outline

This section demonstrates the characteristics of the sciences through the study of ten issues. These have been chosen because of their importance to contemporary life. General Studies encourages an active awareness and concern for these issues. In the future, new issues will become current. The ten described here provide a basis for the issues of the future.

Greenhouse gases and global warming

Can global warming be blamed for recent climatic disasters? Floods in Mozambique, famine in Ethiopia and storms in the UK during 2000 are three recent examples.

Climatic change

Climates are continually changing. Rocks, fossils, pollen analysis, tree ring dating and historical records all show how changes have taken place. In the UK, evidence of ice ages is spectacular proof of climatic change. A little ice age happened in Britain between AD 1500 and 1700. Since 1980 the British climate appears to be getting warmer. Some scientists suggest that this is part of global warming though others say it is just another fluctuation.

Warming the earth

During the day the earth is warmed by incoming short-wave radiation from the sun (whose surface temperature is over 5000°C). This radiation passes through the earth's atmosphere, which contains some natural greenhouse gases at a height of about six miles. At night the earth cools as it emits longer-wave radiation. Not all of the heat reaches space. Some is reflected back by clouds, and the gases trap heat in the way that a greenhouse would in a garden. Hence they are called 'greenhouse gases'.

Increasing greenhouse gases

These greenhouse gases occur naturally and they keep the temperature of the earth 33°C higher. (Note: during the Ice Age the temperature only fell by 4°C.) These natural greenhouse gases include water vapour, carbon dioxide (CO_2), methane (CH_4), nitrous oxide (N_2O) and CFCs (chlorofluorocarbons).

The amounts of carbon dioxide, methane, nitrous oxide and CFCs in the atmosphere have been increasing as people burn fossil fuels, burn and clear rainforests, increase landfill sites, drive more miles and use refrigerators and aerosol sprays. This increase in greenhouse gases is trapping more of the outgoing long-wave radiation and reflecting it back to the earth. More and more heat becomes trapped in the atmosphere of the earth. However, the amount of carbon dioxide in the atmosphere is

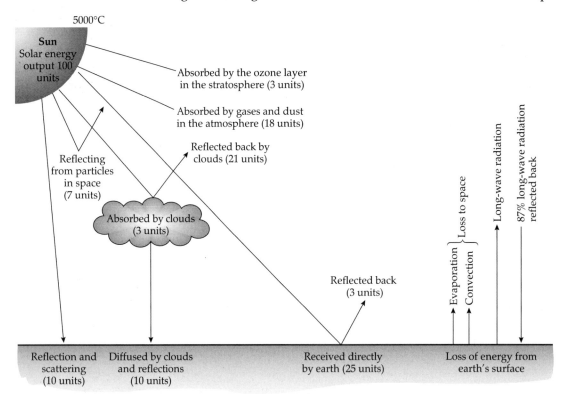

Balance
Of the original units of solar energy:
45 are received by the earth
24 are absorbed by the stratosphere and troposphere
31 are reflected into space.

Figure 7 *What happens to solar energy?*

not constant. Bubbles of CO_2 up to 160,000 years old have been retrieved from ice cores drilled in Antarctica. They show variations in the amount of CO_2 in the atmosphere but with an increase of 25% since 1850.

Carbon dioxide (CO_2) and global warming

All living things contain carbon compounds. Carbon dioxide is the source of carbon compounds for all living plants. Plants take in carbon dioxide from air and water during daylight hours to make glucose sugar by photosynthesis. This takes place in the plants' leaves and needs heat and light from the sun. Plants then convert the glucose to starch and proteins for the roots, stem and leaves. Animals obtain carbon compounds by eating plants and humans eat plants and animals. During photosynthesis the plants give back oxygen into the air. The carbon dioxide gets into the air through respiration by plants and animals, the decay of dead animals and plants, and by the burning of wood, coal, oil and natural gas.

Many scientists believe people are putting too much carbon dioxide into the atmosphere for the plants to absorb, hence the build up of greenhouse gases. The problem increases as people clear forests of trees and plants. Scientists believe this has been the case for the last 200 years, since the Industrial Revolution. We are adding the carbon dioxide to our atmosphere that has been locked away in coal, oil and gas for the last 350 million years.

Fossil fuels, pollution and global warming

The burning of fossil fuels such as coal, gas and oil produces carbon dioxide. Additionally the exhausts of cars release hydrocarbons into the atmosphere. Power stations release sulphur dioxide (which dissolves in rain water to produce acid rain and carbon dioxide). Car exhausts and power stations produce another greenhouse gas: nitrous oxide. Ozone is another greenhouse gas, formed by a reaction of car exhaust gases to sunlight.

Global warming: the evidence

Scientists point to rising average temperatures and a series of hotter years since 1980 as evidence that the greenhouse effect is producing global warming. Some predict a rise of 5°C in the next 100 years.

Possible effects of global warming include:

- rising sea levels, as the oceans expand at higher temperatures and the ice caps melt. Areas at risk would include the east coast of England, Bangladesh, the Nile delta and the Netherlands
- greater evaporation and increased rainfall, with increased snow to replenish the polar ice caps
- increased plant growth to some areas where higher temperatures and water are available
- tropical and sub-tropical diseases such as malaria, yellow fever and dengue fever spreading north and south
- increasingly changeable weather with storms and storm surges becoming stronger, with greater danger to coastal cities like New York
- low-lying areas such as Florida, the Netherlands and Lincolnshire under threat from rising tides and storms.

No one can be certain that global warming is taking place. The higher temperatures could be another natural climatic variation.

TASKS

1 Use newspapers, the library and the Internet to prepare a table of evidence for and against the existence of global warming.

2 How might governments and local authorities reduce the risks arising from global warming?

KEY SKILLS: *Application of number*

1 A company selling thermometers makes a profit of £752,476. In its annual report the figure is rounded to the nearest £100,000. The rounded figure is:

    a £700,000   **c** £752,000
    b £750,000   **d** £800, 000   (*Level 2*)

2 The annual average temperature of a country has increased by 1.2% when compared with 5 years ago when it was 22°C. What would be the annual average temperature now? (*Level 3*)

Energy

Energy in living things

In an ecosystem, such as a woodland, there are producers, consumers and decomposers. Green plants are producers, using inorganic nutrients and energy from sunlight through photosynthesis. Animals depend on the organic nutrients in plants. Herbivores feed directly and exclusively on plants. Carnivores feed exclusively on other animals. As plants and animals die they are consumed by detrivores (feeders on dead organic material). These food chains show the way in which energy is transferred in the ecosystem.

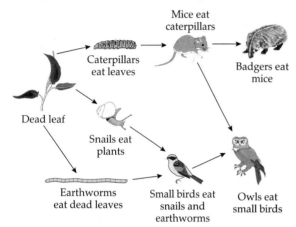

Figure 8   *The food web of a woodland*

To produce energy in the human muscle system the blood supplies glucose, fatty acids and oxygen. In addition, the energy for the use of muscles comes from aerobic respiration to produce adenosine triphosphate (ATP). ATP is a store of chemical energy in cells for use by the body. It is involved in most energy-demanding activities. It is like a store of money the body can spend as energy. ATP acts as the intermediary between energy-requiring actions and energy-yielding activity. ATP is common to all living things and is the source of energy for most biological processes. Muscle fatigue occurs when oxygen, glucose and fatty acids are being consumed faster than they can be supplied. As the ATP is used up lactic acid builds up to cause fatigue and pain.

Energy for living things

The growth in the world's population, and its increasing use of technology, places great demands upon the energy-producing industry. There are two basic types of energy sources:
- renewable
- non-renewable.

Non-renewable sources, which include coal, oil and natural gas, have been the traditional sources of power for industry, transport and domestic users. Concerns about their environmental impact and long-term availability have led to searches for alternatives. At current rates of use, known reserves will last about 50 years for gas, 220 for coal and 30 for oil. If you are under 20 years old you could live in a world without petrol.

Renewable sources include using the power of waves, wind, tides and the sun, hydro-electricity, and biological sources. The technology for many of these is not fully developed and high levels of investment will be needed before these sources make a significant impact. The desirability of building dams for hydroelectric power is being questioned because of their impact on the environment, and the subsequent development of large lakes.

Nuclear power

The production of power from nuclear sources is a contentious issue. There are considerable public misgivings about its development.

Nuclear fission of uranium-235 produces heat which can be used to produce steam to drive turbines that generate electricity.

Advantages and disadvantages in the use of nuclear energy

Advantages	Disadvantages
Treatment of cancer	Disposal of radioactive waste
Sterilization of medical equipment	Environmental disasters following accidents
Carbon-14 dating of archaeological items and sites	Spread of nuclear weapon capability
Nuclear power generation	High set-up costs
Precise measurement	

A glimpse of the future

The escalating demand for energy, particularly with the development of IT, has placed greater demands on power supplies. For example, in California they have experienced blackouts and 'brownouts' (localized, small-scale, temporary blackouts).

Scientists are predicting that fewer large power stations will be built and instead homes will be fitted with their own power generators using heat from the house, natural gas and hydrogen. If that is hard to believe, remember that only a few years ago, many people couldn't have imagined a telephone without a wire.

Transport

Characteristics of different forms of transport

	Types of transport				
	Ships	**Trains**	**Cars and lorries**	**Aircraft**	**Pipelines, e.g. for oil and gas**
Speed	Slow	Fast for distances up to 200 miles	Fast for short distances	Fast for long distances	Very fast
Delays	Few, possibly weather	Regular due to track and signals. Commuter overcrowding	Traffic jams	Weather and airport problems	Very few
Costs	High fuel and harbour costs. Very high initial expenditure. Very low per mile costs	Quite high with track and buildings to maintain but relatively low per mile costs	Relatively low cost for short journeys but increase rapidly with distance. High cost of road building	Very high costs for aircraft and airports but low per mile for passengers	Expensive to build but low costs to run
Alternative routes	Few ports	Mainly to main cities and towns, large areas not served	Very flexible	Not very flexible	Restricted to key routes
Effects on the environment	Some pollution of sea by tankers. Ports occupy large areas for warehousing	Noise and fumes from diesel engines plus visual pollution from overhead lines. Modest use of land	Noise and air pollution. Links to health problems and global warming. Use large amounts of land	High levels of noise pollution. Use large areas of land for airports	Disruption during building but little when buried. Damage may cause major disaster

Road transport

Cars and lorries are very flexible, offering door-to-door convenience. However, their sheer popularity threatens their success. Studies have shown that to meet future demand for road space in cities, much of the urban fabric would have to be demolished. New road building appears to defeat its own object as more vehicles congest the roads. Increased fuel prices, higher vehicle taxes, better public transport and the introduction of charges to use urban roads are all ways to reduce road use. Governments plan to have an integrated transport policy that will reduce car use by single travellers, increase the use of public transport, move freight to the railways, increase the use of bicycles and demand cleaner emissions from road vehicles. The great problem is how to get people out of their cars. Cars are clean, warm, safe and contrast with the perceived delays on trains, dirty stations and inconvenience.

Changes to public transport include bus and taxi lanes, new underground and light railway systems and supertrams.

TASKS

1 A private car costs at least 30p per mile to run. The average motorist covers 12,000 miles per year at a cost of £3600. Despite its expense it remains a widespread ambition to own a car. Suggest reasons for this.

2 Plan a journey from your home to a holiday destination. Use the criteria of cost and environmental effect to assess the impact of your journey on other people.

3 Using the headings given in the table, suggest reasons for the low levels of use, in the UK, of canals, hovercraft and cycles.

KEY SKILLS: *Application of number*

1 *Billions of miles travelled by UK transport (1952–92)*

Year	Car	Train	Bus	Cycle
1952	36.2	24.4	75.5	14.4
1992	365.6	23.8	26.9	3.1

a Which method of transport increased its travel mileage between 1952 and 1992?
A cycle   B bus   C train   D car

b Which method of transport had the most stable figures from 1952 to 1992?
A cycle   B bus   C train   D car

c The estimated approximate increase in car use between 1952 and 1992 is:
A 10 times   B 20 times
C 100 times   D 12 times
(*Level 2*)

2 A minibus with 2 staff and 7 students leaves a Sixth Form centre for an excursion to London. One student is late and misses the minibus by 10 minutes. A friend offers to drive a car and catch the minibus. They set off 30 minutes after the minibus. The car travels on average 10 mph faster than the minibus and catches up in 2 hours. What was the average speed of each vehicle? (*Level 3*)

An interesting number puzzle

An express train leaves London for Glasgow. At the same time a slower train leaves Glasgow for London. If the express train averages 70 mph and the slow train 40 mph, which train will be nearer to London when they pass?

Space exploration

- What do we know about the universe?
- Where did the universe come from?
- Did the universe have a beginning?

Look at the night sky. The brightest objects are likely to be planets such as Venus, Jupiter, Mars and Saturn. The nearest star is Proxima Centauri about 4 light years away (23 million million miles). Our sun is 8 light minutes away. Each month some newspapers print a map of the sky at night. Try having a look one dark, moonless night – if possible, find a place away from streetlights.

Developing ideas about space

Aristotle (340 BC)	Argued that the earth was a round sphere. He based his ideas on the shadow of the earth on the moon during an eclipse and the variable height of the North Star when sailing from north to south. He thought the earth was stationary with the sun, moon, planets and stars moving around it.
Ptolemy (AD 100)	Thought the earth was at the centre of eight spherical orbits (geocentric view). The theory worked well, with one or two adjustments and was adopted by the Christian Church.
Copernicus (AD 1514 and 1543)	Suggested that the sun was stationary, with the earth and moon orbiting around it (heliocentric view). Few believed the idea.
Galileo (AD 1609)	Used the newly invented telescope to support Copernicus.
Kepler (AD 1610)	Worked out that the orbits of the planets were ellipses and not circles and worked out the mathematics of planetary movement.
Newton (AD 1687)	Published *Philosophia Naturalis Principia Mathematica*, including the law of gravity to prove elliptical orbits around the sun.

Our modern picture of the universe dates back to 1924 when the American astronomer Edwin Hubble showed that ours was not the only galaxy. He worked out the distances to nine other galaxies and today we know there are some hundred thousand million galaxies, each of which contains some hundred thousand million stars. Our galaxy is one hundred thousand light years across and is slowly rotating every several hundred million years.

The characteristics of the light from a star allows us to find its temperature, the composition of its atmosphere and whether it is moving towards or away from us. Hubble catalogued many stars and found that the majority are moving away from us. He found the more distant galaxies were moving away faster. Scientists recognized this expanding universe and believe it will continue to grow for at least another ten thousand million years.

Theoretical physicists and astronomers have explained this expanding universe, with galaxies moving away from each other, as the product of a 'big bang' that occurred ten to twenty thousand million years ago. They begin their count of time with the 'big bang'.

Creation and the beginning of time

Debates about the creation of the universe range across a wide spectrum of subjects. They include religious views of the Creation, which are the inspiration for many works of art, and scientific arguments about big bangs and steady-state universes. The topic brings out the connections between these areas, and is truly synoptic.

Scientists now believe it all began with a big bang. They have collected evidence from astronomy and theory, including relativity, to support their ideas. At the big bang moment it is thought that the universe had zero size and was infinitely hot. One second after the big bang the temperature is thought to have fallen to about ten thousand million degrees (about a thousand times the temperature at the centre of our sun). Temperatures as hot as this have been reached in H-bomb explosions. About one hundred seconds after the big bang, temperatures would have fallen to one thousand million degrees.

When the earth was created it was very hot, with no atmosphere. Gases from the rock began an atmosphere and eventually the process of evolution began. Scientists acknowledge there are still unanswered questions about the big bang. One question you might ask is, 'What about before the big bang?' They would reply that that's a singularity and needs no answer.

Space exploration

The early space flights, especially those containing people, gained great public attention. One of the largest television audiences watched the landing on the moon. The problems facing Apollo 13 gripped the attention of the media across the world. Since then the Viking landing on Mars and the Voyager 'flybys' to outer planets have gained less attention. The emphasis in space has switched to the deployment of telecommunications and surveillance satellites in near-earth orbits. The available finance has been used to develop the modest flights of the space shuttle, and unmanned flights to explore outer space have been cut back.

The costs of missions to space are high. For example, the unmanned Voyager mission launched in 1977, and now heading out of the solar system, has cost £1.5 billion so far and the Galileo mission to Jupiter cost over £2 billion.

The future for NASA is smaller, cheaper and better spacecraft with less ambitious payloads. Plans are in hand for probes to Mars, Mercury, Pluto and Venus.

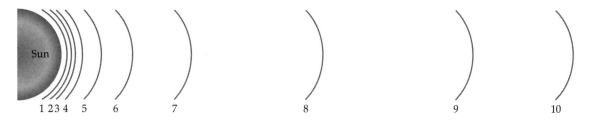

Name	1 Mercury	2 Venus	3 Earth	4 Mars	5 Asteroids	6 Jupiter	7 Saturn	8 Uranus	9 Neptune	10 Pluto	
Mean distance from sun km.	58	108	150	228	—	778	1427	2870	4497	5590	

Figure 9   *The planets in our solar system*

Population dynamics

Populations, be they human or animal, if they are well adapted to their environment, increase their numbers in a similar pattern. They tend to follow an S-shaped curve (see Figure 10).

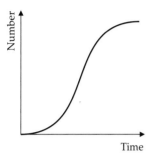

Figure 10 *Population growth*

At first they increase slowly, and then very rapidly (exponentially). After a time, growth slows and numbers become steadier.

Human populations and demographic transition

Changes in the total population in a place can be accounted for by the following equation:

$$\text{population change} = \text{births} - \text{deaths} + \text{in-migrants} - \text{out-migrants}$$

Demographers (scientists studying population change) have noticed that many countries follow the same four stages in the growth of their population. The rate at which they progress through the stages appears to be quickening.

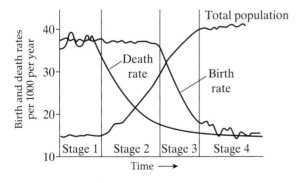

Figure 11 *Demographic transition*

Improvements in medicines (especially antibiotics), central heating and the air-conditioning of buildings, better hygiene and diet have increased life expectancy in many parts of the world. Additionally, birth rates have been high in some areas and especially in many less economically developed countries (LEDCs). During the 1990s, alarming projections for the population of the world were made. However, there are signs that with the education of women and the availability of contraception, birth rates are falling. Many women wish to marry later, follow a career, have more material possessions and recognize the very high costs of a growing family.

However, in some countries, traditional values such as the desire for a son to carry on the family name, the need for farm labour and a lack of knowledge mean that birth rates are still high.

World population, from 1 to 6 billion

Year	Billions	Year	Billions*
1830	1	1974	4
1927	2	1987	5
1960	3	2000	6

*One billion equals one thousand million (10^9)

Optimism or concern for the population of the world

Optimism	Concern
In many economically developed countries the population total is growing slowly and in some it is even falling.	Some countries are encouraging more births to ensure a labour force and consumer market for their economy.
Some less economically developed countries are showing signs of reduced population growth as the education and emancipation of women takes place.	High growth rates are still found in the poorer rural areas of some less economically developed countries.
Technology has increased the supply of food to produce surpluses in some countries.	Lack of funds and ways of distributing food leave famine and high death rates in some areas.
Self-help schemes and alternative growth poles are spreading population throughout countries.	Rural-to-urban migration is still strong in many countries, with shanty towns spreading around city peripheries.

Genetic engineering and biotechnology

Have you ever been greeted by an elderly relative with the words, 'Oh, you do remind me of your father/mother'? Do you sometimes find yourself wondering about the connections between your appearance, opinions and lifestyle and those of your parents? It can be a shock to find your individuality and all that education being overwhelmed by hereditary factors.

A little history

Gregor Mendel (1822–84) experimented with peas to study the way characteristics were passed from generation to generation. He noted the plants' height, flower colour and seed shape. The study of this process is called genetics. Mendel wrote the first four rules of genetics.

1   Organisms get their characteristics from their genes.
2   A pair of genes controls particular characteristics, one from each parent.
3   Genes may be dominant or recessive.
4   Dominant genes decide characteristics over recessive genes.

The genetics of eye colour

What colour are your eyes? Check on the colour of your parents eyes.

Suppose **B** represents the brown-eyed gene and **b** the blue-eyed gene. Each parent has a pair of genes that determine their eye colour.

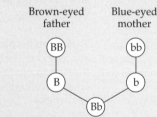

Baby with brown dominating gives brown eyes

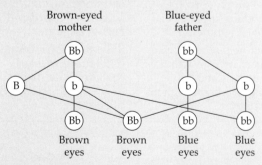

Figure 12 How parents' genes determine the colour of their baby's eyes

James Watson was 72 in 2000. In 1953, working with Francis Crick, he discovered the molecular structure of DNA. Some have called DNA the secret of life and some have described it as the greatest scientific discovery of the twentieth century.

Chromosomes

Everyone inherits some characteristics through the genes they receive from their parents. Every cell in the body contains enough information to make a copy of the person. The information is stored in the nucleus of the cell in long thin strands called chromosomes. Chromosomes are made of DNA (deoxyribonucleic acid).

Humans have 46 chromosomes in each cell, chickens 36 and peas 14. These chromosomes are arranged in pairs with 23 from the father and 23 from the mother. In the last fifteen years ways have been discovered to change the genes in a chromosome. This is called genetic engineering and has been used to produce antibiotics, insulin and growth hormones. When scientists start to replace faulty genes that cause hereditary disease important moral questions are raised.

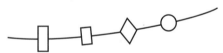

Double helix chain DNA

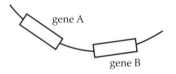

An enlarged section of DNA

An enlarged section of a gene containing four units

Figure 13 Diagram DNA under the microscope

Two examples of biotechnology

The stem cell debate

This is a technique with great potential yet there are objections to it. Stem cells differentiate to become particular cell types such as blood cells or brain cells. Embryonic stem cells are called pluripotent because they can turn into any of the cell types found in animals. In the foetus or adult they are called multipotent because they can produce a more limited set of cells. Stem cells from the embryo have been induced to develop into specialist cells for the liver or brain. Scientists are finding ways to inject heart cells generated in the laboratory into damaged hearts. This type of technology may yield a way of treating Parkinson's disease, cystic fibrosis, diabetes, leukaemia and other diseases of the blood, as well as burns and fractures.

Rejection is a problem that has to be faced in transplant surgery, but it is not thought to be a problem when stem cells from the donor are planted in the same host.

Objectors wonder when life begins. Eggs and sperm are alive and are destroyed by nature. Now scientists will be able to determine which eggs and cells survive and grow. Traditionalists see life as a gift from God to be treated with reverence.

Designer babies

A number of recent developments in genetic technology have allowed scientists to influence the characteristics of babies while they are still in the womb. The following examples show just how difficult the decisions that arise can be.

- A couple has a young son whose life can be saved if a matching donor from the family can be found to donate bone marrow. All 20 members of the family are tested and no matches are found. Doctors tell the parents that if they had another child it might have bone marrow that matches. However, they also tell the parents that this new child has a one in four chance of having the same disease as the first child. The mother decides to take the risk, knowing that she can have an abortion if tests show the new child has the disease.

- A couple has four sons and a young daughter. Suddenly the daughter is killed in a car accident. The couple asks doctors if they can have a child in conditions where the scientists can select the sperm to ensure the unborn child is female.

- Scientists have perfected a technique to check for abnormalities in the foetus. The technique is also able to check the level of intelligence of the unborn child.

Health and fitness

Mens sana in corpore sano – a healthy mind in a healthy body.

Start out positively. This page is about 'health and fitness' when so many are about health and disease. The World Health Organization (WHO) defines health as 'a state of complete physical, mental and social well being, and not merely the absence of disease and infirmity.'

Ways to health and fitness

(Be sure you start with a healthy body and take note of any medical conditions.)

- Exercise the body and push it to its safe limits from time to time, this could add ten years to your life.
- Avoid getting unfit, it's harder to get back to fitness.
- Jogging may help with weight and heart problems but use good running shoes to protect your knees and ankles.
- Avoid TV watching unless the programme has been chosen deliberately.
- Join a local gym/fitness centre and get a personalized programme from the expert there.
- Eat and drink wisely, avoiding too much junk food and beer. Drink 2 litres of water per day and stop smoking.
- Eat small healthy meals every 3 or 4 hours.
- Avoid weight reduction pills.
- Cycle to work, school or the shops whenever it's feasible.

How to survive AS level studying

1. Use a rucksack to carry study materials and not a shoulder bag.
2. Sit with your bottom higher than your knees.
3. Ditch the diet unless it is recommended on medical grounds.
4. Take twenty minutes exercise at least three times per week (every day if possible) – brisk walking will do.
5. Try to get seven or eight hours' sleep every night. Wind down before you sleep, switch off the TV, video and computer in your bedroom 30 minutes before sleep.
6. Study in short bursts (30 minutes maximum) and set a target for each burst.
7. Avoid direct sunlight unless you are protected by sun-cream.
8. Avoid being recruited as a smoker – it's bad for your health as well as mine.

Health, fitness and weight

Fashion currently indicates that we should all lose weight. There is always someone who has lost lots of weight very quickly. Beware, as they have probably done one of four things: eaten a drastic diet, taken diet pills, used diuretics or eaten almost no food. None of these are safe or reliable ways to long-term weight loss.

Fitness can be estimated by how quickly your heart rate recovers to normal after exercise. If H is a measure of fitness then

$$H = \frac{P_0 - P_6}{P_0 - P_R}$$

where P_R is the pulse rate after 10 minutes' rest, P_0 the rate after four minutes' of strenuous exercise and P_6 the rate again after 6 minutes' rest following the exercise.

Values near to 1 indicate fitness, with higher values indicating decreasing fitness.

Health, fitness, drugs and sport

In 1993, a group of Chinese athletes won major athletics races and claimed new world records. Their coach, Ma Junren, claimed they had taken turtle blood and caterpillar fungus. However, in 2000, in Sydney, the athletes coached by Junren were banned from the Games when they tested positive for banned substances.

Drugs in sport

Anabolic steroids

These are synthetic substances related to testosterone, the male sex hormone. These drugs have their medical uses, including treating delayed puberty and impotence. Using these drugs, women develop more masculine characteristics such as a deepened voice and body hair.

Anabolic steroids were used in sport until the 1970s when effective tests were introduced. Ben Johnson lost his Olympic 100 metres' gold medal when he tested positive, and recently nandrolone, a steroid, has been detected in some élite athletes.

Erythropoietin (EPO)

This drug dramatically increases performance in stamina events such as cycling, distance running and rowing. The drug is produced naturally in the body but has been manufactured since 1987 to treat kidney disease. EPO stimulates the production of red cells to transport oxygen around the body. EPO can be fatal if it thickens the blood too quickly and there are reports of the death of 20 cyclists because of this drug. Testing was introduced for the 2000 Sydney Olympics.

HGH (Human Growth Hormone)

Costing £1500 for an eight-week cycle, this muscle-building drug has been popular with sprinters and swimmers. It is a naturally occurring substance, currently undetectable through tests. However, a detection test is expected soon.

Oxyglobin

This is the latest drug to outwit the testers. It is an energy-boosting protein, used to treat kidney problems in cows. Rumours suggest that cyclists and distance runners are using it but, at the time of writing, it is not on the list of banned drugs. Its side effects are not known.

Health and fitness.

KEY SKILLS: *Application of number*

A recent study of the fitness of young people in Japan concluded that youths are spending too much time playing video games. The average 19-year-old male student now takes 6 minutes and 38 seconds to run 1500 metres, which is 34 seconds slower than in 1979.

1 How long did the average 19 year old take in 1979?

2 By how much has their average speed (in kph) decreased since 1979?

3 By how many metres would the average male student in 1979 beat the average male student today?
(*Level 3*)

Organ transplantation

Some of the issues

It is possible to transplant about 25 different organs and tissues including bone and cartilage, bone marrow, cornea, heart, lung, heart-lung, kidney, liver, pancreas. Acceptable donors can range in age from newborn to senior citizens. Ideal donors are people who have just died, maybe in an accident, who were in good health, and have been declared brain dead. In such cases the brain has ceased to function but the heart and lungs continue with the use of life support machinery.

Kidney transplants are quite successful if there is a good match. This saves the patient many hours per week on a dialysis machine. The main problem is rejection by the host's body. This used to be reduced using drugs that suppressed the body's immune system but left the patient very open to infection.

How do we increase the supply of organs for needy patients who are in the queue?

An Internet discussion

JT, 15 Aug: I do not believe medics should just be able to take organs from dead people without consent. However I work in a kidney dialysis unit and see the suffering of people and their families waiting for an organ for transplantation. I have told my family that all my organs are available after death. Let's educate people to give organs freely.

CP, 16 Aug: I think that after death usable organs should be harvested unless the family objects on religious or moral grounds. Education could go a long way to increase the number of donors.

JH, 17 Aug: Suppose we had a 'presumed consent' law so that people who did not want to donate would have to opt out.

SC, 17 Aug: Is it right that people with money can jump the queue. I hear there are people in the Third World selling live organs to richer countries. I know we can spare a kidney but is this right?

DC, 19 Aug: I believe we should have legalized organ harvesting at death. With more organs donated we increase the chances of a speedy match. But who gets the organ first?

EH, 19 Aug: No, I do not believe we should allow that to happen. There should be no competition for organs. Suppose I am dying and I put out for offers on my organs. It would benefit my heirs. That is my right. It might be good to sell them and have a last fling. I might be in a fix if I didn't then die.

CH, 19 Aug: I work in health care and think it great if we could give someone else the gift of life. Selling organs takes away the gift of love for another human being.

PT, 20 Aug: I like the idea of carrying a donor card and if you do not have the card they take what organs they need.

CH, 20 Aug: Forcing people is not going to work. You could have millions of families objecting. Suppose it was a new baby that had died.

NV, 21 Aug: I feel we should have a register so people can make their wishes clear.

The cases for and against organ transplantation

For transplantation	Against transplantation
No risk for dead patients	Defining death: brain dead?
Benefit to recipient	Some risk for live donors.
Recipient benefits society by being healthy	Against Hippocratic Oath of doctors: *primum non nocere* (first do no harm).
Last chance solution	May be against religious beliefs on mutilation.
Donor contributes to society	Problem of donation by minor or incompetents.
Donor and family may gain income	Difficulties over consent.
Aids medical advance in other fields	Selling of parts of their body by poor people.
	What is 'free consent'?
	Draws resources from the rest of the health service.

TASKS

1 In two paragraphs summarize the cases for and against organ transplantation.

2 In what circumstances should a family refuse to allow the organs of a dead relative to be removed?

KEY SKILLS: *Application of number*

In the USA, eight people die each day while on the waiting list for a transplant. A new name is added to the list every 16 minutes. At what annual rate do organs need to be donated to hold the list to its current length? (*Level 3*)

Conservation

In the past, human activity has caused environmental damage. There is a need for positive action to reduce and even reverse the damage being caused. Ecological studies show us how the damage is caused and conservation is action to restore and maintain the environment. Conservation is active; it is more than preservation.

Strategies for environmental conservation

Natural habitats, untouched by humans, no longer exist on the earth, so all habitats are semi-natural. Conservation is aimed at preserving and maintaining these semi-natural habitats. Currently there are three strategies being used:

1 **Protection of areas and sites**. In the UK these include:
   - National Parks
   - Areas of Outstanding Natural Beauty (AONB)
   - National Nature Reserves
   - Sites of Special Scientific Interest (SSSI)
   - Environmentally Sensitive Areas (ESA)
   - Special Areas of Conservation
   - National Trust (NT)
   - Royal Society for the Protection of Birds (RSPB)
   - County Wildlife Trusts.

2 **Sustainable use of resources**. These include:
   - limiting commercial fishing
   - managing use of forests for farmed timber.

3 **Conservation of endangered species**. These include:
   - genetic conservation
   - International Union for Conservation
   - Red Data Books
   - Convention on International Trade in Endangered Species (CITES)
   - use of botanical gardens
   - breeding programmes in zoological gardens.

Case Studies of Conservation Strategy

1 National Parks

National Parks were created in England and Wales in 1949 to preserve the landscape of some of the most beautiful parts of the country. It was intended that farming would continue alongside increasing use by people for recreation. There are ten National Parks plus the Norfolk Broads, which has equal status.

The New Forest in Hampshire is about to become the eleventh National Park. The parks are a success and receive large numbers of visitors throughout the year. The most popular sites, called 'honeypots', are under great pressure. Demand can be so high that there are queues and traffic congestion. The more popular footpaths are becoming heavily eroded and appear as scars on the hill and mountainsides. Litter is a problem as well as the trampling of vegetation. Within the National Parks in England and Wales some economic activity continues. Quarrying, especially for limestone for the manufacture of cement, takes place and employs many local people, but it creates noise, dust, heavy lorry traffic, and spoil heaps.

Yellowstone, in the USA, set up in 1872, was the world's first National Park. The area was established because it contained hot springs, geysers, lava flows, rugged scenery and canyons. It was also rich in wildlife, including bears, elk and buffalo. The area has to be carefully managed, with well-made roads and hotels, to meet the demand from visitors. Other famous National Parks in the USA include Yosemite, Grand Canyon, Zion, Bryce and Rocky Mountain. Arguments about their management focus on such issues as the type of landscape to be conserved. Some people believe that the areas should be allowed to return to wilderness, whilst others see the areas as places of recreation.

National Parks have also been established in some less economically developed countries (LEDCs), such as Kenya. They are provided to protect wildlife and land as well as encouraging the development of tourism.

2 Managed use of resources

This requires commercial users to take a long-term view of resources. For example, some countries have very large areas of natural or planted forests. These forests employ many people and provide much-needed income. This can be the key to the development of a country and the improvement in the quality of life of people living there.

The conservation strategy for these areas recognizes that mature trees can be removed but that surrounding trees should not be damaged. Where necessary, new sapling trees can be planted. Whilst this conservation farming of timber does take place in the UK, it is less successfully managed in some of the tropical rainforest areas.

3 Conservation of endangered species

In 1900 there were 100,000 tigers in India. Today it is estimated that between 2000 and 3000 remain. Such is the attraction of the Indian tiger that several Indian game reserves advertise that they have tigers, and tourists come to take photographs. In fact they have no tigers in the reserve. On current trends there will be no tigers in the wild by 2010. The main problem is that some parts of the tiger are believed to cure disease. This belief is especially strong in Japan. Governments are taking joint action to protect the Indian tiger. The Japanese government has passed laws banning trade in tiger products. China has the death penalty for tiger poachers and the United Nations is paying the Indian government to protect its endangered tigers.

TASKS

1 'Are National Parks museums, sanctuaries or playgrounds?' Discuss this question using experience from the UK, USA and an LEDC.

2 Are you in favour of the keeping of 'wild animals in zoos?' What are the arguments for and against this practice? What criteria would you use to assess the design of a zoo?

3 Find an example of a local conservation project and assess its success.

4 Find an example of a site in need of conservation. Make a case for the allocation of funding. Draw up a plan for its conservation.

5 What are the arguments for conservation when there are so many other priorities in health and education?

KEY SKILLS: *Application of number*

The table shows the ages of buildings in a recent conservation study.

Age	Number of buildings
pre 1400	1
1400–1599	7
1500–1699	10
1700–1899	8
1900–	4

1 How many buildings were more than 300 years old?

   A 8   B 18   C 26   D 28

2 What percentage of the buildings was less than 300 years old?

   A 30%   B 40%   C 50%   D 60%

   (*Level 2*)

Environmental pollution

There are several different types of pollution including air, water, noise and visual pollution. This page looks at air pollution in some detail.

Sources of air pollution

Carbon dioxide   Burning fossil fuels in power stations, industry and transport. Burning rainforests.

Methane   Decaying vegetation, farming (animal dung and rice growing), sewage disposal and landfill sites.

Nitrous oxide   Vehicle exhausts, fertilizer, nylon manufacture and power stations.

CFCs   Refrigerators, aerosol sprays, solvents and foams.

Effects of air pollution

1 Damaging the ozone layer

About 25–30 km above the earth, in the area of the atmosphere called the stratosphere, the concentration of the gas ozone increases. Ozone is a form of oxygen that contains three atoms of oxygen combined together (O_3). The ozone is formed by the action of the sun's ultra-violet (UV) radiation on oxygen (O_2). The ozone layer protects the earth from UV radiation from the sun. UV radiation reaching the earth causes harm to living things and the maintenance of the ozone layer is important to the survival of life. Scientists monitoring this gas have noted that, over Antarctica, its concentration has fallen to about two-thirds of its 1970 level. Similar reductions are now being noted over the Arctic. These reductions allow greater concentrations of UV radiation to reach the earth and have been linked to an increase in skin cancer, damage to the skin's immune system and cataracts in the eyes. For example, it can cause pre-existing moles on the skin to change into malignant melanoma.

The reduction in concentration of ozone has been referred to as the 'hole in the ozone layer' and has been linked to the release of CFCs (chlorofluorocarbons) into the atmosphere from aerosol sprays, refrigerator coolant and the manufacture of foam packaging. The CFCs move slowly into the atmosphere and breakdown to release chlorine. The chlorine breaks down the ozone molecules. This process can take five years and was happening for a long time before scientists realized the damage. The EU is enforcing its ban on the use of CFCs in member countries. The use of UV filter sun-creams is recommended by doctors for visitors from the UK, particularly to countries such as Chile, New Zealand and Australia.

2 Increased incidence of asthma

Car exhausts generate ozone close to the earth's surface. This causes damage to plants and affects the breathing of humans and animals. When the weather is hot and still, during summer, health warnings may be broadcast, especially in cities, when air quality deteriorates because of traffic fumes. People suffering from asthma are badly affected by this pollution.

3 Poor air quality in urban areas

There can be up to seven times more dust particles in cities than rural areas. Much of this air pollution comes from the burning of fossil fuels and car exhausts. The gases forming part of this pollution include sulphur dioxide, nitrogen oxide, hydrocarbons and carbon dioxide. This pollution can cause urban areas to have more cloud, higher temperatures and less sunshine. If you take a tile and smear it with light grease and put it outside for a few days you may find clear evidence of air pollution. The collars on shirts and blouses also show the pollution in the air.

Los Angeles has the worst air pollution of any city in a more economically developed country (MEDC). The city is very spread out and people travel long distances in their 25 million vehicles to get to work and to reach shops and other services. Los Angeles has tough laws against emissions from vehicles but because the number of miles travelled per day continues to rise the pollution problem remains. The sunny weather adds to the problem as photochemical fog is produced. On over 100 days per year pollution levels are above the standard set for safe health. This pollution costs lives and many billions of dollars in health care.

Pollution levels are falling in many MEDCs due to the introduction of lead-free petrol, the closure of old factories and the use of cleaner power plants. In cities in LEDCs, air pollution is worse, with conditions in Mexico City particularly poor.

4 Damage caused by acid rain

In recent years pollutants – mainly from coal-fired power stations, heavy industry and vehicle exhausts – have been detected in rainfall. The two main chemicals found are sulphur dioxide (SO_2) and nitrogen oxides (NO_2 and NO). When mixed with rainwater they form sulphurous or sulphuric and nitric acid. The rain becomes more acidic and may fall locally or the pollutants may be carried across international boundaries before mixing with rain water.

Acid rain can cause damage to soil, plants and fish life. It has been linked to the damage of forests in Scandinavia and Germany. There are also suggestions that Alzheimer's disease, bronchitis and lung cancer may also be produced by acid rain. Some famous buildings, including St Paul's Cathedral, the Acropolis and the Taj Mahal, have also been damaged by acid rain.

Because of the damage caused, the emissions from power stations are now 'scrubbed' and catalytic converters fitted to cars. The use of diesel fuel, which is low in sulphur, also helps.

Reduction of air pollution

Policies to reduce air pollution include:

- introduction of lead-free petrol
- use of catalytic converters on cars
- use of electric powered vehicles
- reduced emissions from vehicles
- redesign of engines
- random roadside checks
- annual vehicle inspection
- improvements in fuel
- replacing old cars and buses
- petrol/electric engines
- increased use of public transport
- fewer new, out-of-town centres
- zero emission vehicles
- reduced on-street parking
- introduction of safe cycle tracks
- bus and tram priority lanes
- improved suburban rail services
- co-ordinated transport planning
- introducing alternate drive days
- relocation of industry

TASKS

1 Carry out a survey of at least 25 people asking them to describe examples of pollution in their daily lives. Classify their responses into air, land, water and others. What actions do you recommend to reduce this pollution?

2 What actions have been taken by car manufacturers and the fuel industry to reduce pollution caused by the products they sell?

3 Make a list of the items in a household that are likely to be discarded and are not biodegradable.

2 Understanding of scientific methods, principles, criteria and their applications

Euclid was asked, 'Is there an easy way to understand geometry?' He replied, 'There is no royal road to geometry.'

Definitions

Experiment
An examination of conditions, usually to test the effects of change in one of the variables. Experiments are used to test theories.

Hypothesis
A tentative explanation of facts. Observations which can be tested by an experiment.

Prediction or forecasting
Future conditions or events may be predicted based upon laws.

Scientific law
A description of a regularity in nature, observed many times with no exceptions found.

Theory
An explanation of a pattern or relationship, by experiments or other observations, with no exceptions found. Laws are built from theories.

Getting started

1 'If you are an optimist you will be willing to "try" more than if you are a pessimist. Optimists do not have the fatigue of self-doubt' (Hoffman).
2 Scientists are human, so can they be objective?
3 Do scientists have imagination or are they just very systematic?
4 Can science explain everything?

Induction and classification

1 Do 'Wait' buttons help to change the traffic lights sooner?
2 Why did Archimedes shout 'Eureka!'?
3 Why is it helpful to group things in a classification?

Hypothesis testing and deduction, theory and law

1 Changing scientific theory.
Ptolemy believed that the earth was at the centre of our system of planets. This became the view of the Renaissance Church. However, Copernicus developed a theory that the sun is at the centre of our solar system. Galileo used his new telescope to collect data on the movement of stars. He published his results, which showed that the view of Ptolemy and the Church was not in agreement with the observations. So strong was the reaction of the Church that Galileo had to recant his conclusions, or face execution.
2 How can shadows from sticks help prove the earth is not flat?
3 How could you generate proof that homeopathic medicine works?
4 How do you feel about the quote: 'In my group, I would prefer an idea not to be thought of than I not be the one who thinks it'?

Modelling, forecasting and reliability

1 How many different types of model can you name?
2 Why is forecasting so difficult in some areas and not in others?
3 Why are some events more reliably forecast than others?

Experimental design and time scales

1 'A novel is a static thing that one moves through, a play is a dynamic thing that moves past one' (Tynan). Using these ideas how would you describe a scientific textbook or a scientific experiment?
2 What happened in the 'first three minutes' and the '100 days of white-hot technology'?
3 Is the past a different country where they did things differently?

Outline

This section introduces some of the methods used by scientists to increase their understanding. It describes the principles with which they work, the criteria they use for proceeding and gives examples of their application. Hindsight is a wonderful thing and when scientists explore the unknown they do not proceed with as much order as some biographies suggest. They use guesses and half ideas as they struggle to unlock a problem.

Induction and classification

Induction

A scientist may collect a mass of data from observation and measurement. As the information is tabulated, graphs and charts drawn, and statistics calculated, the scientist begins to note a pattern or relationship. As more observations are made at different places or times, the scientist looks again to see if the pattern or relationship is present. As cases continue, so the scientist begins to develop a theory. Further observations may support the theory and the scientist prepares a law, though the inductive scientist may never be certain. If observations do not fit the theory some revision of it may be necessary or the theory may even have to be abandoned.

This process of building theory from observations is called **induction.**

Classification

An important part of the inductive method is the classification stage. As a large number of observations are made – for example, fossils, plants, birds or insects – it becomes helpful to divide them into groups. This is called classification and gives the mass of information some sense of order. The main features of a good classification are:

a maximum similarity within group
b maximum difference between groups
c observed members for all groups and few groups with only one member
d only use relevant measures
e there should be no duplication with members in only one group or class.

However, no classification is likely to be perfect.

Devising a classification is not easy. If the information to be classified is numerical, it can be split into classes using quantitative methods. A dispersion graph is one way in which information measured using one or two variables can be divided into groups. This method can be extended in research to include more variables using Pythagoras' theorem. When the data is not numerical the classification becomes more subjective. Classifications can be used to distort the message in information through the careful selection of class boundaries.

TASKS

1 Suppose you were going to classify shops, here are some of the problems you would face:
   a How have you defined a shop? Does the definition include garages, bookmakers, banks? What would be the other marginal shops?
   b Would you classify shops selling uncooked food, fast-food outlets and restaurants in the same group?
   c How would you classify empty shops?

2 Here is a list of shops. Begin to build a classification using four or five groups/classes. Give each group/class a name.

Greengrocer	Hardware
Antique shop	Cleaner
Jeweller	Photographic materials
Women's shoes	TV and radio
Women's clothes	Men's clothes
Bank	Travel agent
Building society	Estate agent
Public house	Gift shop
Butcher	Book shop
Baker	Fish and chips shop

Hypothesis testing and deduction, theory and law

Hypothesis testing is a popular method for conducting a scientific investigation. During hypothesis testing the investigator follows a series of stages. These are shown in the hypothesis testing model (Figure 14).

Stages of hypothesis testing

1 Formulating a hypothesis

The dictionary describes a hypothesis as an idea that is suggested as a possible explanation for a particular situation or condition, but which has not yet been proved to be correct. So a hypothesis is more than speculation. It is the expression of an idea with possible variables that account for the situation or condition.

2 Planning the investigation

2.1 Set up clear definitions of the terms used.
2.2 Read literature about the topic, including textbooks, articles and the Internet. Make notes and keep good references.
2.3 Note the time and resources available (the inexperienced tend to underestimate).
2.4 Design the experimental procedures, keeping in mind health and safety.
2.5 Consider whether the work has any ethical implications, for example, for living organisms or the environment.

3 Keeping records

3.1 Organize the way the investigation is to take place, including the size and method of collection of sample materials.
3.2 Design your recording sheets.
3.3 Carry out a pilot study and reconsider plans.
3.4 Keep records of results and a diary of activity (the diary is a chore but it will be essential).

4 Analysis of results

4.1 Tabulate results very clearly.
4.2 Inspect the tables for possible explanations.
4.3 Data entry and processing on the computer may come here.
4.4 Check on the significance of any statistics calculated.
4.5 Draw any necessary graphs, maps and charts, but only use them if they show new information beyond the tabulation.
4.6 Ensure all tables and visuals are clearly labelled.
4.7 Propose tentative conclusions.

5 Draw conclusions

5.1 Write down tentative conclusions.
5.2 Check the conclusions are supported by the evidence.
5.3 Refine and finalize conclusions.

6 Writing up

This section can be a real challenge. Do not let the investigation go cold on you. Insert title, abstract or synopsis. The main chapters will be:

6.1 Introduction, aims, definitions, scope and literature review.
6.2 Description of the project activity.
6.3 Commentary on the findings.
6.4 Presentation of tables, charts and so on, and results.
6.5 Conclusions.
6.6 Evaluation of the investigation including its reliability, potential sources of error, success of the techniques used, recognition of limitations.
6.7 Suggestions for changes and ideas for further work.
6.8 Bibliography and acknowledgements.
6.9 Appendices if really needed.

The hypothesis testing model

The model works well for investigations in sciences such as physics, chemistry, biology and physical geography. For investigations where behaviour is involved the model has to be modified. Sometimes this is done through the formation of a control group of people or through tests where the participants are not aware of the purpose of the study. For example, in the testing of a new medical treatment one group make be given a placebo (a harmless inactive treatment) alongside other patients with the same illness receiving the new treatment. This helps to eliminate psychological effects of patients believing they are receiving a better cure.

In an investigation of values and attitudes individuals may be given pairs of words so that they can select ones to meet their views.

These types of investigation, where the data collected is less certain than that in the physical sciences, tend to have more tentative conclusions.

A key influence to eliminate in any investigation is your own set of attitudes and values. Inevitably you ask yourself 'What do I think?' 'What reasons can I give for my observations?' Be careful to ensure that your conclusions are based upon the evidence. Concluding that there is no definitive conclusion is better than a biased or wrong one.

Models 'of' and models 'for'.

Scientific enquiry does not always follow the neat stages of Figure 14. Sometimes data has been collected before a hypothesis emerges. At other times theory produces a solution that awaits experimental proof for many years. So the diagram should be seen as a 'model for' checking on the steps in an investigation rather than an exact match of a route to follow.

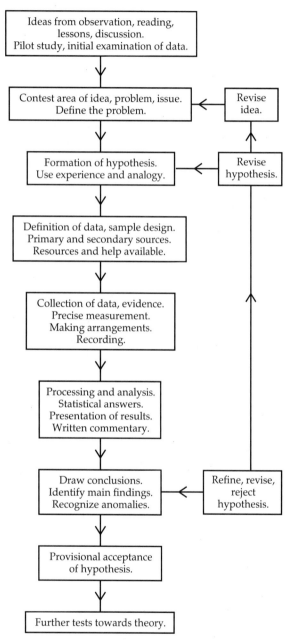

Figure 14 *Hypothesis testing model*

Theory and law

A theory is a set of ideas that are intended to explain something. It is based upon evidence and reasoning, but has not been completely proved. As more evidence confirms a theory, it becomes a law. A law is a set of rules by which a system is seen to work.

Caution

In 1874, John Stuart Mill, in his important book *Systems of Logic* placed great emphasis on the 'method of residues' when he wrote of the 'insufficiency of the obvious causes to account for the whole effect'. This cautions us not to claim too much for our investigations.

A key test asks whether the conclusions would be the same if repeated by the same researcher on another occasion or by a series of other researchers. That is why it is so important to specify carefully what took place.

Modelling, forecasting and reliability

Imagine standing above a crowded beach. Through the day people arrive. The weather is good and the beach becomes busy. Not all parts of the beach are crowded and groups of people use different parts for activities that do not mix. The shallower sea areas are for families with young children, whilst the area with high breakers is for surfers. As you come to know the beach you recognize patterns. Certain times of the day, types of weather and seasons influence the pattern. You become able to forecast, approximately, the level and pattern of use of the beach. A key role for scientists is to understand events, like the day at the beach, and then to forecast, with some reliability, what will happen.

The real world is more complex and to understand events scientists simplify. They take away factors that have less relevance. This is called building a model. The model is a simple version of reality or an idealized version of what they wish reality to be. A map is a model where traffic and weather have been removed. Once the scientist has a successful model they are able to use it to make forecasts. Here are three models that are linked to forecasting.

Weather forecasting

Before satellite images allowed us to see the weather coming towards us, scientists used to make detailed recordings of weather. Ships in the Atlantic added to this data. Meteorologists then drew maps to show the pattern of weather. As sequences of these maps were drawn, patterns emerged identifying waves of warmer, wetter air moving towards the British Isles. They called the front line of this air a warm front and the cooler air behind a cold front. These could be drawn on the map and the sequence of weather noted. When the pattern repeated the forecasters had an idea how the weather would change (Figure 15) though these forecasts are not totally reliable.

Earthquakes and plate tectonics

There are about 500 active volcanoes. They occur in lines across the globe and earthquakes follow a very similar pattern. In trying to forecast earthquakes, scientists monitor any tremors of the earth. Scientists are not able to forecast an earthquake – this is one case where they are still working to refine the model.

Diffusion, contagion, succession

When new land is exposed, it is colonized. This is called an ecological succession. On dry land pioneer plants such as surface algae, lichens and mosses are followed by small, rooted plants, then grasses, small shrubs, trees and finally woodland. This colonization has temporal and spatial components. Scientists note the stages in this colonization by identifying and mapping the plants.

Social scientists note similar patterns when people adopt an innovation. The spread of infectious disease has also attracted research. In some LEDCs studies have included the arrival of family planning, and the spread of AIDS.

In building models, scientists note the characteristics of adopters of innovations, barriers to adoption and chance events.

Recent studies show the spread of the computer taking a decade but the adoption of the mobile phone being very fast.

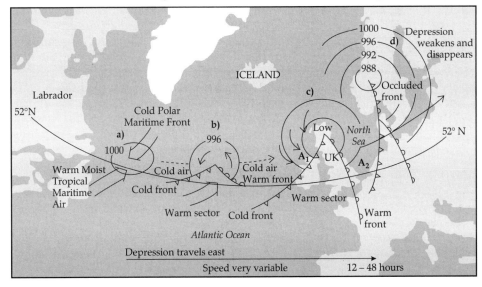

Figure 15

A depression across the Atlantic

Experimental design and the role of time scales

Scientific researchers approach investigations in a variety of ways. They design experiments to suit their purpose with as much accuracy as possible given the resources and state of knowledge. They include precise notes and records of results, which can be checked by others. Here are four examples of the different approaches. Note the alternative designs and the way time scale figures in each.

1 Investigating in the laboratory

In an electrical circuit, an ammeter (A) measures the current (I) in amps. A battery drives current around the circuit that includes a fixed resistance (R) and a voltmeter (V). When the switch (S) is closed, voltage and current can be measured (see Figure 16). The voltage from the battery can be varied. You have been asked to find any link between V and I if R is constant.

In the laboratory you build the circuit, check the voltmeter and ammeter are reading correctly and then vary the voltage. You have two different resistors (measured in ohms) to use. Here are your results.

R = 6 ohms

A	0.1	0.2	0.3	0.4	0.5
V	0.6	1.2	1.8	2.4	3.0

R = 8 ohms

A	0.1	0.2	0.3	0.4	0.5
V	0.8	1.6	2.4	3.2	3.8

Note how you have one anomalous result which will need to be checked.

In fact the relationship you find is $V = I \times R$, which is called Ohm's Law.

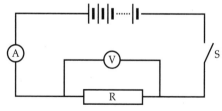

Figure 16 *Investigating the relationship between voltage, current and resistance*

2 Investigating people's thinking

A group of psychologists investigated how people solve problems. To do this they used the 'Missionaries and Cannibals' problem and the 'Jealous Husbands' problem.

Three missionaries and three cannibals want to cross a river. Their boat only carries two people. They can all navigate. If the number of cannibals exceeds the missionaries on either bank the missionary will be eaten. How can they all cross safely?

The Jealous Husbands problem involves three husbands and their wives crossing the river. This time no husband is to be left alone with another man's wife.

Six groups of people were asked to solve the problems. Group 1 was given the Missionaries problem, and a little time later the same problem again. Group 2 had Missionaries followed by Jealous Husbands. Group 3 had Jealous Husbands followed by Jealous Husbands again, and Group 4 Jealous Husbands then Missionaries. Group 5 had Missionaries then Jealous Husbands, but with a hint that they were the same problem. Group 6 had Jealous Husbands then Missionaries with the same hint. Groups 1, 3, 5 and 6 improved on the second task.

Note how the repeat of the same problem or the hint of similarity improved performance. Note also the experimental design used to gain some insight into problem solving.

3 Investigating behaviour and attitudes

Social scientists look at circumstances where people's behaviour is being investigated. A problem is that the presence of the investigator, as observer or questioner, may change behaviour. Questionnaires are a very popular way of collecting information. The questionnaire collects information about age, gender, marital status, occupation, car ownership and so on, and cross-tabulates these with aspects of behaviour such as purchasing habits, voting behaviour and attitudes to controversial issues. The semantic differential is a useful tool for this research. In this approach people have to select one of a pair of words, for example, beautiful/ugly or agree/disagree with a sentence. If words and sentences are selected carefully the respondent can be asked the same point twice to see if they have a secure position.

4 Investigating in the field

This investigation is of changes in temperature down a 500-metre slope with a height difference of 300 metres. Start by noting the location of the slope on a map, its aspect and vegetation cover. A visit will be needed to plan your observations. You need to decide how many and what type of thermometers you need. One design would be to follow two lines (called transects) down the slope. You have to decide the time or times of day for recording and the duration of your study. Access, health, safety and security need checking. Undertake a pilot survey to check all procedures.

Keep careful field notes and prepare for wet weather. Your results can be tabulated, graphed and conclusions drawn. Always include notes of any reservations you have or concerns about readings at any of the stations.

Some unsettling thoughts about time

Experiments in the laboratory and field rely on accurate measurements that frequently include a time element. You may feel a little insecure by the news of the following experiment.

In 1962 a pair of very accurate clocks was fixed at the top and bottom of a water tower. The clock at the bottom was found to run slower. This can be explained, though not here, using the theory of relativity. The findings become very important now that satellites are used for navigational purposes.

This variation in time becomes fascinating if you consider two people one of whom goes to live at the top of a mountain (or, even more extreme, in a spaceship). For the person going to the top of the mountain the clocks would run faster, they would be ageing faster. What a paradox!

KEY SKILLS: *Application of number*

1 Plan an experiment using one of the example designs above.
- Plan your approach to obtaining and using information. You should include a data set of at least 50 items.
- Choose appropriate methods for obtaining the results.
- Justify your choice of methods.
- Carry out calculations using your data set.

- Look for and use a formula to develop your experiment.
- Select and justify a way of presenting your methods and explaining the results of your calculations.

The key point is to plan and carry through your experiment.
(*Level 3*)

③ Mathematical reasoning and its application

Some people reading this will know they find numbers and arithmetic a puzzling chore. This page attempts to bring some interest to them and to those who find the beauty of numbers as intoxicating as poetry and Shakespeare.

'Mathematics is the most original creation of the human spirit' (A. N. Whitehead)

'A mathematician is a machine turning coffee into theorems' (Erdos)

© Nick Newman/*Times* Newspapers Limited, 8 September 2000

Getting started

1 How good at maths are you? Why is maths so unpopular? When people argue against mathematics check their own best subject.

2 Can you solve two simultaneous equations in algebra such as

$x + y = 5$
$3x + 4y = 25$

even if you have no idea why you should?

3 Have you reflected upon the teaching of mathematics you have received? Are the mathematics teachers any different from those in other subjects? Are the methods they use any different from those in English and media?

4 Why is it so important to the economy, universities and the future, for young people to have good mathematics teachers?

5 Why not train as a mathematics teacher? There are plenty of jobs and career promotion prospects are excellent.

6 Why not be a mathematician? Unlike other scientists they need no laboratory equipment.

7 Is mathematics created or discovered? Are the truths there but we do not know them? 'Mathematics is there. It's beautiful. It's the jewel we uncover. Mathematics is the search for lasting beauty and ultimate truth' (Hoffman).

Layout of data sets

1 What is a singularity? Mathematicians find it very difficult to deal with infinite numbers, so the point where theory breaks down, because of these infinite numbers, is called a singularity.

2 What is the difference between quantitative and qualitative data?

3 Can you use a spreadsheet such as Microsoft Excel?

4 Check your data. Remember the old saying 'Garbage in, garbage out'.

Amounts and sizes

1 Have you noticed how a pack of cards fits with the calendar? Jostein Gaarder did in his book *The Solitaire Mystery*. There are 52 cards in a pack, one for each week of the year. Each week has 7 days, so $7 \times 52 = 364$ days, with one day left over called 'Joker' day. The year is divided into four seasons, one for each suit of cards: spades, clubs, hearts and diamonds. Each suit has 13 cards, one for each week of the year. So Joker day is only played one year in four.

2 Why do we think 7 is lucky and 13 unlucky? (It may be something to do with the cycle of the moon.) Why is James Bond 007?

3 Why does a cricket umpire stand on one leg when the score reaches 111 and mutter 'Nelson'?

4 Why does the Astronomer Royal think the five most interesting numbers are omega, $n = 10^{36}$, 0.007, $Q = 1/100{,}000$ and lambda? Any ideas? He suggests these are the numbers to put in a space capsule.

Scales and proportion

1 By a graph, mathematicians do not mean a chart, like a bar chart. They mean a group of points connected by lines. A rectangle is a graph of four points connected by four edges. Think of a group of friends as points and join them with a line if they are friends. Graphs of this type can be analysed. Try it with a group of friends or colleagues.

2 Only in the idealized world of the mathematician do the angles of a triangle add up to 180°

3 Our metric system of length uses a base of 10. There are 10 lots of 10p to 1 pound, 10 millimetres to 1 centimetre. Other number systems use different bases. Computers use base 2 (the binary system of two numbers: 0 and 1). For the computer, 1 means on and 0 means off. The Babylonians used a base of 60 (60 seconds in a minute, 60 minutes in an hour). The eighteenth century weight system used a system of 8 (16 ounces in a pound, 32 ounces to 1 quart).

Statistics

1 Why are statistics used so much to persuade?

2 Why are people so suspicious of statistics?

3 Why are some statistics said to be vital?

4 All statistics have an origin. Are you always told the rules by which they were collected?

Formulae

1 Why do we have pi to understand the circle? Pi, written π in mathematics, is equal to 3.14159265358979323846264338327950288419716939… So what went wrong?

2 How is your algebra? Can you rearrange and solve equations?

Outline

Scientists include a valued group of colleagues called mathematicians. Sometimes they work ahead of the experimental scientist and develop theory that has to be tested through observation in the field or laboratory. At other times they follow the scientist and provide a proof for a set of observations that have been made. Some mathematicians are working on theory that has no immediate application. At times their creativity is closer to the world of the arts than science. They produce such beauty.

This section examines five aspects of the work of the applied mathematician. It begins with two views of the way scientists plan, and then looks at the ways in which they analyse and present their findings.

Layout of data sets

Different types of data

During an investigation, observations are recorded as data. Data should be clearly defined, precisely taken and accurately recorded. Other investigators should be able to understand the context of your investigation, know the definitions and units used and read your recordings. There are two basic types of data:
- quantitative
- qualitative.

Quantitative data

Quantitative data is numerical – such as counts, dimensions, and timing. It includes, for example, dimensions of plants, pH of soil, temperature, velocity, current and concentration.

Quantitative data may be discrete or continuous. Discrete data is in the form of whole numbers such as counts of population or eggs in a nest. Discrete data is also known as discontinuous data because it has no intermediate values between the counts or classes. Continuous data has any value within the limits of the study. For example, people can have any height and temperature, and velocity can be measured to hundredths of a division. You could graph discrete data, such as measures of the counts of people, using a bar graph, whilst for continuous data, such as temperature, you would use a line graph. When deciding what type of graph to use you need to decide whether the data is discrete or continuous.

Qualitative data

Qualitative data is descriptive of observations – for example, nesting behaviour of birds, shopping habits and views on a planning application. Photographs can be seen as qualitative data. Scientists often attempt to transform qualitative data into quantitative data because of the statistical manipulation possible.

Recording your data set

During an investigation the researcher needs to plan a way of recording the readings that are taken. A recording sheet such as a table is the best way to make a record. This may be in the form of a spreadsheet on a computer or it could be hand-written. The value of the computer spreadsheet is that it allows further analysis to take place immediately.

The usual layout is to use a row for each event or station and a column for each variable. Units of measurement need to be defined.

Displaying data

When data is stored in a computer spreadsheet, it is very easy to generate a large number of graphs and other images. In an investigation, the displaying of data in a visual form is only valid if it allows greater understanding of the data or it reveals new insights. Graphs should not be drawn for their own sake. Any graphs drawn must be relevant to the investigation. Useful ways of displaying data include:
- graphs to show the relationship of two variables
- bar charts for discrete data such as counts
- kite diagrams for showing information from transects
- scatter graphs linked to correlation and regression (trend line) analysis
- pie charts to show proportions.

KEY SKILLS: *Application of number*

The table shows railway journeys between two cities that are 160 kilometres apart.

Dep. A	07.27	08.23	10.24	11.50	15.00	17.00	20.00
Arr. B	08.50	09.55	11.59	13.18	16.45	18.50	22.00

(Times are shown in hours and minutes.)

You may use a calculator for these exercises.

1 Calculate the average journey time between the two cities.

2 What were the average speeds of the fastest and slowest journeys?

3 Suggest reasons for the pattern of train times shown.

4 Suggest reasons for the variations in journey time shown.

5 A daily user of the line notices that there are a number of ticket prices for the return journey. Which of the following packages would you recommend for the next year (52 five-day weeks)?

A A season ticket giving five return journeys per week for 13 weeks for £900.

B A Senior Railcard involving an annual fee of £20 and daily return tickets of £14.

C Drive the car to B costing 16p per kilometre but with free parking.

(*Level 3*)

Amounts and sizes: units, area, volume, diagrams, perimeter

Amounts

Light travels at a finite, very high speed and was first measured by the Danish astronomer Christensen Roemer in 1676. His observations of the moons of Jupiter indicated a speed of light of 140,000 miles per second (corrected using modern equipment to 186,000 miles per second). Following the theory of relativity (Einstein, 1905) the law emerged that nothing can travel faster than the speed of light. This is because, as the speed of an object increases, so does its weight.

We would know if the sun ceased to shine about 8 minutes after the event. This is the time it takes light to reach the earth from the sun. The light we see as stars from distant galaxies left them millions of years ago.

What is the approximate distance of the earth from the sun? If your calculator cannot cope with these large numbers, the rest of this page will be a help to you.

Very large and very small numbers

Frequently in science, mathematics and technology there is a need to deal with very large numbers. Indices are used to help write these numbers. For example:

- 100 can be written as 10×10 or 10^2 (pronounced 'ten squared')
- 1000 can be written as $10 \times 10 \times 10$ or 10^3 (pronounced 'ten cubed')
- 1,000,000 (1 million) can be written as $10 \times 10 \times 10 \times 10 \times 10 \times 10$ or 10^6 (pronounced 'ten to the sixth')
- one tenth can be written as 10^{-1} (pronounced 'ten to the minus one')
- one hundredth can be written as 10^{-2} (pronounced 'ten to the minus two').

This means that £1.5 billion could be written as £1,500,000,000 or £1.5×10^9 and that 2.4×10^{-3} is a way of writing 0.0024.

Area, volume, diagrams and perimeter

It can be useful to know the volume and area of the following:

Square	Rectangle	Triangle	Trapezium	Circle
Area $= a^2$	Area $= a \times b$	Area $= 0.5b \times h$	Area $= \dfrac{(a+b)}{2} \times h$	Area $= \pi r^2$
Cube	Rectangular prism	Cylinder	Trapezoid	Sphere
Volume $= a^3$	Volume $= a \times b \times c$	Volume $= \pi r^2 h$	Volume $= \left(\dfrac{(a+b)}{2} \times h\right) \times l$	Volume $= \dfrac{4}{3} \times \pi r^3$

KEY SKILLS: *Application of number*

1 The diagram shows the outline plan for a new swimming pool.

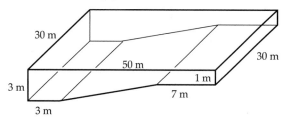

a What is the surface area of the pool (be sure to include the units with all answers)?

b What is the volume of the pool?

c The sides and bottom of the pool are to be covered in tiles. What area of tiles is needed?

d The pool is to be filled using a source providing 50 litres per minute. How long will it take to fill the pool? (1 litre is equal to 1000 cubic centimetres.)

2 A car is travelling along a main road in France where the speed limit is 110 kph. Is the car exceeding the speed limit if it is travelling at 70 mph? You may assume 5 miles is equal to 8 kilometres.

3 a Unleaded petrol is sold in litres. Sales literature for a new car suggests an average consumption of 45 miles per gallon at a steady speed of 50 miles per hour. How many miles will the car travel per litre of fuel? (1 gallon is equivalent to 4.5 litres.)

b If unleaded fuel costs 85p per litre, calculate the fuel cost of a 90-mile journey at a steady 50 mph.

4 a Air travellers are allowed luggage weighing 50 lbs. If 1 kilo is 2.2 lbs, what weight in kilos are they allowed?

b Some people measure their body weight in kilos, others in pounds and some in stones and pounds. What would a 14-stone man weigh in each of these systems? (1 stone is equal to 14 lbs.)

5 A supermarket chain has recently responded to customer feedback by selling its goods using imperial (pre-metric) weights. Which would be the best buy?
A 250 g of butter costing £1.00
B ½ lb of butter costing £1.00

6 Car manufacturers are reducing the prices of new cars. Here are a few examples from Mazda:

Premacy 1.8 Gxi	£15,000	now £12,905
323 1.5 GSE	£15,500	now £12,500
626 1.8 Gxi	£17,500	now £13,400
Dento 1.3 Gxi	£7,500	now £6,250

Which was the greatest percentage reduction?

7 Arrange these numbers in size order, with the smallest first.

1/3   0.3   33%   3/12

(*Level 3*)

Scales and proportions

Reading and understanding scale drawings, maps and charts

If you wanted to build an extension to your home, you would need Building Regulations permission. You would be required to submit a plan. The plan would be to a scale of 1:100. You would also need to produce drawings of the elevation (to the scale 1:100) from two different directions. For the detail of the building and its layout you would probably use a scale of 1:50. This means that every centimetre on the drawing represents 50 centimetres on the building.

Ordnance Survey maps are also drawn to scale. The most popular maps for walking are the 1:25,000 series. This means that 1 centimetre on the map represents 25,000 centimetres or 250 metres or 0.25 kilometres on the ground. Walkers are able to pick out local features such as field boundaries on these maps. The Ordnance Survey Landranger series is good for cycling and the study of urban areas. It is drawn to a scale of 1:50,000 so that 1 cm. on the map represents 0.5 kilometres on the ground. An atlas map of the British Isles would fit an A3 page if drawn at a scale of 1:3,000,000 and could show counties, principal towns and motorways. An A2 sized map of the world would need to be drawn at a scale of 1:80,000,000.

Explanation depends on scale

Another way of looking at scale is in terms of its effect on the explanation you give. Every change in scale will bring about changes, and there is no basis for presuming that associations existing at one scale will also exist at another. For example, the factors influencing the choice of where to live will vary with the scale of consideration. You may have decided to live in the south-east of England because of the number of jobs available. Selecting the actual house will depend upon such factors as price, schools, garden and shops. This means that when you analyse a problem you have to take scale into account.

Ratio and proportions

The most common uses of ratio and proportions are in advertising and marketing. The usual strategy is to show that 1 in 10 people are using the product. Another use for ratios is to show the proportion of people or items having a particular characteristic. One example would be 2 out of every 5 people visiting a garden centre were over 60 years of age.

Calculations of density are a form of ratio. A population density figure gives an average of the number of people per unit of area. In science, density of a substance is the ratio of its mass to its volume.

Another way in which ratios are used is to express the average number of children or cars per family.

KEY SKILLS: *Application of number*

This scale drawing shows the front view of a greenhouse.

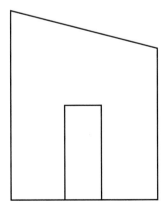

Scale 1:80

1 What is the width of the greenhouse?

2 What size is the greenhouse door?

3 If the greenhouse is 4 metres long, draw a scale diagram of the side view of the greenhouse.

4 During the holidays two students agree to paint a fence and to share their earnings in the ratio 3:2. How much does each receive when they earn a total of £130?

5 The land area of the earth's surface is about 4×10^{11} square kilometres. The population of the earth is about 6000 million. Calculate the approximate population density in people per square kilometre.

6 Six of the twenty-four teams in the Second Division of the Football League changed their manager during a season. Express this information using ratio and proportion in at least two ways. Now compose a headline to include the fact in a sensational way. (Level 3)

Statistics

Statistics is a branch of applied mathematics that has proved very useful to psychologists, sociologists, economists and geographers. Two interesting quotes about statistics are:

> 'There are three kinds of lies: lies, damned lies and statistics.'
>
> 'Statistics are like a bikini, very revealing but hiding the more interesting parts.'

It is said that the Chinese developed statistics but their modern use is linked to the French mathematician Blaise Pascal (AD 1650).

Averages

Did you realize that there are three types of average: the mean, median and mode? Frequently the media use the term average but do not specify which of these three they are using. Let us look at some data.

The mean average

Consider the part-time earnings of someone serving in a restaurant (see table). The mean is found by adding the earnings for the five weekends (£320) and dividing by 5. The mean is therefore £64. This gives an impression of the earnings over the five-week period, but note that three of the five weeks were below this figure. The mean average can be disturbed by the inclusion of very high or very low figures. Nevertheless, it is the most used of the three averages. In mathematical formulae the mean is shown as $\bar{x}$ (pronounced 'x bar').

Part-time earnings for five weekends at £4 per hour plus tips

Weekend	Earnings (inc. tips)
1	£48
2	£48
3	£60
4	£80
5	£84

The modal average or mode or norm

This is the figure that appears most often. In the case of the part-time earnings, £48 appeared most often. This average is frequently used when quoting earnings. 'Most people earned … .' One of its disadvantages is that data may contain several figures that occur more often or that no figure appears twice. In this case the data can be grouped into classes.

The median average

This is the figure that appears in the centre of the figures when they are placed in rank order. In the case of part-time earning the median is £60. Two weeks are above the median and two below. Problems can emerge for the median if there is an even number of cases; for example, with six items, counting from the top and bottom figures leads you to the third or fourth figures. The median is then half way between these two figures. Though not as popular as the mean, and frequently difficult to calculate, the median does give a useful middle figure. Using a computer-based spreadsheet makes it quick to find the median once the data is entered.

Other statistics

Another useful statistic is the **range**. This is found by noting the highest and lowest values. For example, the mean daytime temperatures during a summer week might be 22 °C, 25 °C, 25 °C, 26 °C, 28 °C, 27 °C and 22 °C. The seven days have a mean daytime temperature of 25 °C and a range from 28 °C to 22 °C. A more sophisticated way to measure the spread of values is to calculate the standard deviation. A low standard deviation shows that the data is clustered around the mean.

Other useful statistical tests include t-test to calculate the significance of the difference between two mean values. Correlation statistics suggest the possibility of causal linkage between two variables. The Chi-squared test can be used to test if observed values match those expected by theory. A good way to understand these statistical tests is to consult examples given in AS and A level textbooks for such subjects as geography, biology and psychology.

KEY SKILLS: *Application of number*

1 The table below shows the number of cars owned by a sample of 50 families.

	Cars				
	None	**1**	**2**	**3**	**4**	**5 or more**
Number of families	3	9	19	15	4	0

a What is the mean number of cars per family?

b Which is the modal class of family?

c One of the families with no car buys a car and one of the three car families reduces the number to two. How do the mean and mode change?

2 This table shows the heights (in cm) of a sample of 50 young men aged 17 to 19 years.

148–153	154–159	160–165	166–171	172–177	178–183	184–190
2	4	8	12	13	6	5

a Calculate the mean, median and modal height of the group.

b Comment on your interpretation of the results

3 You have been asked to question a group of 25 people to investigate their attitudes to science. Devise a table including at least five statements in addition to the one shown.

	Strongly disagree	Disagree	Neutral	Agree	Strongly agree
Most scientific innovations are good					
Your five statements					

a Calculate the mean attitude of the group to each statement.

b Which statement showed the strongest support for science?

c What conclusions can you draw from your investigation?

d In the light of the experience which statement would you redraft? Write down the redrafted version.

(*Level 3*)

Formulae

Many scientific investigations involve the use of a formula. Usually the investigator inserts their observations into the formula to obtain a result. On this page a number of formulae are introduced and some practice with substitution in them is offered. The use of formulae is included in the Application of Number Key Skill and some examples are included.

Some useful formulae

Area of a circle (A)	Area $= \pi r^2$ (where r is the radius of the circle)
Volume of a cylinder (V)	Volume $= \pi r^2 h$
Pythagoras' Theorem	In a right angled triangle the length of the longest side the hypotenuse (a) is given by $a^2 = b^2 + c^2$ where b and c are the other two sides.
Volume of a sphere (V)	$V = \frac{4}{3}\pi r^3$
Converting Fahrenheit (F) to Celsius (C)	$F = \frac{9}{5}C + 32$
Miles to kilometres	I kilometre is approximately $\frac{5}{8}$ of a mile
Litres to gallons	I litre $=$ 1.76 pints or 0.22 gallons
Kilograms to pounds	I kilogram (kg) $=$ 2.2 pounds (lbs)

Using formulae

In General Studies and the Application of Number Key Skill, you are expected to be able to use formulae. For example, Level 3 of Application of Number asks you to plan and carry through a substantial and complex activity where you rearrange and use formulae. Examples of the type of formulae expected include solving simultaneous equations with two variables or rearranging formulae to change the subject of the formula.

Solving simultaneous equations

Suppose $\quad 2x + 3y = 2$
and $\qquad x + 6y = 10$

- Multiplying the second equation by 2 gives $2x + 12y = 20$.
- Subtracting the first equation from the second therefore gives $9y = 18$. So $y = 2$.
- Substituting $y = 2$ in the second equation gives $x = -2$.

- Check by entering $x = -2$ and $y = 2$ in the first equation to confirm your result.

Rearranging formulae

If $a = \dfrac{b^2}{c}$ then write down the formula for b.
The answer is $b = \sqrt{ac}$.

A very difficult yet fascinating number puzzle involving a formula

Here is a formula puzzle well beyond A level and Key Skills Level 3. In fact, in 2000 a publisher announced a $1m reward for anyone who could solve it. The puzzle is included here to encourage enjoyment in the world of mathematics. All you have to do is prove that an even number greater than two (we will call this n) is the sum of two prime numbers (we will call them $p1$ and $p2$). So the formula to prove is:

$n = p1 + p2$

Let us try it for some numbers: $6 = 3 + 3$; $20 = 3 + 17$; $52 = 5 + 47$.

In 1999, a computer scientist checked the formula up to 400,000,000,000,000. Now the publisher wants a proof. This puzzle is the work of Christian Goldbach (1690–1764) who put it in a letter to a famous Swiss mathematician Leonard Euler. Try some of the following prime numbers 3, 5, 7, 11, 13, 17, 19, 23, 29, 31 and 37, or even larger ones.

Another fascinating puzzle

Twin prime number are consecutive odd numbers that are primes. Examples include: 3 and 5; 5 and 7; 71 and 73; 1,000,000,000,061 and 1,000,000,000,063. Can you find another pair of twin primes below 30?

Did you know

The largest proven prime number is $2^{3021377}-1$.

Percentages

Percentages are a very useful and popular way of dealing with amounts and proportions, especially when change is taking place. Though they are used a great deal they need to be handled with care. You also need to be wary when reading percentages.

Beware percentages

- Is it true that percentages are always less than 100? No, it is not true.
- If two amounts both increase by the same percentage, have they increased by the same amount? No, they have not.

KEY SKILLS: *Application of number*

1 The formula $V^2 = U^2 + 2fS$ shows the relationship between velocity, acceleration and distance travelled. In the formula U is the initial velocity in metres per second (m/s), V is the velocity at the end of the period (m/s) and f is the acceleration in metres per sec per sec. Use the formula to calculate S if $U = 20$ m/s, $V = 40$ m/s and $f = 10$ m/s/s. Be sure to include the units of the distance travelled.

2 In the study of optics in physics a useful formula is $1/f = 1/u + 1/v$, where u is the object to lens distance, v is the lens to image distance and f the focal length of the lens. Find the focal length of the lens if $u = 4$ and $v = 6$.

3 The number of vehicles that a road can carry is given by the formula:

$$Q = \frac{3600VN}{C}$$

where   Q = number of vehicles per hour
        V = average vehicle speed in m/s
        N = number of lanes
        C = distance between vehicles in metres

a What is the capacity of a two-lane highway where the average speed is 10 m/s and the distance between vehicles is 50 m?

b What is the capacity of a three-lane motorway with traffic moving at 50 kilometres per hour and the distance between vehicles is 30 metres?

c The route of a new road passes through a line of hills that contain important environmental sites. Money and important sites could be saved if the cutting through the hills had only two lanes. Projections for vehicle number per hour are as high as 5000. Are two lanes enough to avoid congestion if an acceptable minimum speed is 40 km/h and vehicles need to be at least 20 metres apart at these lower speeds?

4 Temperature can be measured on the Fahrenheit and Celsius scales. The formula to change Fahrenheit readings to Celsius is:

$$C = \tfrac{5}{9}(F - 32)$$

A physics student and a geography student argue that there is a point where the two readings are the same. Does such a point exist and what would be the reading on the two scales at this point?

5 The population of a country is increasing at 3% per year.
a How many years will it take for the population to double?
b What factors could affect this forecast?

6 If you had £100 in the bank and it gained 5% interest in a year, you would have £105 after twelve months. Now take 5% of your money away. Will you be left with £100? No, you would have £99.75. Can you explain this?

7 a The VAT on a car tyre costing £50 (including valve and balancing) is charged at 17.5%. How much did the tyre cost in total?
b The total cost (including 17.5% VAT) for a car exhaust was £87.50. How much did the exhaust cost before VAT?
(*Level 3*)

Further study suggestions and example questions

Further reading

Doxiadis, A. (2000) *Uncle Petros and Goldbach's Conjecture*, Faber and Faber, London. (M)

Gaarder, J. (1990) *The Solitaire Mystery*, Phoenix, London.

Guedj, D. (1999) *The Parrot's Theorem*, Weidenfeld, London. (M)

Hawkins, S. (1988) *A Brief History of Time*, Bantam Books, London.

Hoffman, P. (1998) *The Man Who Only Loved Numbers*, Fourth Estate, London. (M)

Nasar, S. (1998) *A Beautiful Mind*, Faber and Faber, London. (M)

Singh, S. (1997) *Fermat's Last Theorem*, Fourth Estate, London.

Singh, S. (1999) *The Code Book*, Fourth Estate, London.

Sobel, D. (1999) *Galileo's Daughter*, Fourth Estate, London.

Trefil, J. (1996) *101 Things You Don't Know About Science*, Cassell, London.

Woolfe, S. (2000) *Leaning Towards Infinity*, The Women's Press, London. (M)

The books marked (M) are called fictional mathematics. Their authors have drawn mathematics into a plot with a human story in such a way that they popularize the wonder of mathematics, though they may lose some of its beauty on the way.

www.cites.org for the Convention on International Trade in Endangered Species.

Questions

1 Scientists disagree about the evidence for global warming.
   a Describe the mechanism by which global warming is thought to occur.
   b Why might the effects on western Europe be less disastrous than for some countries in north Africa?
2 a Make an audit of the energy requirements of the house in which you live.
   b How could your daily demand for energy be reduced?
3 a Should motorways be built by private companies who could then charge users a toll?
   b Should the price of petrol be used as a weapon in the war against pollution?
4 a How could you measure your own fitness?
   b Is dieting a good thing?
5 a Define the terms organ transplantation and genetic engineering.
   b Identify and justify your choice of the medical discovery that you wish would take place.
6 Why not visit the Natural History Museum and the Science Museum? Take your General Studies file with you.
7 Carry out an evaluation of solar, tidal, wave and wind power in terms of their costs, potential for energy generation, and environmental effects.
8 Noise pollution comes mainly from road, rail and air traffic. Try an experiment. In a quiet area, play one of your favourite tapes or CDs on a portable player. Adjust the volume so that you can just hear the music at 3 metres distance. Now take the player into a selection of locations near to where you live and note the average distance at which you can still hear the music. Remember to use the same music set at the same volume level. Note the sources of noise pollution.

KEY SKILLS: *Application of number*

1 This formula predicts the height of a man from the measurement of his forearm (wrist to elbow):

$$h = \frac{10f + 256}{3}$$

   a Carry out a survey of at least five male colleagues to assess the accuracy of the formula. Tabulate your results.
   b How would you improve the formula in the light of your results?
   c How well does the formula work with female colleagues?

Preparing for AS coursework in science

The OCR General Studies specification (it used to be called the syllabus) includes the opportunity for candidates to complete a piece of coursework (called internal assessment) during their AS studies.

Completing pieces of coursework instead of taking an examination paper is attractive to some candidates because it relieves them of the pressure of a timed examination paper, and allows them to develop a project over a period of time. In the OCR specification you can complete a 2000-word project on a topic from science instead of sitting the AS science domain paper (Unit 2962). In 2001, the topic chosen by OCR was 'Matters of weight' and candidates were given the following topics as guidance:

1 Weight and fitness

For example:
- health dangers of obesity
- the importance of diet, exercise and fitness to quality of life
- weight reduction in the short and long term.

2 Weight and balance

For example:
- bridges
- levers
- domestic equipment
- sports equipment.

3 Weight and movement

For example:
- vehicle design
- transport of oil
- vessel structure
- sports analysis
- light-weight materials
- weightlessness.

4 Weight and cost

For example:
- productivity
- miniaturization
- soil fertility
- air travel
- space exploration.

To complete the project, candidates are invited to see that as part of work experience with a national newspaper they have been assigned to promote National Technology Week. They have been asked to compile a report on one of these topics.

Building a response

When a report on a project like this one is needed, you are recommended to include the following:
- a clearly stated title, for example, 'An investigation of the correlation of fitness with height and body weight'
- a short synopsis of your findings
- a review of the literature on the chosen topic so that you are able to focus on a specific question, issue or hypothesis
- a clear plan of how the project proceeded (it is helpful to keep a diary or log of the activities you did since they are easily forgotten if you have a rush at the end) – for example, your intention to measure the fitness, height and body weight of 30 members of Year 12, of which 15 will be male
- clear definitions of the things you are investigating and measuring – for example, definitions of height, body weight and how you plan to measure fitness, including details of the units being used
- clear tabulation of data collected – for example, a listing of the fitness, height and body weight of all 30 people taking part in the study, with mean scores and their range given, using a spreadsheet here would be recommended
- analysis of the issues raised – for example, your analysis may reveal that when the data are plotted as graphs there appears to be a relationship between certain variables, though anomalies do exist; the more statistically competent can include correlation coefficients at this stage and consideration of their significance
- appropriate graphs, charts, statistics and photographs – for example, try to include a range of different presentational techniques but never repeat the same data with different presentational techniques unless it gives additional insights; try to move beyond bar graphs and pie charts; one or two photographs to show important points would be valuable
- clarification of the problems you came across, including those where there was not a right way forward and you had to make a choice or compromize

- critical analysis – for example, consider your earlier plans in the light of experience; reflect on the accuracy of your measurements; review the things people have said to you during the project
- relevant conclusions – for example, a simple statement of what has been found, even if you discovered no link; do not overstate findings, they can only be speculative with such a small sample
- list of all sources used – for example, correct titles of books and articles with their all-important date. Show some scholarship by the accuracy of your listing.

Points to remember

- Number your pages when all is finished and include a contents page.
- A very important step is to leave time for at least two proof readings of your report.

- Make plans for the way you are going to bind the report. Ring files are not recommended.
- Add your name, centre number and candidate number.

Marking the project report

An experienced examiner will mark the report using the following mark scheme.

1	Selection and interpretation of sources and evidence	20 marks
2	Understanding of the concepts involved	10 marks
3	Communication in a clear, reasoned and effective way	15 marks
4	Demonstration of awareness of different types of knowledge	10 marks
5	Demonstration of the ability to use problem-solving skills	20 marks
6	Drawing of relevant conclusions	15 marks

KEY SKILLS

Your General Studies report can also be used to generate Key Skills evidence for your portfolio. Many AS students are attempting to achieve Level 3 of the Key Skills of Communication, Application of number, and Information technology. To do this they have to complete a 1.5-hour test in each and produce a portfolio of evidence.

The General Studies Coursework Project has been designed to produce the evidence for you. As you work through your project you can plan your work to produce evidence of the all three Key Skills at Level 3.

Here is your checklist:

Communication

C3.2 Read and synthesize information from two extended documents about a complex subject (one document should include at least one image).

C3.3 Write two different types of document about complex subjects.

Application of number

N3.1 Plan and interpret information from two different sources, including a large data set.

N3.2 Carry out multi-stage calculations to appropriate levels of accuracy, showing methods.

N3.3 Interpret results.

Information technology

IT3.1 Plan and use different sources to search for, and select, information required for two different purposes.

IT3.2 Explore, develop and exchange information and derive information to meet two different purposes.

IT3.3 Present information from different sources for two different purposes and audiences.

In addition you need to:

C3.1a Contribute to a group discussion about a complex subject.

C3.1b Give a talk about a straightforward subject, using an image.

You can use the preparation of your General Studies project to provide opportunities for C3.1a and b. For each of them you will need a group of colleagues to join you. All of the work you do for your Key Skills has to be signed off by you and your teacher as being your own work and up to Level 3 standard.

1 Political systems, processes and goals

Definitions

Consensus	Coming to a general agreement.
Controversy	When people disagree about important issues that affect world affairs and how people live. Disagreement that turns to conflict.
Goals	What politicians are aiming to achieve.
Opinion polls	A statistical method used by social scientists to record the views of a sample of people about particular issues.
Political parties	Groups of politicians who share similar beliefs about political issues. Individuals who come together to provide group strength.
Politicians	Representatives of the people. Representatives of political parties.
Politics	How resources are raised and allocated to meet priorities.
Processes	The ways in which politicians make their ideas and policies work. The routes used to make decisions.
Referendum	A device, not often used in the UK, that allows the voter to express an opinion on a specific question of national importance.
Voting	How those with the vote elect their representatives at local, national or international level. How those with a vote choose their representatives, using a process which keeps their choice a secret.

Getting started

Politics and political processes are often dismissed as 'boring', but it is difficult to think of anything in daily life that isn't 'political'. Here are some examples:

1 Student grants should be restored.
2 The national minimum wage should be the same for everyone over eighteen.
3 Comprehensive schools have proved a failure.
4 If you want to know about sleaze, ask a politician.
5 Leave the European Union and save the pound.

Outline

This topic, which concerns political systems, processes and goals, is very large. The first section covers the names of the main political parties and what each believes in and what their main policies are. It examines the ways in which the aims of the political parties differ and describes who the leading politicians are and what they do.

In a second section we look at how people vote and what influences them. This includes the role of opinion polls and how much we can rely on them.

Finally, we look at what government attempts to achieve.

Throughout this section, the points are illustrated through the main political issues – the things that are often 'in the news' because they are high on what is called 'the political agenda'.

The political parties in the UK

There are lots of political parties but the UK is often described as a 'two-party' system. This means that, since 1945, either the Conservative or Labour Party has been the majority party in the House of Commons, forming the government. There are other parties in the Commons such as the Liberal Democrats – the third biggest group of MPs. There are also nationalist parties which have MPs in Westminster elected by the people of Wales, Scotland and Northern Ireland. Devolution means that, although Wales, Scotland and Northern Ireland are still part of the United Kingdom, power has been devolved from Westminster to give the three countries an opportunity to run some of their own affairs through assemblies (Wales and Northern Ireland) and a parliament (Scotland).

Did we really want the Welsh Assembly?

THE Welsh Assembly is surely yet another product of public apathy and indifference.

Disillusioned with the continual deception of politicians, who are always going to do great things for the public but never do, fewer and fewer people now vote.

Even so, a staggering 50% of the electorate turned out to vote on the Assembly issue. Out of these apparently 51% voted for this expensive and wasteful bureaucracy.

Did the people of Wales really want another luxury for a minority at the expense of the majority? This was by no means a decisive vote of confidence, yet the politicians in waiting immediately saw it as an overwhelming victory.

Despite this dubious victory, they could not wait to get started whether it was popular or not.

Since its inception it has been not just a talking shop but also an arguing shop, with the usual incessant bickering, and political point scoring.

Two people have already been kicked out for trivial reasons, and guess who is paying for all this?

No premises were ever suitably luxurious enough and, as expected, they soon voted for a new grand palace which is estimated to be costing £71 million, but which will undoubtedly cost considerably more, as always.

Will we ever know the actual cost of all this? All this luxury when much of Wales looks so forlorn and uncared for, but then there are always unlimited funds for the wrong things.

It has soon become apparent that this is to become another tax burden on an already overtaxed public. This Assembly has already forced council tax payers in all counties to pay extra for the inefficiency and waste of irresponsible councils in the valleys.

Why should the public be continually forced to pay for the luxury, bureaucracy and waste of a minority?

M F Dixon
Carmarthen Journal,
18 October 2000

Past and present

UK governments from 1945–2000

1945–51	Labour
1951–64	Conservative
1964–70	Labour
1970–74	Conservative
1974–79	Labour
1979–97	Conservative
1997–2001	Labour

Figure heads

When Labour won the 1997 General Election with the biggest majority ever seen in modern British politics, the 'old' image of the Labour Party had been given a political makeover. It had become 'New Labour'. When William Hague replaced John Major as leader of the Conservative Party, the leadership of the two main parties reversed a popular myth. Labour, the so-called 'people's party' was led by a man educated at one of Scotland's top independent schools. The Conservatives, seen as the party of the middle and upper classes, though it has always attracted working-class voters had, as their leader, a young man educated at a Yorkshire local authority school.

TASKS

1 Find out what powers have been devolved to the Scottish Parliament and the Welsh Assembly.

2 How well does the letter featured above make the case against the Welsh Assembly?

KEY SKILLS: *Information technology*

The local political party secretary has developed a computer list of all members. The system breaks down, losing the computer list. What should the secretary have done to ensure that the list of members could still be found?

A   labelled the disks
B   saved the files regularly
C   kept the original membership forms
D   used a password to protect the list

(Level 2)

What the two main parties stand for

What the two main parties stand for may not always be clear. Political parties have long-term aims that are driven by an ideology. However, they need to be in power, in government, to be able to move forward with their longer-term aims. Some government decisions may appear out of line with their ideology, but are intended to allow them to retain power at the next election.

Parties in opposition strive to deflect government policy towards their own aims as well as to discredit those in power.

Making sense?

William Hague used the words "common sense" more than 40 times yesterday in a speech which marked a clear lurch to the right

Hague's highlights
- Keep criminals in prison longer
- Lock away with life sentences dealers who sell drugs to children
- Reduce size of the cabinet and cut European parliament by 100 members
- Abolish Labour's regional agencies and assemblies
- Guarantee a waiting time based on a NHS patient's need for treatment

- Parents able sack school's management if they think it's failing
- A transparent tax system, and tax cuts
- Restore recognition of marriage in tax and benefit system
- Two-thirds of new development to be built on brownfield sites
- Restore role of Territorial Army
- Forcing foreign lorries who use our roads to pay a levy
- Issues that only affect England should be voted on only by English MPs
- New EU treaty must contain a flexibility clause

The Guardian, 8 October 1999

The shape of things to come at Westminster

What's in:

Centrepiece crime bill — permitting mandatory drug testing of people under arrest and reform of probation services

Justice bill — removing defendants' rights to choose jury trial

Sexual offences amendment bill — lowering gay age of consent to 16, plus measures to prevent abuse of trust by adults

Race relations bill — updating the race relations act to cover police and other public services

Electoral procedures bill — improving democratic participation through measures such as voting in supermarkets and rolling electoral registers

Party funding bill — tighter controls, including cap on election spending, following the key recommendations of Lord Neill's committee, plus ban on blind trusts

Freedom of Information bill — amended version of much-criticised draft bill extending openness and public's right to know

Social services bill — enforcing tough scrutiny of children's and old people's homes through a new independent inspectorate

Social security bill — reform of child support agency to streamline processing of cases and chasing up of absentee parents

Transport bill — introducing congestion charging in towns and cities. Railtrack to be stripped of standards

Local government bill — creating elected mayors in cities outside London and cabinet-style local government and ethics

Countryside bill — giving walkers the long-awaited right to roam in open countryside. Will include other measures such as wildlife protection and creation of two national parks

Education bill — reforms to post-16 education and training, including creation of learning skills council to replace further education funding council (the colleges quango) and training and enterprise councils

Deregulation bill — Cabinet office bill to reduce red tape burden on business

Leasehold bill — reforming widely criticised leasehold restrictions

Post office bill — implementing part-privatisation of the post office

E-commercial bill — easing use of internet and email for business and improving security

Utilities bill — strengthening powers of utilities regulators with the aim of lowering electricity and gas prices

The Guardian, 18 October 1999

TASKS

1 Draw up a three-column table and write Conservative, Labour and Liberal Democrat at the top of the columns.

Enter the name of the leader of each party and list five of the party's goals. You could write to the main political parties, use the Internet or take extracts from newspaper reports of the most recent party conference.

KEY SKILLS: *Information technology*

A student wishing to study the election of the President in the USA decides to set up a spreadsheet file containing the names of all the states of the USA, the state capital and political affiliation.

Create a spreadsheet file with a suitable file name. Ensure that the spreadsheet has columns for the name of the state, its state capital and its political affiliation in 2001.

(Level 3)

Leading political figures

Begin by asking yourself how many leading political figures in the UK you can name. Can you name the Prime Minister and the Leader of the Opposition? Can you name the Chancellor of the Exchequer, the Foreign Secretary and the Home Secretary? Do you have any idea what roles they play within the government? Is your local MP male or female? What is their name and which political party do they represent? You will probably know the answers to some of these questions. Ask yourself how you came to know some of them and not others. Even more important are their beliefs. What do they stand for in their roles as politicians?

Politics has probably never been the same since the intervention of television from the late 1950s. 'Party' political programmes are not popular but a lot of people watch the news and, in an age of global communication, favourable coverage and flattering headlines are often thought to be the keys to the door of political success. Politicians are always trying to deliver 'a message' but they rely heavily on their advisors, usually cast as villains in the form of 'spin doctors', who are often accused of trying to 'manipulate' the media.

British politics is strongly influenced by American ideas and one of America's most successful Presidents of recent times was Ronald Reagan – a former film star. Now, one of the main requirements for success in politics is the ability to be 'telegenic' – perhaps if you look good, what you say is of rather less importance. However, as Ken Livingstone proved in the battle to become Mayor of London, success is most likely when you have 'charismatic appeal', a sort of personal magnetism, usually associated with film and pop stars.

Only a few politicians make the news, and not always for the 'right' reasons. According to the judgement of 20 prominent politicians, historians and commentators for BBC Radio's 'The Westminster Hour', the greatest Prime Ministers in the twentieth century were the following:

The Premier League Top Five

Winston Churchill (Conservative, 1940–5, 1951–5)
David Lloyd George (Liberal, 1916–22)
Clement Attlee (Labour, 1945–51)
Herbert Asquith (Liberal, 1908–16)
Margaret Thatcher (Conservative, 1979–90)

Politics, though is not a science and there are usually many more opinions than facts. Third placed Attlee, a man not known for wasting words, said of table-topping Churchill: '50% genius, 50% bloody fool'. Modern politicians, aware that no one gets more publicity than 'celebrities' in the performing arts, are often seen in their company. It doesn't always work.

TASKS

1 Nationally and internationally, a few politicians are fairly well known and sometimes even easily recognizable. They are often known as 'big hitters'. Try to identify the 'big hitters' in the UK government and in different political parties. Discuss your choice and seek to justify it. Which of their ideas and policies cause the most controversy? Who are the statesmen with lead roles on the world stage?

2 Make a careful study of the television images of the Prime Minister and Leader of the Opposition. Note the clothes they wear, their body language, facial expression and the way they greet people. They need to remain popular. They have been coached about their appearance.

KEY SKILLS: *Information technology*

Open a computer file and record the names of the following people, their political affiliation and the constituency they represent:
the Prime Minister, the Leader of the Opposition, the Chancellor and Shadow Chancellor of the Exchequer, the Ministers of Education, Defence, Agriculture and the Environment and their shadows.
Print the file in alphabetical order twice, once by surname and once by constituency. (*Level 3*)

Areas of political controversy

How free are we when we vote? Has the media manipulated our decision? Are we too influenced by the images we see, rather than the detailed political philosophy of each party?

Vote for me

Two of the most commonly voiced criticisms of politicians are 'it doesn't matter who you vote for, they're all the same' or 'don't talk to me about politicians, you only ever see them at election time'. Despite the ingenuity of programme makers and presenters, party political broadcasts are likely to be found in the bottom, rather than the top, ten programmes. Some people may make very rational choices, reading the manifestos (a 'promise to do' or a 'wish list', depending on how you interpret them) issued by parties at election time and making an informed choice about which party offers the 'best' for the future. Many voters are likely to be more 'intuitive' – what we sometimes call being guided by a 'gut feeling'. It's very unlikely that anyone is free from outside influences. From our earliest days we are socialized (given advice, guidance and direction which helps to form our beliefs and values). Any of the factors listed below might influence the way in which people vote.

Key factors in the decision to vote

age	Older voters may be more conservative.
economy	Perceived competence of parties is likely to be important.
ethnicity	Labour appear to poll better with most minority groups.
gender	Only 20% of MPs are female but 50% of electors are women.
home	Family and friends.
issues	Things that might be particularly important at the time for example, asylum seekers.
location	There are still both local and regional patterns, with, for example, less Conservative votes in Scotland and the Liberal Democrats polling well in the south-west.
occupation	Many of the traditional 'heavy' industries have gone but working in the public sector or private sector may influence voting.
religion	Less important than it used to be, except in Northern Ireland where it is extremely significant.
tradition	How strongly someone is aligned to a particular party.

Families 'mirror' TV sitcom models
Julia Hartley-Brewer

The modern British family may not live up to the happy ideal of the 1950s sitcom, but the truth is closer to the fictionalised families on our television screens than most of us would care to admit, a psychologist claims.

While few households would confess to having any similarities with the couch potatoes in the Royle family or with the clean-cut Waltons, both are remarkably similar to many families in Britain, he says.

Even if your life may not revolve around a comfortable armchair on a Manchester council estate or, indeed, Walton Mountain, this does not mean that your closest family relationships are not mirrored in another popular sitcom.

Guy Fielding, a social psychologist at Oxford University, has argued that there are five basic family-types and all of these are accurately depicted by five of the best known television families.

As well as the Royles and the Waltons, typical British families are also mirrored in the cartoon the Simpsons.

Dr Fielding said: "These are extreme family types but most families are sitting somewhere in the middle of that grid. None of the types are better or worse, they are just different."

The Royles, according to Dr Fielding, represent families aiming to strike a balance between the needs of the family and individuals, with strong ties to each other as well as to the daily routine. The Waltons, meanwhile, enjoy routine, always putting each other first while valuing loyalty.

For the Simpsons, who value independence, the needs of the individual always come first.

The Guardian, 29 March 2000

TASKS

1 How much do television series like 'The Simpson's' and 'The Royle Family' tell us about family life and the way people think and behave?

2 Ask a small sample of friends to rank the list of factors influencing the way they vote. Be sure to include an 'other reason' category. What do your results show? What are the reasons people are not likely to reveal their intentions to you?

Voting trends

The UK currently uses a 'first past the post' system to elect people to public office. This means that, at an election, the voters select one candidate. When the votes are cast the person with the largest number of votes is elected. This happens at local and national elections. There are other systems, for example, proportional representation, where voters place the candidates in rank order.

Who to target?

Politics has a vocabulary of its own. Such jargon may be convenient for 'insiders' but it may be one reason why people claim not to be interested. One of the most over-used words is targets. Schools, hospitals, social workers, government agencies – all have targets! The maximum period between general elections is five years. The Prime Minister chooses the date for the election, but voters become targets well before elections as we edge towards the world of pollsters.

Trust the people and let them decide: using a referendum

Much is done in the names of 'the people'; often reflecting something called 'public opinion'. The word 'democracy' comes from Ancient Greece and the Greeks were among the most advanced of early political societies. Their direct democracy did allow a lot of men to participate in decision making. Modern industrial societies are much bigger. We now elect representatives to run our democracies – we elect our MPs as our representatives, although they also have to represent the views of their party, outside groups, and their own views.

Because politicians are our representatives, they make decisions on our behalf. Just occasionally, we hear the 'voice of the people' in the form of a referendum – a 'one-off' vote on an issue of national importance. Countries like Switzerland use referenda frequently, as do many American states though there they call referenda 'initiatives'. In the UK they are rare (there was one in 1975 to test public opinion on whether or not the UK should remain in what was then the European Economic Community).

Most people have opinions but they don't always think very carefully about them, nor do they analyse what they are thinking about or the decisions that they take. That could be left to politicians, but the referendum is a way of 'letting the people think' – the voting equivalent of a gigantic phone-in.

Arguments for referenda

- If we live in a democracy people should be allowed more opportunities to contribute to decision making.
- Politicians don't know what the people think, they merely think they do.
- There will be less apathy and more participation in politics.

Arguments against referenda

- The question used in a referendum needs to be clear but the arguments for and against may not be.
- Wealthy groups can use their cash to persuade people to vote in a particular way.
- The result may not be clear. For example, the 1998 referendum over a Welsh Assembly saw a 51:49% split among voters.

TASKS

1 Describe three systems for electing representative and list their advantages and disadvantages. How do the different systems affect the numbers elected by large and small parties? Which system is most likely to lead to one party having overall control of the elected body?

2 Are referenda a good thing? On what issues do you think there should be a referendum?

KEY SKILLS: *Information technology*

When the economic conditions are right, the UK will hold a referendum on membership of the European Monetary Union.

Using IT, design a referendum form to assess people's view of continued membership of the EU and the move from the pound to the ECU. Sketch your form and then translate your draft into a well-designed form using a computer. Try the form on three people and make amendments in the light of their responses. (*Level 3*)

Voting trends in UK elections: why people vote in a particular way

The voters

People who write books on voting trends rarely reach the same conclusions. Almost everyone over eighteen who puts their name on the electoral register is eligible to vote. Many don't. In general elections in the UK around 70% of those eligible to vote actually cast their vote. It is usually at least half that in local elections and lower still in elections for the European Parliament. Indeed, one question you might ask is should voting be made compulsory? It isn't in the UK, and politicians are worried. Instead of uninviting halls with temporary booths, where voters use a pencil on a piece of string to mark a cross against their choice, we may see voting taking place in supermarkets, via the phone or Internet, or on Sundays – a widely used procedure in Europe. In Australia voting is compulsory, but the problem is what penalty to apply to those who do not vote.

Understanding why people vote how they do is a complex social issue. What we have to remember is that voting is secret. Nobody knows how you voted unless you tell them, and you might not tell them the truth. Some people tend to vote for the same party at every election, but this is becoming less common. Increasingly, people see themselves as floating voters without a strong allegiance to one party. These voters are more open to persuasion than party partisans who rarely, if ever, change the way they vote. The floaters will be the target for those who operate the party information machines and who decide where to focus key party workers.

Politicians themselves are much in demand at election time. This applies particularly to well-known names and faces – party leaders and senior members of the cabinet or shadow cabinet. These 'bit hitters', especially if they are deemed to have appeal on television, may be used in campaigns to influence floating voters.

TASKS

1 Nobody can say why groups of people vote in a certain way, or why they often change their vote at each election. This is where you need to apply some Key Skills. There is a problem to solve and you need to work with others to get the best solution. IT is increasingly important in gathering databases of political information and number skills help in interpreting the results. We need to communicate our findings, perhaps both orally and in writing. Just as politicians have goals – and their main one is to persuade enough electors to vote for them in the next election – the final goal of the student is to improve their own learning and performance.

Discuss with other members of your group how you would vote at the next general election. Identify the reasons for your choice.

2 Turnout in general elections is falling. In the 2001 General Election it was 59%. In local elections, by-elections and European elections it is much lower. Discuss why people seem more apathetic about elections, and the measures that might be taken to increase voter turnout.

KEY SKILLS: *Information technology*

Make an Internet search to find out about voting patterns at the most recent election in the UK to the parliament in Westminster. Keep a note of a least three useful websites that you found and print a selection of their material.

(Level 3)

Public opinion

Government achievements and the mystery of public opinion

Another oft-quoted phrase is 'public opinion thinks …'. The sentence is probably best left unfinished. Politicians invariably claim to have insights that everybody else, except newspaper editors, lacks in terms of knowing what 'public opinion' thinks. Asked to define it, they are usually evasive. In fact, there is no such thing as public opinion – but that doesn't mean to say that we can ignore what people think and, in terms of what governments achieve, the public are the voters. At election time, they will decide whether the governing party keeps its majority.

How do we know what people are thinking?

1   We listen to what they have to say.
2   We listen to chat shows and phone-ins on radio and television.
3   We use chat rooms on the Internet
4   We read the letters columns in newspapers.

Interestingly, or infuriating as this might be, these aren't very scientific. We are left with 'impressions' and what we hear is often 'anecdotal' (based on personal experiences).

Both are too easily dismissed but we do need to think and analyse rather more deeply in an effort to uncover more reliable information. Another way of finding out what people think is:

5   We listen to focus groups.

These are comparatively new in British politics. Groups of people are asked to 'focus' on a particular issue and to advise politicians – or at least the advisers who advise the politicians. As a parliament moves towards a general election, the political parties use focus groups to target 'floating voters' – people whom, with a little persuasion, are most likely to choose them when they next vote. Politicians caricature the view of 'floating voters', who they must win over, as Essex Man, Essex Girl, Mondeo Man, Worcester Woman and Florida Woman. In 1997, Essex Man was seen to have always voted in London for the Labour Party until he moved to a suburb, became a house owner, enjoyed a more affluent lifestyle and raised his aspirations. Essex Girl was his fashion-conscious, accessory-conscious, female companion. Margaret Thatcher successfully targeted them in the 1980s. Focus groups apparently helped the Labour Party to identify the new 'floating voters' as Mondeo Man and Worcester Woman in 1997. By 2001 a 'pebble dash' equivalent was being identified.

Most wanted: the floating voters they tried to woo

Florida Woman
Name: Glenys, Anthea or Geeta. Married to Melvyn, Rod or Ajay.
Age: 33–55
Earnings: Combined income of £20–50,000, mostly brought in by Melvyn, an accountant or plumber.
Habitat: A semi-detached or former council house in East Anglia, the London suburbs or the north-west.
Markings: Two kids, an estate car and some Asda carrier bags. Hall table laden with PTA letters, a programme from a recent trip to Miss Saigon and brochures for package holidays in Disneyworld.
Politics: Naturally Tory, but wooed and won by Labour in the last election. Glenys now worries about class sizes and NHS funding — and occasionally asks Melvyn if the Tories might be worth another try.

Essex Man
Name: Derek or Barry
Age: 25–45
Earnings: £12–20,000 from the day job as a builder, though he may top this up moonlighting on Fridays as a bouncer at Sparkz nightclub.
Habitat: Housing estate in Basildon.
Markings: Ford Capri with go-faster stripes, furry dice and a personalised plate. Used to wear shell-suits but now prefers to dress down in jeans and West Ham shirt. Sports gold jewellery bought in duty free on the flight back from Benidorm.
Politics: Formerly a Labour voter, he swung firmly to the Thatcherite right in 1979. He calls the former PM "Mrs T" and laments that the country has gone to the dogs since her departure. Strongly in favour of Clause 28, though may not know much about it.

Worcester Woman
Name: Debbie, Paula or Carolyn
Age: 25–40
Earnings: £15–18,000 from her job as a clerk at the Halifax, but stopping work to have kids put a serious dent in the family finances.
Habitat: Three-bedroom detached Barratt house in Worcester.
Markings: Never leaves the house without makeup and has her highlights done every two months. Reads the Daily Mail.
Poli... ..ever voted Labour in h... ..l 1997, when she deci... ..ony Blair looked pretty genuine. The Conservatives had gone a bit far with the poll tax, after all. Beginning to wonder whether Labour are all they are cracked up to be, and strongly believes they need to spend more on the NHS.

Mondeo Man
Name: Gary, Martin or Brian
Age: 30–55
Earnings: £18–30,000 from his job as a medical rep or estate agent.
Habitat: Semi-detached house at a new development in Didcot.
Markings: Enjoys polishing the car at the weekend, dressed in jeans and a T-shirt from Burton. Feels like he spends much of his life stuck in traffic jams on the M25, when he passes the time listening to Pink Floyd CDs and Capital Gold.
Politics: Naturally suspicious of anything too lefty, but decided New Labour really had changed and might just be worth trusting on the economy.

Esther Addley

The Guardian, 4 April 2000

TASKS

1 Study the newspaper extract about floating voters. List the characteristics of Essex Man of the 1980s. Do the same for Mondeo Man, Worcester Woman and Florida Woman in 1997. Finally, find out what you can about 2001 'pebble dash' voters.

2 What are the disadvantages of using caricatures of this type?

6 We use opinion polls.

One of the most controversial issues of recent years has been the selection of candidates for the London Mayor. Adverse publicity about his private life led the official Conservative candidate, Jeffrey Archer, to be replaced by Steve Norris. Labour, using a complicated 'electoral college' system that made the votes of politicians much more valuable, proportionately, than members of the London Labour Party, chose Frank Dobson. However, another Labour MP, Ken Livingstone, once the leader of the Greater London Council until it was abolished in the mid-1980s, decided to stand as an independent after he had narrowly lost the vote for the official Labour nomination. One article claimed that Livingstone would get 61% of the vote – far more than the Labour, Conservative and Liberal Democrat candidates put together! But remember, it was only a claim.

Race for London mayor Guide to the main candidates

Ken Livingstone Independent	**Frank Dobson** Labour	**Steve Norris** Conservative	**Susan Kramer** Lib Dem	**Darren Johnson** Green
Slogan Ken4London	Frank and to the Point	Action not Politics for London	Kramer Can Do It	A strong green voice for London
Poll rating Unstoppable at 61%	Facing humiliation at 16%	Tough battle in a Labour city, on 13%	Struggling on 8%	1%
Transport No tube sell-off. Would raise money through bonds issue. Promises four years fare freeze and fully enforced bus lanes.	£8bn of investment into tube through public-private partnership. Performance pay for tube managers. Free bus passes for under-18s.	Privatise tube to invest in infrastructure; no fares rise above inflation. Priority for buses and 24-hour services. No congestion charges.	Keep the tube publicly owned, by selling revenue bonds. Congestion charges on cars and lorries during working hours on weekdays.	Reduce traffic in central London through congestion charges. Money would be used to help pedestrians and cyclists.
Crime Root out "corrupt and racist minority" from the Metropolitan police.	Named police officer – like a named GP – for everyone.	Police to tackle crimes that "make life a misery" for Londoners, including mugging, car theft and burglary.	New community constabulary to support Metropolitan police. Push for reversal of cuts in police numbers.	End prosecutions of cannabis users. Tackle police racism through new complaints and disciplinary unit.
Headline grabber Return of bus conductors	New weekly London lottery to raise £50m for health and education	Quotas of one third ethnic minorities and 50% women in cabinet and mayoral staff.	Walking every high street in London during campaign. Owns cat called Whittington.	Would love to be Ken Livingstone's deputy.

The Guardian, 4 April 2000

Influencing public opinion – views on drinking

Opening hours in British pubs have long been criticized. They are much more flexible than they once were but unfavourable comparisons are being made with European countries. It is possible that parliament might seek to change the law to permit pubs to open 24 hours a day.

'Real' opinion polls claim to be scientific and, to a large extent, they almost certainly are. Even from a thoroughly unscientific, unrepresentative and extremely limited sample, we can get some idea about what the 'person in the street' thinks about the proposal.

Streetwise... ...about 24-hour drinking

The government is currently considering controversial plans to scrap last orders and give certain pubs and clubs the chance to remain open 24 hours a day. We asked people in Ammanford what they thought.

Lin Walters, Gwauncaegurwen
Personally, it doesn't really bother me one way or another. I don't think it will have much of an affect on people's drinking habits at all.

Robert Evans, Saron
24-hour opening times probably would be a good idea. People would pace themselves a lot better and not feel under pressure to binge-drink before last orders.

Phil Jones, Cwmgors
I think it should be up to individual landlords to decide when they want to open and close. Most other European countries are a lot more liberal when it comes to opening times and they do not seem to have had problems.

Daniel Robert Gibbons, Ammanford
I have to admit that I think it would be a bad idea. Having 24 hour drinking times is only going to encourage a lot of people to spend more and more time in the pub.

Nicky Powell, Pontardawe
There are probably good and bad reasons for having 24 hour opening times. I am sure a lot of people would be happy to have the chance to stay in the pub for a few extra hours, but it might cause problems for the police.

Leann Harries, Ammanford
I am sure that having all-day opening times would stop a lot of people from binge-drinking. It would allow people the chance to take their time and not feel quite so rushed.

South Wales Guardian, 16 March 2000

CAMRA (The Campaign for Real Ale) is one of the most successful consumer pressure groups. It exists to promote the interests of drinkers of draught beer. Drink is a very political issue. Taxes and duties raise huge sums for the Exchequer. Wide-scale smuggling reduces the government's income and has a devastating impact on pubs, particularly in Kent. There are many breweries up and down the country and public houses employ a lot of people. Employment, or the loss or lack of it, is a highly sensitive political issue. Churches, temperance groups, and local residents may all wish to voice their opposition. The battle for public opinion is on and the CAMRA magazine *What's Brewing* speaks for the drinkers.

CAMRA was aware how quickly opposition to the government's plans could be mobilised
CAMRA branches must give top priority to instant rebuttal of misleading coverage of the government's proposed licensing reform. That's the message from CAMRA HQ as opponents of the long-overdue reforms resort to scaremonger tactics in a bid to whip up public anxiety. CAMRA branches and newsletter editors should expect headline-hungry local journalists, egged on by the temperance lobby, to squeeze as much shock-horror value as they can out of the story.

What's Brewing, April 2000

TASKS

1 Find out the *actual* results of the elections for London Mayor held in May 2000. Why did an 'independent' (Ken Livingstone) win, beating well-known candidates from the major political parties?

2 Which of the six ways described on pages 78–9 do you feel is most effective in gauging public opinion?

3 Comment on the way in which CAMRA has planned to influence public opinion.

KEY SKILLS: *Information technology*

During a recent data entry session your computer developed a fault. The best way of ensuring that the data file you had just completed in not lost is to create:

A a back-up file
B a hard copy
C a soft copy
D an empty file.

(Level 2)

The use and value of opinion polls

Opinion polls are carried out on a carefully designed and scientific basis in order to estimate public opinion on a particular issue. MORI and Harris are two well-known companies that carry out these polls for clients. They do not ask all of the people but a representative sample. Because they are efficient organizations and only ask a relatively small number of people, the opinion poll results can be produced very quickly. In the months, weeks and days before a general election many polls are commissioned by the newspapers and political parties to estimate the likely pattern of voting behaviour. Sometimes the poll covers the whole country, whilst at other times it focuses on voting intentions in marginal constituencies. Concern has been raised about the daily publication of opinion poll findings in the days before polling because they may influence the outcomes of the election.

Opinion polls are very important between elections. Tony Blair's vision of the 'New Labour Party' was designed to appeal to voters in what has become known as Middle England which, presumably, lies somewhere between the North–South divide. Many will be 'floating voters' – people who voted Labour in 1997 and 2001 but might not do so in future elections. They do not want to see a 'tax and spend' Labour Party, heavily influenced by the trade unions and 'freely' handing out social benefits to the 'undeserving'. They do, though, want good schools, a high quality National Health Service, less congested roads and a reliable system of public transport. These are the people who may change the way they cast their vote at the next election. They are of major interest to the political parties who need to know what these undecided voters want in return for their vote. One way of finding out is to use an opinion poll (see the newspaper extract below).

Core voters give Blair a warning

ICM interviewed 1,011 electors it had first questioned during election week in 1997. The raw data has been weighted to ensure that the sample represents the electorate of Britain as a whole, both demographically and politically (according to the 1997 election result). Interviews were conducted by telephone between 20 and 22 September.

HOW LABOUR IS SHAPING UP ON THE KEY ISSUES

Q. On balance do you think Labour is or is not keeping its promises to:

	All	Labour voters in '97
KEEP TAXES DOWN	%	%
Is	48	61
Is not	42	27
Don't know	11	12
IMPROVE BRITAIN'S STATE SCHOOLS		
Is	39	57
Is not	44	29
Don't know	16	13
IMPROVE THE HEALTH SERVICE		
Is	37	55
Is not	53	36
Don't know	10	9
REDUCE POVERTY		
Is	36	50
Is not	46	38
Don't know	17	13
STOP SLEAZE		
Is	33	55
Is not	47	34
Don't know	20	21
IMPROVE PUBLIC TRANSPORT		
Is	22	34
Is not	65	55
Don't know	13	12

Q. Do you agree or disagree with the following statements:

a) 'Tony Blair has become too arrogant since becoming Prime Minister'

	All	Labour voters in '97
	%	%
Agree	47	34
Disagree	49	63
Don't know	4	3

b) 'Tony Blair does not care enough about Labour's traditional working-class supporters'

	All	Labour voters in '97
Agree	52	46
Disagree	42	49
Don't know	6	5

c) 'Tony Blair pays too much attention to rich people who give Labour large donations'

	All	Labour voters in '97
Agree	50	42
Disagree	39	49
Don't know	11	10

Q. Gordon Brown is likely to have extra money to spend next year. Which two or three of these would be best for you and your family?

	All	Labour voters in '97
More spent on the health service	76	79
More spent on education	56	62
Higher retirement pensions	44	41
Lower income tax	34	30
More spent on public transport	32	33
Higher child benefit	15	18

The Observer, 26 September 1999

Opinion poll health warnings

Perhaps opinion polls should carry some sort of health warning. Even with the best and most scientifically structured polls, four points need to be remembered.

- Polls have a margin of error, which can be a great as +3% to –3% (this means you may think 52% are going to vote for you but the figure could be 49% or 55%).
- Some opinion polls contain a high proportion of 'don't knows'.
- When asked their opinion, or even how they just voted, some people might not tell the truth.
- Journalists often interpret and extrapolate from opinion polls, especially in writing an eye-catching headline.

There is probably no such thing as 'public opinion'. There are 'public opinions' – lots of them – but they may often change. On one day we have a snapshot. The next day the snapshot may be a little different.

What governments and political parties in the UK seek to achieve

General elections always generate a lot of interest and publicity. The campaign usually lasts for about four weeks and the news media usually provide saturation coverage. More than anything else, politicians seek power. There have been many debates about the British electoral system, mostly because it favours the two main parties and does not give fair representation (in terms of the ratio of votes to seats) to smaller parties. (Unlike many European countries, Britain does not use proportional representation in general elections.) Whichever party wins a majority in the House of Commons, which is greater than the combined number of seats of all the other parties, is likely to form the government. (Coalitions between parties, which are common in European politics, are rare in Britain.) Having offered a manifesto to the electorate prior to the election, the party with the overall majority will assume a mandate (permission to carry out its manifesto promises). In fact, this mandate is unlikely to represent the views of more than 43% of those who voted so a government cannot claim to represent the 'majority'.

The issues

There are times in political life when there is a distinct gap between the ideology of the two main parties. (This was particularly marked in the 1980s when Margaret Thatcher was Prime Minister, favouring free market economics at a time when Labour, though slowly changing, was more sympathetic to state intervention and the public sector.) The gap between the Labour and Conservative parties in the twenty-first century is probably less wide but, on some issues, differences may be observed.

- **Personalities**: following the American pattern, there is now a 'presidential' style to British politics. Much of the media focus is on the leaders of the parties and their 'approval rating' among the public.
- **The economy**: Bill Clinton spent eight years (the maximum period allowed by the American Constitution) as President of the USA. When asked about the reasons for his success he is reputed to have said, 'It's the economy, stupid'. Ability to handle the economy competently, and to get the balance of taxation right, is a key factor.
- **Social policy**: social policy affects the lives of almost everyone. It represents 'big issues' such as crime, education, social security and the National Health Service. All are sensitive political issues and all are massive consumers of resources, whether publicly or privately delivered.
- **Transport**: as the 'petrol crisis' of late 2000 revealed, petrol prices are important politically. People may care about the environment but most still need a car and the personal mobility it offers. Millions also rely on public transport. Both privatised buses and, in particular, the rail system have come in for much criticism because of the standard of service they sometimes offer.
- **Europe**: Labour is often seen as being mainly 'pro Europe' while the Conservatives often attract those who are critical of the role the UK plays in the European Union and who might seek to 'defend the £' against the threat of the Euro.
- **Special issues**: each general election will bring with it 'special issues' which do not fit easily into any category. One such issue in 2001 is likely to be the question of 'hunting with dogs' and what is seen as a threat to the rural way of life.

2 The nature of objectivity in social sciences

Definitions

Facts   Statements which can be proved on the basis of accepted facts.

Objectivity   Impartiality. The ability to make a detached analysis. Avoiding subjective judgements. Dealing with outward things, not thoughts and feelings.

Opinions   Viewpoints for which there is not an agreed body of factual evidence.

Social sciences Subjects commonly associated with the study of people, systems and ideas in society – for example, sociology, philosophy, politics, economics, human geography and psychology.

Subjectivity   A personal feeling, perhaps influenced by feelings and emotions.

Getting started

1 Are the implications of the findings of social scientists far too important to be left to social scientists?
2 Are social sciences really no more than social studies?
3 'If someone tells me they're completely objective, I think they're either a fool or a liar.' Do you agree?
4 There's nothing scientific about the social scientists.
5 The problem with social scientists is that they're all left wing.
6 Social science provides us with the tools to analyse social and economic problems. It's invaluable if we want to understand society.

Outline

You need to know something of how social scientists operate and how they present their research findings. The social sciences are full of questions to be answered and disagreements with plenty of claims and counter-claims. Pure objectivity, the ability to remain completely uninfluenced by personal feelings, thoughts and emotions is not easy and the work of anyone who claims to be 'truly objective' should be examined and analysed as critically as possible. Sometimes it is easy to distinguish between a factual statement and one that is an opinion. Sometimes the dividing line between the two may not be easy to identify. Social scientists try hard to use scientific methods and to present an objective view. We are the ones who make judgements on social, political and economic issues.

Diary of a diaster
From bragging to bail-out

February 1996
Greenwich, in east London wins the battle to host Britain's flagship millennial exhibition. It is planned to incorporate contributions from several cities, but Birmingham city council, which had proposed a rival bid, is angered at the decision.

January 1997
Deputy prime minister Michael Heseltine appeals to opposition leader Tony Blair to pledge support for the exhibition after business interests refuse to back the project without his endorsement. Blair agrees with some preconditions.

June 1997
Blair, now prime minister, gives the go-ahead to the millennium exhibition to be housed in a giant dome designed by his friend, Richard Rogers, at a cost of £750m. It is expected to attract 12m visitors.

January 1998
Stephen Bayley, the dome's creative director, walks away from the project in disgust at its lack of "vision". His successor, the former Channel 4 boss, Michael Grade, says that doubters will be left with egg on their face "as more than 12m people pour in".
  Peter Mandelson, the minister responsible for the project, goes on a highly publicised tour of Disney World in Florida to pick up ideas on how to fill the vast space. He accuses critics of having a vendetta against the dome.

February 1998
Mandelson promises a "strong spiritual element" to the dome, sparking a row over the focus of the millennium celebrations and criticism from religious leaders.

December 1999
The last station on the £3bn Jubilee Line extension of the tube, linking central London to the dome, opens.

It had been dogged by rising costs and delays and is one of the few ways of reaching the Greenwich site.

New Year's Eve 1999
Three thousand invited guests spend much of the night queuing at Stratford tube station as embarrassed dome organisers are unable to cope with the crowds.

February 2000
New Millennium Experience Company chairman Bob Ayling tells Jennie Page, the firm's chief executive, that she is sacked. Pierre-Yves Gerbeau, from Disneyland Paris, is brought in and an extra £60m is given to the NMEC.

May 2000
Mr Ayling, formerly chief executive of British Airways, resigns as part of £29m refunding deal agreed by the millennium commission, in favour of David Quarmby, chairman of the British tourist authority.

Lord Rogers, who had previously called the dome "a huge vote of confidence in the people", condemns the attraction. He says it lacks "a ringleader with a vision... We tend to go for what we call 'popular' and people don't fall for it", he says.

July 2000
A Japanese investment bank, Nomura, buys up the dome and proposes to transform it into a theme park from January 1 2001. The NMEC is given £43m as an advance against the sale of the dome.

September 2000
The NMEC is granted another £47m of public money, and David James takes over from Mr Quarmby as chairman. Millennium commission says an external review has revealed serious failings in NMEC's financial management.   **Simon Bowers**

The Guardian,
6 September 2000

Who can best pass judgement on the Dome?

Disagreements in the social sciences

Distinguishing between facts and opinions: objective physical science and subjective social scientists?

People tend to have more respect for the findings of physical scientists than they do for social scientists. They see physical scientists – studying physics, chemistry, biology, geology and physical geography – as more objective, with less involvement of their feelings and opinions. But what do we mean by their being more objective?

Science is a word that suggests certainty; people in white coats conducting experiments in laboratories, following defined routes, to reach clear precise conclusions. The process is widely deemed to be secure and respectable. If objectivity can exist then it is in the laboratory that we are likely to find it. Social scientists seek to use scientific methods to study society even though they are unlikely to wear white coats. Social scientists use observation and measurement and their laboratory is the world in which we live. Their findings are usually based upon statistical probability. They therefore have less certainty than the physical scientists do. They can only say that people probably behave in a certain way because of the factors tested. As a result, the social scientist at times lacks the authority of laboratory physical scientists.

The public perception is often that the work of social scientists is influenced by their own feelings and political beliefs, or that they consume a lot of time and money merely to confirm what, to most people, is common sense and obvious. Laws cannot predict how people will behave or react to a certain situation in the way that laws can be used to predict, for example, the expansion of a metal. In short, social science has less status than the physical sciences because of its subjective nature and lack of objectivity.

The headline 'Hope for Hunt Ban', in the article from *The Mirror*, is not objective because the word 'hope' shows that the newspaper wants a ban on hunting to take place, even though opinion on the subject is sharply divided.

HOPE FOR HUNT BAN

THE House of Commons is to get a new chance to ban fox-hunting.

In an unusual move, MPs are expected to vote on a four-option Bill.

The Bill would let them choose between an outright ban; the licensing of hunts; local referenda to vote on hunting; or keeping existing hunting laws. A final decision will not be taken until a report into the economic impact or hunting from Lord Terry Burns is published.

A Home Office source said: "The Burns report will contain recommendations on how a ban could be implemented.

"We are still a long way from a decision.

"But this suggestion is a sensible option."

A Bill giving MPs a choice is based on the strategy the Tories used to get round the issue of Sunday shopping when they were in power.

Labour has been looking for a way out of its problems over fox hunting since Tony Blair vowed last year he would ban it.

His promise seemed at odds with ministers who had refused to help backbenchers bring in a fox-hunting ban.

Some MPs fear a new Bill may fail in the Lords. A previous one failed in the Commons.

But MP Michael Foster said: "This new Bill may be a way a ban could be brought in by minimising obstruction from the Lords."

The Mirror, 6 April 2000

Making judgements on social, economic and political issues

Governments face a range of social issues. There are very few groups in society who don't try to influence governments in some way. Farmers in the UK have experienced severe difficulties in recent years, not least because of the ban on the export of British beef to some countries and the devastating impact of foot and mouth disease. The farmers and others have organized lobbies of parliament to try to influence government policies on rural issues. Governments have needed to balance these rural pressures against those arising in urban areas.

Governments also face decisions on a range of economic issues. Regional differences in the quality of life in different parts of the country, variations in levels of employment, imbalances in the skills needed for the future, the control of inflation and the retention of the confidence of the financial markets are all economic issues.

Some farmers have a low opinion of the government

Finally, governments face a range of political issues. They wish to retain power and achieve their aims. However, parliamentary time is limited, the House of Lords is still active in its scrutiny of new legislation, public opinion can be volatile and international pressures can be strong. Each minister has to face a range of political issues on a daily basis.

Governments use expert advisers to help them resolve some of these issues. These are likely to include expert physical and social scientists. The issues are complex and governments often have to choose between conflicting pieces of advice from their experts. Social scientists have additional challenges as advisers because their knowledge is less certain than that in, for example, engineering.

The objectivity of scientists

So far, the objectivity of social scientists has been questioned. However, there are those who also criticize the objectivity and role of the physical scientists.

In the extract below, George Monbiot warns us that 'real' scientists may not be quite the genuine article that we may have first imagined – but remember, it's just another subjective judgement made by a journalist.

The proliferation of papers means that some fields, however small, have become almost impossible to master. It is hardly surprising that so many readers fail to see that no scientific issue is only a scientific issue. Many nuclear physicists, for example, still insist that nuclear power is safe. In a world governed by science, they would be correct. But people, not principles, run the world. Their inability to perceive the wider consequences of their work has led some scientists to treat the anxious public with contempt. Just as science graduates can't understand the concerns of the laity, the laity can't understand the scientists.

George Monbiot, *The Guardian,* 24 February 2000

TASKS

1 Discuss the meaning of 'objectivity'.

2 Study the article 'Hope for Hunt Ban'. In what ways can it be said not to be objective? Rewrite it in a more objective form, using the same number of words.

3 'Indents' can be used in text to:
A identify the correct piece of text
B make space for bullet points
C move text in from the margin
D identifying a file that is lost.   (*Level 2*)

4 Present the following as an A5 sheet, using different size fonts to emphasize key points.

Vote for Sarah Faulkener as student president. Talk to Sarah in the Centre at 4.00 p.m. Friday.

How would you improve the flyer for members of Years 12 and 13?   (*Level 3*)

KEY SKILLS: *Generating evidence*

■ Using the theme of 'disagreement in the social sciences', agree, as a group, on a specific problem to discuss.
■ Choose a topic that is controversial – nationally, locally, or even within your school or college.
■ Take the roles of two leading, but opposed, social scientists and their supporters.
■ Construct a framework that involves identifying some basic research methods to test your hypothesis.
■ Identify the key arguments.
■ Both sides present their findings and express their views.

■ Formulate some conclusions.
■ Did the group reach a consensus or did the discussion end in disagreement?
■ Evaluate, as far as you can, the process. How scientific was it?

This activity will allow you to generate evidence of the Key Skills of Communication, Working with others and Problem solving. Depending on the issue chosen, Application of number and IT could easily play a part. The final and most difficult part of the process is to discuss the extent to which you have improved your own learning performance.   (*Level 3*)

③ Social and economic constraints

Definitions

Community Any defined, identifiable social group in a specific location or building.

Constraints Factors that limit what can be achieved. Obstacles to success.

Economics The framework embracing employment and unemployment, income and spending, taxes and commerce, finance and business. The interaction between agreed priorities and scarce resources.

Leisure Activities undertaken for pleasure and relaxation beyond work, school or college.

Private transport Any form of personal transport owned by an individual.

Public transport Any form of transport that, on payment of fares, carries passengers.

Social Connected with any aspect of society, individuals, groups and activities. The different social classes in society. The structure of how we live.

Social benefits Payments made by public bodies, such as central government and local councils, to those who qualify to receive them – for example, old-age pensions, child benefits, income support payments, housing benefits.

Social classes Different groups within the social structure, often divided on the basis of factors such as birth, wealth, residence, education and accent.

Social Services Public services – for example, education, housing, health and social security – provided by public bodies such as central government and local councils.

Getting started

1 'If you want a real education, you won't get one in school.'
2 'The fact that such a rich country as Britain has homeless people begging is a public scandal.'
3 'No matter how much money is poured into the National Health Service it won't be enough.'
4 'Most of those on Job Seeker's Allowance are just idle scroungers.'
5 How far do men and women have equal employment opportunities?
6 'The problem with communities is that everybody keeps falling out with each other.'
7 'As last we're living in a classless society.'
8 'Some people get paid a lot more than others because they have skills and need incentives.'
9 'The only taxes we should have are those that pay for defence and the police.'
10 'Public transport is what's used by commuters and those who can't afford anything better.'

Outline

This section begins with a consideration of how education, housing provision, health services and social benefits affect the lives of different people. It then addresses the problems in providing the four social services. The section then examines the worlds of work and leisure, changes in the jobs people do, unemployment, the world of work and work experience, how people spend their leisure time and the facilities for leisure in different communities. This leads on to a consideration of the division of wealth among social classes, wage and salary levels for different jobs and why they vary. The section concludes with an examination of travel and transport in the community: provision and quality of bus and rail services, the use of private transport, and how people travel to work.

In each of these topics the emphasis is upon the way in which social and economic constraints condition provision.

Social and economic constraints: introduction

A quick look at the essentials

It has often been said that we 'work to live, not live to work'. Bear that in mind when thinking about the content of the social sciences. There are four main social services: education, housing, health and social benefits. Of these four main social services, we experience something to do with education and health from an early age. Our parents receive one of the social benefits (it used to be called family allowance) and we all become aware of the issues connected with housing. For young people, education and training is probably the most important of these. Getting a good job brings rewards in terms of job satisfaction, personal fulfilment and financial reward. Each age group places different demands upon the social services.

It's not easy to sum up a large part of our lives in a single paragraph but sometimes, 'synthesis' (the ability to summarize in a way that just brings out the most important points) is invaluable. Here are some further pointers that might be helpful before we look at social and economic constraints in more detail.

- 'Topical' issues change quickly, but you should try to identify those associated with education, housing, health and social benefits. You do not need a detailed knowledge of the services that are run, but you need to be aware of areas of controversy. These could include criticisms of what schools do or do not achieve, the number of the homeless young people on the streets, the costs of raising standards and meeting demand in our hospitals and how to meet the needs of people like the unemployed or asylum seekers.
- Work patterns are changing and most people should expect to change careers and therefore be flexible and adaptable. Most students will have undertaken some work experience and are better prepared to enter the world of paid employment, increasingly influenced by ICT.
- Leisure patterns are changing dramatically with a wider range of recreational facilities available locally and less expensive holidays allowing mass tourism at home and abroad.
- There used to be three main social classes (upper, middle, working). Although no longer mentioned as often as it was, social class remains important and was never as straightforward it appeared. (New classifications appear in the 2001 census.)
- Travel is essential to our lives. We are much more mobile and we have higher aspirations.

TASKS

1 'Since we have paid our taxes to have the four main social services there should be no beggars.' Discuss whether you think we should give money to beggars.

2 Find out how patterns of employment and unemployment changed your community and why the changes have taken place. Which people are most likely to be unemployed? What is it like to be without work? What sort of support can be given?

3 Find out what leisure facilities are available in your area for people of all ages and incomes. Suggest additions that appear to be needed. Assuming there is no extra money available, which facilities could be cut to make way for your recommendations?

4 What role does social class play in your life and the lives of your friends?

5 Carry out a survey of public transport in your area. In addition, ask some users of public transport for their ideas on ways in which it could be made more attractive to car users. Ask if criticisms of public transport are really justified.

6 'The economy is the key' is how many people have come to interpret election results. The reasoning is that people will vote for a party that they think is competent to run the economy.

KEY SKILLS: *Information technology*

Which spreadsheet tool would you use so that information is shown in alphabetical order?

A File   C Chart
B Sort   D Format   (*Level 2*)

Money matters

Without the necessary financial resources we will have no services and, in our own lives, we can have only what we can afford. Even if we use credit cards, as millions do, we have to pay in the end. It is the same for governments. They raise money in taxes to pay for the services they provide. In the UK, everyone pays taxes – for example, income tax, VAT, duty on fuel, tobacco and alcohol. The income from these taxes is spent on, for example, health,

education, transport and the armed services. Some countries spend more than their taxes bring in and get into debt. They borrow money from banks to fund development projects that they hope will increase their income.

The person who is closest to the nation's purse strings, at least in politics, is the Chancellor of the Exchequer. He has to compare what the government spends on services with what it receives from taxes. A wrong move, in a global economy where there are some very powerful players, will 'send shock waves through the City' – 'the City' being the major financial networks in the City of London. The Chancellor and his advisors must somehow try to reconcile conflicting interests. The first extract gives us a glimpse behind what is described as 'The Chancellor's fridge door'.

The second extract ('If it's burning a hole in his pocket') creates a lot of scope for study and use of some of the Key Skills. Towards the end of 1999, it was widely believed that the Chancellor had a 'surplus' of £20 billion to spend. The extract identifies eight options for Gordon Brown, ranging from the doubling of spending on schools, to sending home £800 in a 'Vote Labour' envelope. You can use most, if not all, of the six Key Skills to look at the options, evaluate them, discuss the outcomes and reach a consensus on how the £20 billion might be spent. Groups, or people within them, are unlikely to agree – which is why the social sciences remain full of controversy.

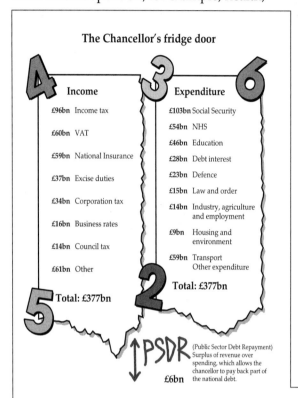

The Chancellor's fridge door

Income

£96bn	Income tax
£60bn	VAT
£59bn	National Insurance
£37bn	Excise duties
£34bn	Corporation tax
£16bn	Business rates
£14bn	Council tax
£61bn	Other

Total: £377bn

Expenditure

£103bn	Social Security
£54bn	NHS
£46bn	Education
£28bn	Debt interest
£23bn	Defence
£15bn	Law and order
£14bn	Industry, agriculture and employment
£9bn	Housing and environment
£59bn	Transport Other expenditure

Total: £377bn

↑PSDR↓ £6bn (Public Sector Debt Repayment) Surplus of revenue over spending, which allows the chancellor to pay back part of the national debt.

Latest prospects for the economy

Percentage change unless otherwise stated	What happened in 1999	November forecast for 2000	Yesterday's forecast for 2000	Yesterday's forecast for 2001	Average latest independent forecast for 2001
Economic growth (Gross domestic product)	2	2.5–3.0	2.75–3.25	2.25–2.75	2.6
Spending by consumers	4	2.75–3.0	3.5–3.75	2–2.5	2.6
Govt and local authority spending	3.5	3	4	2.75	2.8
Investment	5.25	2.25–2.5	3.25–3.75	3.75–4.25	3.6
Stockbuilding	−0.75	0.25	0.25	0	1.9
Exports	2.5	6.5–6.75	5.5–6	5.5–6	5.6
Imports	7.25	6–6.5	7.75–8.25	5.5–6	5.9
Balance of payments (current account, £bn)	−12.25	−10.25	−20.5	−21	−17.9
RPI (4th quarter, excluding mortgage interest)	2.25	2.5	2.25	2.5	2.3
Money GDP (total value of economy, £bn)	901	–	946–951	990–1,000	–
PSNB* (excess of spending over revenue, £bn)	−11.9	−3	−6	−5	−7.5

*Fiscal year
After allowing for inflation except retail prices, current account and where indicated. Calendar years except PSNB and money GDP: (financial year)

The Guardian, 22 March 2000

If it's burning a hole in his pocket...

What Brown could do with £20bn

Double spending on schools.

Raise defence spending by 100 per cent.

Cut the basic tax rate to 15 per cent, or scrap the higher rate.

Cut VAT to 11 per cent.

Abolish petrol and diesel duty.

Scrap all taxes on cigarettes, drink and gambling.

Repay 5 per cent of the national debt.

Send every home £800 in a 'Vote Labour' envelope.

The Observer, 19 September 1999

Building a fairer society...

Budget 2000 takes further steps to support families and pensioners, ensure a fair tax system and protect the environment:

- an extra £4.35 a week for the under 16 child credit in the **Working Families' Tax Credit** from June (and for the child allowance in Income Support from October) and an extra 50p a week on the **Children's Tax Credit** when it is introduced in April 2001. The value of the Children's Tax Credit will be more than twice the married couple's allowance (withdrawn from April 2000) which it replaces.
- a £100 increase in the Sure Start Maternity Grant to £300 from the summer;
- as a result of measures announced in this Parliament, 1.2 million children will be lifted out of poverty;
- support for **pensioners** including a further increase in the winter fuel payment from £100 to £150 for every household with someone over 60;
- a boost for **savings**, with the current £7,000 Individual Saving Account (ISA) contribution limit retained for 2000–01;
- a 5% real increase in **tobacco duty**, with the additional revenue raised going towards investment in the National Health Service;
- a freeze in **spirits duty**, while increasing **alcohol duties** in line with inflation; and
- protecting the **environment** through reforms to **vehicle excise duty** including an extension of the reduced rate to cars with engines up to 1,200cc from March 2001 – benefiting 2.2 million more cars; increases in **road fuel duties** in line with inflation; reforms to **company car tax** to increase in **landfill tax** to promote better waste management; and a new levy on the extraction of **aggregates** from 2002.

This is how the Chancellor spent some of the 'surplus'

HM Treasury, March 2000
Crown Copyright is reproduced with the permission of the
Controller of Her Majesty's Stationery Office.

TASKS

1 Study the tables of income and expenditure in the extract 'The Chancellor's fridge door'. How far do you agree with priorities for spending?

2 Compare the 2000 Budget with the Budget of 2001.

3 What do you think the Chancellor of the Exchequer should do with £20 billion? On what basis might he need to decide priorities?

4 Discuss what is meant by the term 'a fairer society'. How far do you think the measures listed above will help to achieve it? What else might be done to reach this goal?

KEY SKILLS: *Information technology*

1 The table below shows the exchange rate of the pound against other European currencies on a day in November 2000.

Euro	1.67	Austria	23.00	Belgium	67.43
Denmark	12.47	France	10.96	Germany	3.27
Ireland	1.31	Italy	3236	Netherlands	3.68
Norway	13.38	Portugal	335.13	Spain	278.14
Sweden	14.49				

Use the Internet to find out the names of the currencies of these countries. Enter the information on a spreadsheet in alphabetical order. Give the spreadsheet a title including in the names of the other currencies.

(Level 3)

2 Using the spreadsheet you have created, rearrange the countries in terms of the value of their currencies. Print out the new table.

(Level 3)

What do we mean by social class?

Society is dynamic. Coping with change is becoming increasingly difficult, not least because of the massive advances in information technology. Trying to attach labels to people is usually dangerous because we are trying to allocate people according to an agreed set of criteria. The problem is that people can't agree what the criteria should be. Traditionally, class has been represented in a pyramid shape, though it is said that, after the 2001 census, the shape will be like an hour glass.

However, things have changed. The former Prime Minister John Major liked to talk about a 'classless' society. Certainly many of the traditional manual jobs in heavy industry have disappeared. More people have merged into the 'middle classes', yet we are also said to have an 'underclass'. These are people who exist on the margins of society, often on large estates, caught in a cycle of deprivation.

Here is another view of the class system:

A who's who guide to the class war

Not sure which class you belong to? Let *Socialist Worker* help you decide. The paper has been running a series of columns in which it defines who belongs to the ruling, middle and working classes

The ruling class

Most of us rarely, if ever, meet or see this ruling class. They flit between their expensive homes across the world, borrowing, living, socialising and eating in a world of their own. They are people who, through their control of the major financial institutions and companies, take the decisions that determine what happens to the rest of us… The ruling class owns and controls the press and TV, education and culture… [They] have their own separate clubs, culture and schools to instill a sense of superiority into themselves.

The middle classes

Firstly, there is the fairly small section which carries out disciplinary and bullying functions for the ruling class. This includes line managers and senior office managers… These ``little Hitlers'' of management play a role in directing the process of exploitation… and demanding that everyone else works longer and harder… These include the higher ranks of the armed forces, top legal figures, consultants and senior hospital managers, college principals, pro-capitalist newspaper columnists, the heads of the bureaucracies in the councils and education… At the other extreme, there are people deemed "middle class" who are teachers, social workers, nurses and ordinary office workers. These people are really part of the working class… Between the two groups we have already identified, there are others who are genuinely in the middle. For example, heads of primary schools are not the same as ordinary teachers, but nor are they like a council's head of education or the headmaster of Eton.

The working class

People say the "traditional" working class of industrial workers, like miners and dockers, is declining. They also deny that white collar workers [are] part of the working class… [In fact,] the number of industrial workers is vastly bigger [than in Marx's time]… [There is] a global working class whose conditions of life and work, and even the way they dress and the music they listen to, are more and more similar… Even in Britain… there are still millions of manufacturing and industrial workers… Every time a social or political crisis erupts, the question, ``What will the workers do?'' is at the centre of debate. This is especially true among the ruling class, who know only too well the power of those they depend on.

From **Socialist Worker**, October 2, 9 & 22

TASKS

1 Using your own community, attempt to determine whether, and in what forms, a class system exists.

2 What does data from the 2001 census tell us about social class in the twenty-first century?

KEY SKILLS: *Information technology*

Population of Japan (1998)		
1	A	B	C
2	Age Group	Percentage male	Percentage female
3	0–14	8	7
4	15–29	11	10
5	30–44	10	10
6	45–59	11	11
7	60–74	7	9
8	75+	2	4

The total percentage of the population that is female can be found using which formula?
  A SUM A1:C8
  B SUM(B3:B8)
  C SUM(C3:C8)
  D C3 + C8

(*Level 2*)

How education affects the lives of different people

When Labour won the 1997 general election, Tony Blair's slogan was 'education, education, education', but as Polly Toynbee, a *Guardian* columnist, suggests 'very large sums of money over many years will be needed to approach anything like the educational nirvana Tony Blair desires'.

The main changes taking place in education are:

- children now start school at an earlier age, as low as three in some areas
- there is more testing of children and school 'league tables' are published showing things like examination results and attendance figures
- most children over the age of eleven go to comprehensive schools, though the parents of about eight per cent of children pay fees for them to attend independent schools
- there has been a dramatic increase in the number of students remaining at school beyond sixteen, and in those going on to some form of higher education
- the links between social class, educational opportunity and achievement remain strong
- more emphasis is being placed on life-long learning, providing opportunities for people of all ages to take a variety of courses, many of which will help to develop their work skills, of which IT is an important one.

We are a long way behind many other countries, as Polly Toynbee reminded us in a *Guardian* article of 3 December 1999. We failed to recognize the growing importance of scientific and technical education in the late nineteenth century, having once been the 'workshop of the world' and, as countries such as France and the USA developed more universities, the British Prime Minister, Gladstone, was arguing that compulsory education was 'adverse to the national character'. According to Ms Toynbee, as we enter the new millennium, 'one in four adults lack basic literacy ... , our 13 year olds fall to 25th place in world numeracy tables and we have the lowest staying-on rates, at 16, in the developed world.'

Britain is failing on education
Our 'divisive' system must end

THIS GOVERNMENT talks a good game when it comes to social inclusion and children. It has produced a catalogue of initiatives – all with names designed to suggest a new dawn. Sure Start for young mothers, New Start for alienated teenagers and Fresh Start for failing schools sounded wonderfully millenarian when introduced. But the cold reality in this first year of the twenty-first century is that our education system remains the most fragmented and divisive in Western Europe. Even those close to Tony Blair know this to be true. Before he joined the Number 10 Policy Unit, Andrew Adonis wrote a series of articles for this newspaper entitled 'The Great Divide' in which he lamented the 'apartheid' in the schools system that Labour had inherited from the Tories. Tragically, all too little has changed. No one should gloat at the failure of Fresh Start, least of all the Conservative Party, itself responsible for two decades of neglect which brought state education to its knees. But the news that only one of the Government's Fresh Start schools has shown any marked improvement in standards comes as no surprise when nothing has been done to tackle the fundamental divide at the heart of British education.

The summer began with a row over elitism at Oxford. Autumn begins with a 'sink-school' crisis. The two issues are interlinked. We have an education system based on elitism. While we continue to find it acceptable that our top universities should be dominated by children who have attended private schools, it is unlikely that we will tackle the so-called 'failing schools' at the bottom. This Government desperately hoped to finesse the politically explosive issues of selection and private schools, and concentrate on improving the rump of the comprehensive system instead. This is clearly not working and the children in need of greatest support are still not receiving enough.

This is a matter of such gravity that the Prime Minister should institute a National Commission to investigate educational underperformance. At the top of its agenda should be the issues of selection, the current poor governance of so many state schools and the unfairly advantageous charitable status of private ones.

The Observer, 3 September 2000

TASKS

1 The budget of your school/college is to be increased. Without going into detailed costing, list your priorities in order of importance and justify your choice. Priorities that you might like to think about could include:

- higher pay for teachers/lecturers to reduce shortages
- better buildings
- a new ICT (or other specialist) centre
- more books and equipment
- better pupil:teacher ratios to cut class sizes
- small grants for post-16 students
- better community facilities within the school/college
- improved facilities for those with special needs
- investing more in the performing arts – music, dance, drama
- other projects of particular relevance to your school/college.

2 Read the article 'Britain is failing on education'. Identify the ways that the newspaper editorial claims that Britain is failing in education. Giving reasons, say how far you agree or disagree with this viewpoint.

How housing, health and social services affect the lives of people

Education is only one of the many 'social services' that people use. Some say it is the most important because it can influence what we achieve throughout our lives. The importance of qualifications is emphasized everywhere.

Other important social services, which can also play an important part in our lives, are housing, health and social benefits. The 'social services' we talk about are mainly those provided by central government (which is often responsible for much of the funding) and local councils – or health care trusts in the case of many health services. Some issues cause controversy that is difficult to resolve.

Examples of these might be:

- choice, and the right of individuals to pay – for example, for private, rather than National Health Service, treatment
- whether or not central government does too much and holds too much power
- if services are provided by the government, does this mean that there is no incentive for individuals to take personal responsibility?
- should benefits be 'universal' (payable to all) or 'selective' (payable only to those in need)?
- is 'choice' just a convenient way of 'jumping the queue' for those who can afford it?

Housing

It is more common for people to 'own their own home' in the UK than in many other countries, but houses are expensive, especially in parts of the country within travelling distance of London. Rented accommodation is often equally expensive, and there are far fewer council houses available than there were 20 years ago. In some cities there are large, local-authority-built estates characterized by poverty, despair and high rates of crime. Rural areas also have areas of poor housing but these are far less concentrated. At the end of the 1990s, it was estimated that over 125,000 people in England and Wales were sleeping rough. Beggars returned to the streets in the 1990s and, in 1991, the magazine *The Big Issue* was set up. It campaigns for better housing provision. Shelter is another housing pressure group. It was set up in the 1960s when there was public outrage after the BBC Play for Today, *Cathy Come Home* used harrowing scenes of insensitive officials and families being broken up.

This short poem by Nicole provides a poignant insight into the life of a homeless person.

LIVING IN THE COLD WEATHER SHELTER

In by six
Out by nine
It's raining and cold
But that's fine
Dodgy food
Cold cups of tea
A messy room
with a view to the sea

So-called resettlement
with help that's too late
Back living on the streets
That's fact, that's fate!

NICOLE

The Big Issue, 3–9 April 2000

Nurseries close as council faces £40m cash gap

At two nursery schools in Stoke Newington, north London, the finger paintings that used to adorn the wall have been replaced. In their stead hang the sort of posters more usually associated with industrial action than early learning. "Stop the council wrecking our lives... stop the cuts," they say.

This outbreak of militancy among the parents of the under-fives who attend the Fernbank and Atherden Road nurseries was sparked last Friday evening when parents collecting their children were told as of yesterday they would have to attend other nurseries within the borough; the two centres would be closed until further notice.

Outraged, the parents announced they would occupy the centres, sleeping over if necessary, so that their children could continue to be cared for in familiar surround-

ings. Yesterday, despite the provision of places for the children elsewhere, the occupation continued.

The underlying cause of the closures is the financial bog in which the local authority, Hackney council, has become mired. Last week the borough treasurer ordered that spending be frozen and told the council to produce a cuts package within 21 days amid fears of an overspend approaching £40m. The closure of Fernbank was an early indication that the emergency measures were beginning to bite.

In a special report to the council, which is run by a Labour-Conservative coalition, treasurer George Jenkins forecast that the overspend would fall between £14.5m and £22m with the worst case scenario seeing the council £40m in the red. No new staff can be taken on and no spending commit-

ments made until a cuts package has been accepted. Before the special measures were introduced the council was already committed to trimming £22m from council spending for the 2000–2001 financial year.

The malaise in Hackney, where gentrification has set some of the capital's most desirable real estate alongside desperately needy estates, is deep rooted. Years of council infighting impeded decision making and a series of high profile projects have ended in overspend and confusion.

A leisure centre in Stoke Newington has run £10m over budget and is still not open, and the council is embroiled in a legal battle after a disastrous attempt to privatise its revenue, benefits, council tax and business rates collection and payment system.

Paul Kelso and Peter Hetherington,
The Guardian, 24 October 2000

The government estimates a need for over 4 million new homes to be built in the UK. The policy is to build on brownfield land where possible, though some new settlements and expansion of existing ones will be necessary. Some of this housing must be affordable to those on low incomes and it should also reflect the changing nature of housing demand, which shows an increase in single occupiers, single-parent families and more elderly couples.

Health

'Choice' always exists. The idea of a 'welfare state' first emerged in the early years of the 1900s for the most needy in society. In 1945, after the end of World War II, a wider service was envisaged, spanning life from 'cradle to grave'. When the National Health Service was first launched in 1948, it was entirely free, but the costs were massive and prescription charges were brought in almost immediately. As expectations and needs have risen over the years, the social services are very costly to provide for the nation. Those who can afford it may choose to contribute to private pensions, pay private school fees and join a private health scheme. Since tenants were given the right to buy their council houses in the 1980s, many more people now own their own houses – although most have large mortgages. Increasingly, voluntary groups help in the provision of services but their resources are much more limited than those of the state or major private providers.

Health services continue to be high on the political agenda, and are likely to be a key factor in influencing voters at future general elections. The UK has an ageing population because of dietary improvement, greater affluence, warm housing and medical advances. New technology, which does things undreamed of in 1948, is often very expensive. The same applies to medicines. We expect more of our hospitals and medical services and demand efficiency gains rather than paying more in higher taxation. Successive governments have significantly increased the amount spent on the health service but we still need more specialist doctors and more nurses. Once it was claimed that the UK had the best health service in the world. Here are some figures that might help you form a judgement.

The best health service in the world?

- Britain has about the lowest number of doctors in the developed world, with one for every 625 people. In the US it's one for every 384, and in France one for every 344.
- Britain spends less on health care than virtually any other developed country. In 1997, we spent £869 per head on health, compared with £1,245 in the Netherlands, £1,490 in Germany and £2,559 in the US.
- Over the last 10 years, the number of acute beds in Britain has fallen by 25,000.
- Men with lung cancer have only a 7 per cent likelihood of living five years in Britain, half the survival rate of France, Spain and the Netherlands.
- Women with breast cancer have a 67 per cent chance of living more than five years, compared to 80 per cent in France, Sweden or Switzerland.
- Every year, 314 of every 100,000 men in Britain die from heart disease, compared with 202 in Australia, 233 in the US and 251 in Germany.
- Britain carries out fewer heart operations of almost all types than nearly any other developed country in the world.
- The amount spent on food per patient per day by the NHS: £1.70.

The Observer, 16 January 2000

Social benefits

Social benefits are paid mainly by government agencies (such as the Benefits Agency) although some, such as housing benefits, are paid by local councils. Some benefits are universal and are paid to all who qualify. For example, parents with children can all claim child benefit, irrespective of their income. Other benefits are selective. These are paid only because people need support, perhaps because their income without support would be very low. This might apply to people with disabilities who are unable to work. Some benefits are funded from direct taxation. Others, such as Unemployment Benefit, may depend on what a person has previously paid into a compulsory government National Insurance fund.

KEY SKILLS: *Information technology*

Flats are offered for rent at the following rates per calendar month.

Central	£120	Cranham Rd	£335
Station	£410	Hewlett Rd	£375
Gretton	£650	Pittville	£625

Enter the information into a spreadsheet and arrange the flats in terms of cost per month with the most expensive at the head of the table. Add a column and calculate (using a formula instruction) the cost per twelve calendar months. *(Level 3)*

Imagine a health service where...

- You can get an appointment with your GP on the day you call
- You can visit a GP either near your home or near work
- You can go to a walk-in clinic anywhere and the doctor can access your medical records on computer
- You have more than six minutes with your GP, so they have time to give you a full explanation and answer your questions
- You can have yearly health check-ups
- You can book an appointment direct with a consultant if you know the general nature of your problem
- You can choose the time of your appointment
- You can choose your consultant and your surgeon
- Operations are never cancelled
- The food in hospital is edible, the toilets are clean, the paint isn't peeling, and the staff aren't harassed
- You don't have to wait more than half an hour to see a doctor at accident and emergency
- You don't have to spend days waiting on a trolley in a corridor if you are admitted to hospital through accident and emergency
- If you have suspected cancer, you can have a scan and a biopsy the next day
- If you are diagnosed as having cancer, you can start treatment immediately and you are treated by a cancer specialist
- If you have a stroke you are treated by a stroke specialist
- If you need a heart operation, you are operated on immediately
- If you have a non life-threatening but painful condition such as severe arthritis, you don't have to wait more than three months for an operation
- You aren't denied life-saving treatment, which you would be given if you lived in another health authority

The Observer, 26 March 2000

TASKS

1 Suppose the target for your local area is 50,000 new houses. What type of housing needs to be built and where should it be located? What will be the main points raised by those who object to these changes?

2 Study the information provided about the health service and suggest what you now think the health service could be like. What are the implications of our 'dream' health service and how could it possibly be achieved?

3 How long should waiting lists be? Should the National Health Service provide treatment on demand? What would be the implications of such a policy?

4 Why are some people resentful of paying taxes to fund social benefits?

Work: changes in the jobs people do

A job for life?

Until very recently, it was widely assumed that many people would do the same sort of job, perhaps even for the same employer, all their lives. Information technology and the growth of a highly competitive global economy have changed that. Increasingly, employees need to be better qualified, flexible (willing to change jobs) and mobile.

The structure of the economy has changed. Traditional, so-called 'staple' industries, such as mining, steel and shipbuilding, have all but disappeared in the UK. Both the primary sector (mostly mining and agriculture) and the secondary sector (manufacturing) have been under great pressure. More and more people work in the service sectors (services range from international finance to fast food). All the time, the emphasis is on a better-trained, more skilled workforce. The balance of this workforce has changed. Many more women work, although many are in part-time jobs. Far fewer people over 55 work than was the case 10 years ago. A national minimum wage was established in 1999 and 'homeworking' is likely to spread as access to information and communication technology increases.

Jobs for life are likely to become a thing of the past and hence the emphasis on 'lifelong education'.

The extracts that follow show the views of three different people.

The Single Mum

'I work full-time for the railways. The thing about being a single parent is you never have time for yourself. I'd love to go to the gym, or even have a drink after work, but I can't. If you do get a spare moment, you spend it with the kids.

'It's all very well people saying that you can use your time more effectively, but you have to be in control of it to do that — and I'm not.'

Jill Milnes, single parent

The Executive

'I never feel I have enough time. Maybe if I didn't need to sleep I could get everything done. By the time you have finished work, got home and wound down, it is time to think about bed to do it all again the next day.

'I fill every hour – if I had more time I would do more nothing. Doing nothing is not an option for people with a career, especially if they commute.'

Simon Burton, single,
senior marketing executive

The Schoolboy

'Things are getting faster. I quite often feel I don't have enough time — at the weekends, too. I do schoolwork every night.

'That can take an hour sometimes. Next year I have to take my Sats exams, so I'll have to study more for them. If I had more time I'd do more skateboarding.'

Arthur Hodder,
12-year-old schoolboy

The Observer, 3 October 1999

TASKS

1 Compare the work pattern experienced by the oldest member of your family with the pattern that you expect to have.

2 Plan a diary over, say, a week showing how you use your time. Ask others to do the same. Compare diaries at the end of the week and discuss the way you use your time.

KEY SKILLS: *Information technology*

A library has introduced a bar code system for the issue and return of books. One advantage of this is:

A more books will be borrowed
B books will be easier to find on the shelves
C books can be purchased automatically
D checking of overdue books will be easier.

(Level 2)

How people spend their leisure time

Time to play

Leisure can mean different things to different people. It can take place relatively cheaply in the home. It can take place at little cost away from the home. The quality of leisure opportunities is increasingly likely to depend on our age, income, where we live, socio-economic grouping, personal taste, access to transport and whether or not we have any disabilities. Leisure usually does mean pleasure in one form or another but, taking areas as diverse as holidays, sport, pubs and clubs, entertainment, gardening and educational opportunities for adults, the changes even in the last ten years have been rapid and far-reaching. For some, at least, 'leisure' has become a 'lifestyle'.

Consider the implication of the changes in lifestyle in the extracts below.

How lifestyle changes have affected spending trends

The home
The south-east property boom has fuelled a 26% rise in prices since 1989. Spending on services such as domestic and garden help has grown by 45% in a decade, while major home improvement is the main spending priority among affluent middle-aged women.

Household goods
The largest area of growth has been in home offices and new technology, a negligible market a decade ago but now worth £2bn. Sales in the brown goods sector have doubled in five years, and the television market is still strong.

Food, drink, tobacco
Convenience foods rose by 16% to 1994 and by a further 17% since. They are particularly important to 15–24 year-olds and "sedentary" females. Wine has seen a 7% increase in sales, testimony to the British consumer's "increasingly sophisticated" palate. Hot drinks out-performed soft drinks in the past five years. Oddly, smokers are keener on music than are non-smokers.

Entertainment
Eating out becomes more popular as prosperity spreads. In 1999 we spent £21.4bn in restaurants and pubs, equivalent to almost half of what we spend on eating at home. Gambling, cinemas and theme parks have flourished at the expense of traditional entertainment such as museums and zoos. The toy market, stimulated by the emergence of computer games, has soared by 75% in a decade.

Travel
Now seen as a necessity, we take more and shorter holidays thanks to cheaper flights and better connections, which have in turn hit the domestic market. Spending on cars is £41bn, equivalent to £1,516 per car on the road. 53% of adults regard their car as important to lifestyle, and 38% would buy a new one as a priority, given financial security.

Personal goods
The clothing market has grown by 38%, with footware and jewellery performing particularly well. Sales of toiletries have increased by 69% in 10 years.

Health
The NHS is still cherished by 37% of people, while 9% want private health insurance. Improvements in diet have seen the consumer base for laxatives shrink.

Financial services
Pensions account for £60bn of gross expenditure, with personal schemes growing by 13% as occupational schemes fell by 28% to 1994. Since then, however, the mis-selling scandals have seen the trend reversed.

Paul Kelso, *The Guardian*, 9 February 2000

TASKS

1 Plan a survey of people's use of their leisure time using a brief questionnaire. Show the results in the form of a graph or a bar chart.

2 Some people say they are too busy to have leisure time. Others suggest it is healthy to work hard and play hard.
a Why is leisure time good for you?

b Using your local newspaper, make a count of the number and range of local clubs in the area. Include sports teams as well as special interest clubs and leisure courses. Comment on your findings.

3 What information can be deduced from the graphs on p. 97?

KEY SKILLS: *Information technology*

Your are preparing a poster to advertise a Christmas disco at your school or college. Any profits from the event will go to the most popular charity of those attending the disco.

You can expect to have at least £300 to donate. Use either clipart, your Centre's intranet or the Internet to select and print a suitable image.

(*Level 3*)

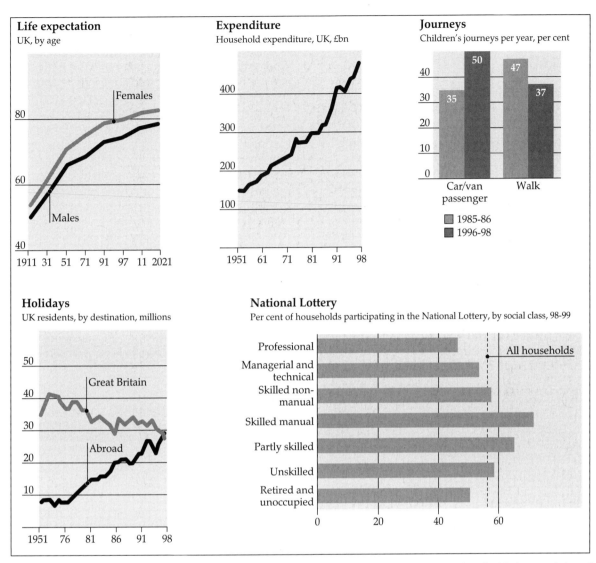

Life expectation
UK, by age

Females

80

Males

60

40

1911 31 51 71 91 97 11 2021

Expenditure
Household expenditure, UK, £bn

400

300

200

100

1951 61 71 81 91 98

Journeys
Children's journeys per year, per cent

40

30

20

10

0

Car/van
passenger   Walk

35   50   47   37

■ 1985-86
■ 1996-98

Holidays
UK residents, by destination, millions

50

Great Britain

40

30

Abroad

20

10

1951 76 81 86 91 98

National Lottery
Per cent of households participating in the National Lottery, by social class, 98-99

Professional

Managerial and
technical

Skilled non-
manual

Skilled manual

Partly skilled

Unskilled

Retired and
unoccupied

All households

0   20   40   60

Crown Copyright is reproduced with the permission of
Her Majesty's Stationary Office.

Social Trends, 30, HMSO, 2000

The division of wealth among different social classes

Incomes: rich and poor

Without some sort of income we are left destitute, and either starve or have to beg. Incomes vary enormously, with some senior executives, entertainers and sports people earning more in one year than many working people earn in a lifetime. Among the poorest groups in the UK are many older people, especially widows, who are dependent on the state pension. Pressure groups seeking to protect pensioner interests challenge governments to maintain the value of the state pension in comparison with average earnings. Governments are cautious because the number of pensioners is rising as life expectancy increases. This means raising the level of taxes, which is unpopular, to pay for the pensions. One way to reduce this tax burden is for more people to invest in private pensions throughout their working lives.

The money earned at work pays for our daily lives as well as our contribution to society through taxes. The majority of people on high incomes have earned their position and carry heavy responsibilities. Higher earners pay proportionally more of their income in tax.

Although Britain is often described as a wealthy country, there are obviously marked contrasts between the spending capacity of the rich and of the poor. Shown below is what happened when a lord became a fixed-income pensioner for a week.

LORD ON A BUDGET

Help the Aged transformed 32-year-old Lord Redesdale into a 76-year-old pensioner with savings of £5,000, and living in rented property. After all his essential outgoing budgeted for, he is left with £28.99 disposable income per week

HIS INCOME

Basic State pension	**£66.75**
Occupational pension	**£12.53**
Disabled living allowance	**£14.05**
TOTAL WEEKLY INCOME	**£93.33**

HIS WEEKLY OUTGOINGS

Rent, mortgage or home loan	**£35.00**
Gas	**£5.00**
Electricity	**£5.00**
Water rates	**£5.00**
Home Insurance	**£3.80**
Council tax (Band B)	**£10.54**
TOTAL WEEKLY OUTGOINGS	**£64.34**

WHAT HE SPENT

TV licence stamp	**£2.00**
Phone bill	**£3.00**
Cat food	**£1.80**
Hair cut	**£3.50**
Light-bulb	**£0.30**
Dog chews	**£0.90**
Beers	**£5.00**
Newspaper	**£0.35**
Food*	**£21.18**
Fizzy drink for nephew	**£1.50**
Laundrette	**£2.90**
TOTAL	**£42.43**
OVERSPENT BY...	**£13.44**

*1 loaf sliced bread 45p, 1 tin dried milk £1.39, 2 chicken legs £1.60, potatoes 40p, 1 swede 50p, fruit (for puddings) £3, margarine 89p, 6 eggs 90p, cheese £1.80, cereal £1, 1 pint milk 35p, coffee £1, mince £1.80, 1 tin tomatoes 28p, 1 tin baked beans 36p, rice 95p, frozen peas 99p, biscuits 85p, jam 47p, pickle 50p, 1 tin sardines 50p, pasta 50p, 2 Mars bars 70p.

TOTAL £21.18

Daily Mail, 10 April 2000

TASKS

Interview an old person and talk to them about how they manage their income. Ask them how they might spend any rise in their income.

KEY SKILLS: *Information technology*

Which of the following should be installed on your computer to protect your files:

A data protection
B virus checking
C spell checking
D floppy disk?

(Level 2)

Wages and salary levels for different jobs

Wages and salaries vary enormously from job to job and even area to area. This may reflect factors like scarcity, training or skills. The differences between people's incomes are often very wide (see table 'Public sector pay: who earns what'). A top professional footballer, even leaving aside lucrative sponsorship deals, can earn significantly more in a week than a fully trained and experienced nurse can earn in a year. Singled out for particular criticism are the senior company directors, often of large organizations, who qualify for large bonuses or generous severance payments when they leave their jobs.

The cartoon below appeared after closures in the Welsh steel industry were announced by Corus in 2001.

Public sector pay: who earns what	
	Starting from:
DSS typist	£7,425
Auxiliary nurse (unqualified)	£8,315
School cleaner	£8,376
Refuse collector	£8,679
Assistant librarian	£12,437
Nurse (newly qualified)	£12,855
Teacher (starting salary)	£13,362
Police constable (starting salary)	£16,050
Ward sister	£16,310
Fireman (after 15 years)	£18,899
Senior nurse	£21,495
Teacher (after 7 years)	£22,410
Police constable (after 14 years)	£25,410
Head of small primary school	£26,733
Police chief inspector	£34,518
Head of large secondary school	£59,580

TASKS

1 Explain the meaning of the 'Chorus' cartoon? How effective do you think it is?

2 Can celebrities justify their high earnings? Why aren't people who provide essential public services, like nurses and teachers, paid more?

KEY SKILLS: *Information technology*

An author using word processing software creates a file for each page of a textbook. When the files are saved the author notices that they do not appear in page order in the folder.

Suggest reasons for the following files being saved out of page order.

HGS page 97.doc   HGS age 98.doc
HGS page 99.doc   HGS 100.doc.

(Level 3)

Travel and transport in the community

Why do we need transport?

Getting to school or college is relatively easy for those who live nearby. The same applies to going to work. The problem is that not many people do live near enough to their place of education or work and so they need private or public transport.

Most of those who can afford it buy a car. However, this is an expensive way to travel if the purchase price, depreciation, running costs, insurance, and road tax are taken into account. They choose a car because of its door-to-door convenience. In rural areas, because of poor public transport, a car becomes essential. In urban areas, especially the large cities, the car is less useful and parking difficult and expensive. The alternative is public transport in the form of trains, trams and buses.

Travel, transport and traffic: the problem

Traffic is seen as a 'problem'. It is never out of the news and a frequent subject for chat shows and phone-ins. Problems, though, don't just suddenly happen. The chart below provides some insight into the longer-term development of a problem that has now become acute.

The petrol crisis

Petrol has become more expensive in the last few years, partly because governments have raised taxes on it to discourage the excessive use of cars and to protect the environment. (By raising this 'indirect' tax it also makes it less likely that direct taxes, such as income tax, will have to rise.) The major oil producers (OPEC) also seek to raise the price of oil by limiting output.

Led particularly by farmers and road hauliers, there were widespread protests in the UK in September 2000, resulting in a major political crisis. Petrol pumps ran dry throughout the country and there was strong public support for the protestors. Eventually, because of the threat to emergency services and essential car drivers, the protest was halted.

It is suggested that people under the age of 30 face the future prospect of travel in a world without petrol. New forms of energy and alternative technology may make this less of a shock than it would at first appear.

The road to gridlock

1960: Transport Minister Ernest Marples orders study into growing car ownership.
1963: Buchanan Report calls for massive road building.
1964: Beeching cuts rail network from 19,000 to 13,000 miles.
1968: Barbara Castle raises tax on heavy lorries and nationalises bus industry.
1970: Ted Heath launches 10-year 4,000-mile road-building programme, most of it motorway.
1971: 80 per cent of seven and eight-year-olds travel to school on their own.
1974: Energy crisis. Petrol prices, train and bus fares all soar.
1975: Plans for Channel Tunnel shelved.
1977: Transport White Paper: Higher rail fares, BR grant cut by 25 per cent. Extra subsidy to keep down bus fares. Rolling motorway building plan frozen but M25 to go ahead 'as priority'.
1981: Tories privatise National Freight Corporation.
1985: Bus deregulation outside London sparks 'bus wars'.
1986: M25 opens. Go-ahead given for Channel Tunnel.
1987: British Airways and British Airports Authority privatised.
1988: Transport Secretary Paul Channon puts privatisation of BR 'firmly on the agenda'. Expansion of roadbuilding to £4 billion over next three years.
1989: Roads for Posterity heralds 'biggest road-building programme since the Romans'.
1990: Margaret Thatcher lauds 'great car economy'. Go-ahead for £1bn Jubilee Line Extension.
1991: First move to promote rail over road. Motorway programme declared 'officially complete'.
1992: £1.7bn Jubilee Line Extension in balance after Canary Wharf developers go bust.
1993: £2.5bn Crossrail project axed. But £2.8bn earmarked for widening part of M25 to 14 lanes. First major road protests over Twyford Down and M11 link.
1994: Rail infrastructure hived off into Railtrack. Signalmen strike throughout summer. Channel Tunnel opens.
1995: Government tells people to use their cars less but Transport Minister Steven Norris says travelling in London is better by car because 'you don't have to put up with dreadful human beings sitting alongside you'.
1995: Transport Secretary Brian Mawhinney scraps M25 widening, but approves Newbury by-pass.
1996: Privatisation of Railtrack. Rail freight industry sold off. Eighty per cent of children own a bicycle but only 2 per cent cycle to school. Only 7 per cent of seven and eight-year-olds now make their own way to school.
1997: Passenger railway split into 25 franchises and sold off in dying months of Tory government. Labour elected.
1998: John Prescott strikes deal with Railtrack to rescue Channel Tunnel Link. Government announces part-privatisation of air traffic control and London Underground. Road-building budget cut from £6bn to £1.4bn over seven years. M25 widening between M4 and M3 junctions to go ahead.

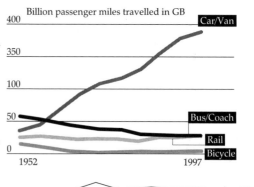

Billion passenger miles travelled in GB

400 — 350 — 100 — 50 — 0

Car/Van

Bus/Coach

Rail

Bicycle

1952   1997

The Observer, 14 December 1999

Provision and quality of bus and rail services

Is the car a devil or an angel?

Increasingly, discussion about transport is polarized. The car is heavily criticized because it contributes to congestion and pollution. The car is strongly defended on grounds of personal freedom and necessity. Public transport is regularly seen as a costly, inefficient and dirty alternative to the car. The arguments are illuminating only because they should serve as a warning against generalization and being dogmatic.

Governments are desperate to find a 'solution' to the 'transport problem' especially in the heavily congested south-east, and in a number of towns and cities. At times, we all suffer, so we look for a scapegoat – someone to blame. It might be a particular bus or train operator, but it's usually the government. In his book *Devil's Advocate*, the journalist and interviewer John Humphrys provides a timely reminder when he suggests that 'seeing ourselves as victims means we stop seeing ourselves as responsible'. Devils and angels are not always easy to identify as we are

sometimes led to believe but, in the interests of increasing electoral support, politicians sometimes make promises that are very difficult to deliver.

The case against:

cars	buses and trains
noise and air pollution	do not run to time
expensive	dirty
create traffic congestion	inconvenient to get to
visual intrusion	do not fit suburban and rural living

The Observer, 22 October 2000

The derailing of Railtrack

The time has come, surely, for Railtrack to be taken back into public ownership. Not only is subsidy being siphoned from taxpayers' pockets to Railtrack shareholders and directors but, worse, no one ever seems to take responsibility for the deaths of increasing numbers of

passengers. If it is not possible to do this without paying for the shares, it should be done at a price that ensures no shareholder makes a penny profit.
Mike Clutten
Leicester

If the failings of private sector involvement in transport turn out to be the cause of the rail crash, will the government halt its privatisation plans for London Underground and the National Air Traffic Control Service?
Jonathan Butler
Glasgow

The Guardian, 19 October 2000

TASKS

1 Study the article covering 'the road to gridlock' and identify what you consider to be the more important dates and developments. How have these influenced changes in transport patterns? Why has there been such a rapid increase in car transport in the last 30 years?

2 What is the difference between privatization and nationalization of the railways?

3 What is the cartoon saying about the state of the railway system?

4 After reading the letters titled 'The derailing of Railtrack', say how far you would agree or disagree with the contents.

KEY SKILLS: *Information technology*

If you want to move a paragraph to a different part of an essay that you have word processed, you should use:

A cut and paste
B copy and paste
C format paragraph
D page set up.

(Level 2)

Moving towards a policy for transport

Successive governments have drawn up plans to relieve traffic congestion and improve public transport. In the interests of co-ordination (or what become known, later, as 'joined-up government') the Deputy Prime Minister, John Prescott, initially took responsibility for transport and the environment. This was big, bold government. It was a worthy but massive task. At the end of 1999, very much with the political analyst Peter Hennessy's theory of 'overload' in mind, Mr Prescott was given some help in the form of Lord MacDonald, who became responsible for transport policy. Devising a transport policy requires problem solving on a macro-scale – a key skill for the best political and civil service brains.

Governments in the UK get a maximum period of five years to meet their objectives. Then MPs must submit themselves to the voters. Most of the problems governments face are highly complex, but they have a relatively short time in which to solve them.

The government, in formulating its policy, has to take into account the views of various pressure groups, including:
- transport users who want the cheapest fares
- operators wanting the best profits for their shareholders
- environmental groups concerned about pollution
- motoring organizations seeking to protect the interests of drivers
- hauliers demanding low taxes and low diesel prices
- car owners wanting less congestion and faster journeys
- travellers looking for clean and safe journeys.

In 2000, the plan for the future of transport included:
- improved railway performance
- half-price bus travel for all pensioners
- a doubling of the number of cycled journeys
- the first privately built toll road, near Birmingham
- investment in London Underground
- a 20% reduction in emissions of carbon dioxide.

TASKS

1 How would you improve public transport? Following de-regulation in the 1980s, most bus companies became privately owned and exist as profit-making bodies. After privatization in the 1990s, railways were franchized to 25 different private operators. They still receive a large government subsidy but this is declining year by year. A separate company owns the railway tracks. Plan your next moves if you were advising the government on what they should do about public transport.

2 What plans would you draw up to cut car and lorry congestion? Your choices include:
- build more motorways and/or toll roads
- provide car-sharing incentives
- tax parking places at work and in city centres
- increase petrol duties annually.
Say why you think these measures may not work and suggest other alternatives.

3 Since people will not give up their cars, can we expect politicians, who are dependent on people's votes, to introduce unpopular anti-car policies?

KEY SKILLS: *Information technology*

Produce a response to the question, 'Discuss the suggestion that all drivers should be expected to pass a driving test every five years.' In your response make sure that you include appropriate use of the following:

- bold text
- italicized text
- two different sizes of font
- bullet points
- an indented paragraph. *(Level 2)*

Summary of the social domain for AS

When examiners and teachers talk about something being synoptic it's a way of saying that ideas need to be drawn together, rather like a summing up at the end of a discussion. That may mean bringing ideas from a very wide range of subject areas.

In the AS unit of the social domain, you have looked at aspects of politics, the ways social scientists explore problems and advise politicians and at some of the cases where social and economic constraints influence the four main social services. Politicians in the UK face many problems that do not have an easy answer. In some cases there is, as yet, no known solution to some of the social problems. Politicians turn to social scientists for advice about the best way forward. Social and economic constraints together with the need for re-election mean that compromize solutions are frequently used. An example of such an issue concerned the arrival of many asylum seekers in the UK.

We can use the subject of asylum seekers to draw together the different strands of what this unit has covered. Genuine asylum seekers are refugees, who have to leave their own country perhaps because of political or religious persecution. Other asylum seekers may be trying to enter the UK for no genuine reason, perhaps even using illegal methods. Enter the politicians with their political systems, processes and goals. There is clearly a humanitarian issue, but public opinion is markedly unsympathetic to many asylum seekers. The number of asylum seekers has increased dramatically and they increase the demand upon the social services. Their cost inevitably falls on taxpayers.

Social scientists are asked to look at this type of problem as objectively as they can. They give advice to the politicians taking into account the international law on asylum seekers as well as the demand they place upon the social services.

The Observer, 16 April 2000

TASKS

1 Study the cartoon carefully. Identify the figures and interpret what it is saying through some extremely clever use of language and imagery.

2 Under what circumstances would you allow asylum seekers to stay in the UK? Explain the demands they place upon the four main social services while they await a verdict on their case.

KEY SKILLS: *Information technology*

1 Give examples of occasions when a spell checker may not be reliable.

2 Why is it necessary to set the language for a spell checker?

3 How would you use a computer to count the number of words you have used in an essay?

4 What use can be made of a mail merge option?

(Level 3)

Further study suggestions and example questions

Further reading

Artis, M. J. (1999) *The UK Economy*, Oxford University Press, Oxford.
Champion, T. *et al.* (1996) *The Population of Britain in the 1990s*, Oxford University Press, Oxford.
Jones, B. and Kavanagh, B. (1999) *British Politics Today*, Manchester University Press, Manchester.
Moore, S. (1999) *Sociology Alive*, Stanley Thornes, London.

AS questions and the social domain

Social domain examination papers cover aspects of society (political systems, processes and goals; the nature of objectivity in the social sciences; and social and economic constraints). There are usually two types of question set for AS papers. The first type is questions requiring short answers. They are usually based upon a brief passage, or a diagram, or some other kind of data stimulus. The second type of question requires more extended writing.

Short-answer questions based on a passage of text

So much for mechanistic solutions. The deeper task, as the women's minister says, is to alter the 'culture of politics'. It is not just too macho; it is often guilty of outright discrimination. The Commons is a prime example – whether it is working hours hostile to family life, or sexual harassment from male MPs. This cultural problem extends to our second revelation: that Labour is shutting out black and Asian candidates as well as women. Last year's MacPherson report into the murder of Stephen Lawrence alerted us to institutional racism even in those bodies that pride themselves on tolerance and anti-racism.

The Guardian editorial, 16 October 2000

Explain briefly the following words or phrases as used in the passage:
a mechanistic solutions [3]
b women's minister [2]
c culture of politics [3]
d macho [2]
e working hours hostile to family life [2]
f Labour is shutting out black and Asian candidates [3]
g institutional racism even in those bodies that pride themselves on tolerance and anti-racism. [4]

Hints on managing short-answer questions

■ Always have time in mind. Read the passage as quickly as you can. Underline the words on which questions are based.
■ Note that each question carries relatively few marks. Keep your answers as short as possible.
■ Be succinct. Write about only what is needed.
■ If you don't know the answer to one of the short questions, move on to the next. Return at the end if you have time.

Extended written answer questions

Wages and salaries paid to people in different types of employment vary enormously. Top sports players, pop stars and television personalities can command huge sums. Millions of others have to be protected by the National Minimum Wage.
a What do you understand by the terms wages, salaries, and the National Minimum Wage? [10]
b Why do some people earn far more than others? Examine the advantages and disadvantages of trying to find ways of increasing the earnings of the low paid. [40]

Hints on managing extended written answer questions

■ Note that the 'lead in' part of the question is only worth 10 marks. Define the three key terms as succinctly as you can.
■ There are two questions within b. Make sure you answer them both. Try to analyse rather than describe and make sure your arguments are reasoned. Give examples of higher and lower wage earners. Remember that you need to provide both advantages and disadvantages of finding and applying ways of trying to the increase the earnings of the lower paid.

4 The nature of scientific objectivity and the question of progress

Definitions

Biography   An account of someone's life written by someone else, as opposed to autobiography, an account of one's own life.

DNA   Deoxyribonucleic Acid, the double helix chromosome that hold the information for metabolism, growth and development.

Gravity   The force causing things to fall to the ground and to remain on the ground. Theories concerning gravity were at the centre of Newton's and Einstein's theories.

Longitude   Position on a map, east or west of the Greenwich Meridian. Ships found it hard to find their longitude without accurate clocks.

Objectivity   The capacity of the scientific observer to see the world 'as it actually is'. Problems arise because the experience, values and attitudes of the scientist 'colour' their perception.

Search engines   Devices on the Internet used to make rapid searches of websites. Famous ones include Yahoo!, Lycos, Hotbot, AltaVista, and alltheweb.

Time   A construct to measure the passing of events, it has at least 30 different uses 'time for', 'at time', 'the time', 'times', 'to time', 'one time' and 'some time' are examples.

Getting started

1 Near the end of his life Sir Isaac Newton wrote:

'I do not know what I may appear to the world, but to myself I seem to have been only a boy playing on the sea-shore, and diverting myself in now and then finding a smoother pebble or a prettier shell than ordinary, whilst the great ocean of truth lay all undiscovered before me.'

2 For the Millennium celebrations, a newspaper carried out an opinion survey of children aged 10–14 years on their view of science. The results make interesting reading.

80%	thought	science is boring
15%	thought	biology the only part of science of any interest
7%	wanted	to take up science as a career
43%	wanted	to become astronauts
23%	wanted	to become footballers
20%	wanted	to become fashion models
99%	knew	Neil Armstrong was the first man on the moon

Some quotes from those interviewed:

'Science is boring. It's all equations, long words, body parts and bad smells.'
'Science is complicated, all about atoms and everything.'
'I like science because you never know what is going to happen.'
'I don't mind experiments but I hate recording results.'

3 'Once or twice I have … asked the company how many of them could describe the Second Law of Thermodynamics. The response was negative. Yet I was asking something which is the scientific equivalent of, "Have you read a work of Shakespeare's?"' (C. P. Snow, *The Two Cultures*, 1959).

Disease control and health

1 Can we ever be sure that what we eat will keep us healthy? Why are some people vegetarians?

2 Why use chemicals to increase yields when we have enough food?

3 Should the National Health Service treat smokers for free?

4 Are men or women healthier?

Gravitational motion

1 What famous role did the humble apple play?
2 How does Jonathan Swift satirize Sir Isaac Newton in *Gulliver's Travels*?
3 In the seventeenth century few could understand Newton's famous book *Principia Mathematica*. Name a book today that you find difficult to understand.
4 How can 300-year-old theories help in a world of sophisticated computers?

Longitude

1 Do you ever need to know your longitude?
2 How does longitude affect you?
3 Why have the Olympic Games in the middle of the night?
4 When we fly west do we gain or lose time? What is jet lag?

The impact of information technology

1 How many search engines can you name?
2 Do you get angry queuing on a helpline?
3 Are you a geek with a WAP (Wireless Applications Protocol) phone?
4 How is your style of writing changing with word processing, email and Internet boxes to fill? How is your handwriting? Do you still use 'snail mail'? Do you write with freedom and exuberance or in compressed staccato? Whose email address would you like to have (alive or dead)?
5 Is the Internet a triumph of hype over content? Does Internet use breed a world of loners? How do you feel about the failure of dot.com companies?
6 Why does everyone talk of pornography when none of the top 20 Internet search words contain pornography?

7 Do you want uncensored anarchy or governmental and corporate control (like on television) to win? Does the Net encourage a two-tier society?

Biography of great scientists

1 Why do we read about the lives of long dead scientists?
2 Who do you nominate as the greatest scientist of them all?
3 Which scientific discovery would you like to have made?
4 Which scientific discovery does the world most need to be made?

Outline

Trying to be objective means putting aside all personal attitudes and values. Scientists wishing to be objective base their judgements on the facts, on events or things that can be observed and measured. The conclusions of the objective scientist are independent of the individual and do not involve his or her feelings. No one can achieve fully objective research but the objective scientist tries to avoid the effects of personal feelings and experience.

As scientists discover new insights they want to make progress, to move towards improved quality of life for people. Scientists are challenged that some of their discoveries have not contributed to progress.

The four topics examined in this section show scientists contributing new insights which have resulted in improvements to quality of life. In a final section, the work of two scientists is described to show how objectivity and progress are part of scientific enquiry.

Disease control and health

Disease

Diseases can be divided into communicable and non-communicable disorders.

Communicable disorders usually communicated by organisms	
viral	influenza
bacterial	tuberculosis
protoctistan	malaria
fungal	athlete's foot
prions	CJD (BSE)

Non-communicable disorders not 'caught' from others	
cardiovascular	blood disorders, atherosclerosis, angina, heart attack and stroke
malnutrition	food deficiency, kwashiorkor and maramus
genetic	Down's syndrome
ageing	eye deterioration
mental	schizophrenia
cancer	cell division and tumours
allergy	asthma
accidents	broken bones
obesity	overweight

This page examines four current connections between disease and health. All four are particular concerns for young people:
- cigarette smoking
- BSE and CJD
- DNA and genetic engineering
- mental illness.

Cigarette smoking

Every packet of cigarettes sold in the UK contains a health warning. The nicotine from cigarettes constricts blood vessels and increases blood pressure, whilst the smoke affects the mucus in the throat to increase the likelihood of carcinogenic particles being trapped in the throat and lungs. Smoking cigarettes doubles the chance of heart and vascular disease, increases by 20 times the possibility of chronic bronchitis and 30 times the possibility of lung cancer. Smoking has become the main cause of premature death in the under-70s.

Smoking also raises moral issues because of the effects on people nearby and the costs of treatment for this self-inflicted illness. Many theatres, restaurants and trains no longer provide facilities for smokers.

Tobacco companies face heavy claims from insurance companies and are being criticized for their campaigns to increase the number of smokers in some less developed countries.

Many people find giving up the habit of smoking very difficult. Aids include nicotine patches, chewing gum, hypnosis and placebos. The addictive nature of the cigarette still makes the decision a major challenge. However, there are many success stories, usually driven by the reduced health threats and financial advantages.

BSE and variant-CJD

By 1999, some 70 people had died in the UK from CJD. Scientists believe that the disease reached epidemic proportions in cattle through feed. At first it was thought that BSE ('mad cow disease') could not spread from cattle to humans. However, this has proved to be untrue. A widespread programme of cattle slaughter was introduced to remove the disease from herds. Those most at risk are people who have eaten infected meat, particularly meat that has been mechanically recovered. No one is certain how many people will develop the fatal variant-CJD (the human form of BSE). Estimates are as high as 150,000. Strict regulations for food, from the farm to the plate, include the fact that no cattle over 30 months can be part of the food chain.

In the case of BSE and variant-CJD, scientists do not know enough about the disease to give clear advice.

DNA

There are 100 trillion cells in the human body. The nucleus of each of these cells contains 23 chromosomes from the mother and 23 from the father. These 46 chromosomes make up the molecule DNA (deoxyribonucleic acid). This is the famous double helix identified by Nobel Prize winners James Watson (an American biochemist) and Francis Crick (a British biophysicist). The DNA molecule in each human cell is composed of four chemicals – adenine (A), thymine (T), guanine (G) and cytosine (C).

These four chemicals are the digital code of life. Every living organism (wheat, fish, trees and chimpanzees) is composed of these four letters A, T, G, and C – the genetic code. Chimpanzees appear to share 98.9% of human DNA. In June 2000, scientists at last completed the code for human DNA, which begins:

ccacatgatatctatccaacccatgccccacatgatatctatccaac
ccatgtccccacatgatatctatccaacccatgtcc …

... and so on, until it fills 500,000 pages of a telephone directory (750 Mb or one DVD disc). It has over 3 billion letters. Over 95% of this human genome is junk – left over instructions from earlier stages in evolution. However, 100,000 of the genes code the 20 amino acids that make up the body's proteins. Everything about our bodies is made from proteins and genes give the instructions.

Now that the code of the human gene is known, it is more likely that conditions such as Down's syndrome, Turner's syndrome, Huntingdon's chorea and cystic fibrosis can be eradicated. The problem is where to draw the line. For example, Alzheimer's disease in old age may be detectable just after conception. There is a danger of medical insurance and health treatments being withheld. Later there will be the desire for designer babies, just as currently scientists can modify plants. Other benefits could include cures for AIDS and malaria. This is the beginning of a gold rush for the pharmaceutical companies.

Mental illness

During heavy study, students can lose their desire to do well. This often happens half way through a course. It may be part of moving on from the security of the known to the challenge of the new. It may be boredom, as the novelty of A level becomes a grind. This happens to lots of people, but do not confuse a little sadness with depression.

Depression

What do you take pleasure in? Do you enjoy a bacon sandwich, a glass of wine, a loving hug, clean cotton sheets, listening to Robbie Williams, or talking to the cat? People suffering from depression (one in five of the UK population lives with periodic depression) lose the joy of any pleasurable experience. Some people do not believe that depression exists and accuse the depressed of not trying, or tell them to get a grip.

Scientists studying depression have been using fMRI (functional magnetic resonance imaging) to try to understand the condition.

Sadness	Depression
Do you: ■ Cry watching romantic films? ■ Mope in bed on Saturday morning? ■ Have no energy for study or clubbing? ■ Only laugh at good sitcoms? ■ Eat chocolate for comfort? ■ Wonder if you will ever feel like sex again?	Do you: ■ Cry at nothing? ■ Find getting up and going to bed difficult? ■ Keep putting off doing vital things? ■ Feel useless and helpless? ■ Wake very early in the morning? ■ Lose and gain appetite for food and sex?

TASKS

1 Using your local newspaper, make a study of the health issues in the news. In addition, look at the announcements of deaths and note the age to which people are living.

2 Conduct a sample survey of about 25 people to obtain their views on the treatment that they have received from the National Health Service. Concentrate particularly upon their understanding of their illness. You will need to conduct your survey with sensitivity and respect their confidentiality.

3 Arrange for an interview with someone working in the National Health Service. This could be a doctor, nurse, health visitor or administrator. Do not expect to use up more than 30 minutes of their time. Concentrate on prepared questions on the ways they help patients to understand their illness and treatment, the provision they have for long-term care, the terminally ill and members of the family of the sick person. Take careful notes.
Prepare a one-page report that lists your findings and recommendations.

Gravitational motion
Sir Isaac Newton (1642–1727)

Albert Einstein never doubted that Newton was the greatest scientific genius. Though Newton's discoveries are good approximations for most purposes Einstein's equations and theory of relativity have replaced them. For example, spacecraft are programmed and tides predicted using Newton. In general they work well for bodies moving much slower than the speed of light, or when the pull of gravity is not strong.

What then were the discoveries of this product of Grantham Grammar School and Trinity College, Cambridge? The answer lies in the three volumes of *Principia Mathematica* published in 1687. This could be the most important book ever published in science. It contains Newton's Three Laws of Motion and a theory of gravity. These laws explain the way things move, bounce off each other and respond to being pushed and pulled. They underpin all things mechanical, from the engineering in building projects to washing machines and the calculations to send spaceships to remote planets.

Newton's laws

Law 1 states that bodies keep moving in a straight line unless something pushes or pulls them. Thus the planets would move in straight lines if gravity did not stop them.

Law 2 states that action and reaction are equal and opposite, so that the thrust of a rocket is counteracted by the rocket moving forward, or the floor pushes back with a force equal to your weight.

Law 3 states that the velocity at which bodies move depends on the forces applied to them. The acceleration of an object is inversely proportional to its mass and directly proportional to the force acting on it. The equation for this is $F = m \times a$ (Force in Newtons, mass in kilograms and acceleration in metres per second per second).

Newton and the gravity model

Perhaps more popularly known is the story of Newton forming the law of Universal Gravity while watching an apple fall. Indeed the tree from which the apple fell is still to be seen, with the eye of faith, in Cambridge.

The gravity model

Newton's findings on gravity can be put into formula form as:

$$F_{12} = G \frac{M_1 \times M_2}{d_{12}{}^2}$$

where
F_{12} is the force between two bodies
M_1 is the mass of one of the bodies
M_2 is the mass of the second body
d_{12} is their distance apart (note the use of the inverse square law)
G is a constant.

Applications of Newton's gravity formula

This model or equation works well for the orbits of planets and stars. One of its famous applications came with Apollo 13 in April 1970 ('Hello, Houston, we have a problem here'). Computer checks at mission control showed failure of the spacecraft's four main systems. The spacecraft was on its way to the moon and had no way of turning around and blasting back to earth. Mission control allowed the spacecraft to proceed on its way to the moon. They then applied Newton's theory to get it back to earth. They used the gravity of the moon to slingshot the spacecraft around the moon. Precise firing of the moonlander rockets brought the astronauts safely back. The outcome of this can be put down to effective application of the Laws of Newton.

Social scientists have borrowed Newton's formula and used it to predict the movement of people between two centres. The formula is rewritten as:

$$M_{ij} = G \frac{P_i P_j}{d_{ij}{}^2}$$

where
M_{ij} is the interaction between places i and j
P_i and P_j are a measure of the mass of the two places
d_{ij} is their distance apart
G is a calibrating constant.

Studies have shown that the formula is helpful in predicting the movement of people between two urban areas and the attractiveness of shopping centres.

TASKS

1 Use the library or the Internet to find out why the UK has two sea tides per day and higher tides in spring and autumn.

2 For this experiment you need a pair of bathroom scales and a lift. Weigh yourself before entering the lift. Now, while inside the lift, stand on the scales. Now press the button to ascend and watch the scales. Do the same as the lift descends.

Longitude

All places on the surface of the earth can be located using a system of co-ordinates called longitude and latitude. The cartographer and astronomer Ptolemy plotted the lines as early as AD 150. He marked the equator as zero latitude.

Longitude

Longitude is measured using a series of circles that pass through the north and south poles. These circles are called meridians (see Figure 17). Longitudinal meridians are the north–south lines on maps (Figure 18).

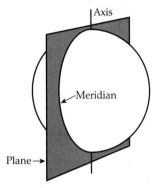

Figure 17 *A meridian is a line that circles a sphere about its circumference*

The longitude of a place is measured in degrees to the east or west of the line of longitude 0° that passes through Greenwich. If you travel 180 degrees east from Greenwich you come to the 180-degree west line of longitude.

Greenwich was not the first choice for the zero (or prime) meridian. Ptolemy used the Canary Islands; later mapmakers used the Azores, Cape Verde Islands, Rome, Copenhagen, Jerusalem, St Petersburg, Paris and Philadelphia.

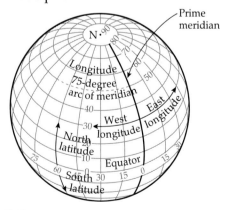

Figure 18 *The geographic grid, showing lines of longitude and latitude*

Navigation depends upon finding your location using latitude and longitude. Latitude could be estimated using the length of the day or the height of the sun. To know one's longitude means knowing the local time and the time at the home port or the zero meridian. Once the time difference is known, and accepting that the earth rotates about once in every 24 hours, the longitude can be found. Each hour represents about fifteen degrees (see Figure 18). Producing an accurate timepiece (clock), especially one that would work at sea, was at one time the greatest of scientific problems. Systems using the stars had been used to some extent but the complex tables involved had to be revised as the earth moved in space. Eventually a clock maker named John Harrison claimed the prize offered by the Queen (Queen Anne) and government for his accurate timekeepers. 'The Harrisons' H-1 (1737), H-2 (1741), H-3 (1759) and H-4 (1759) can be seen in the National Maritime Museum in Greenwich, London. Today, global satellite systems inform sea and air transport of its position.

The international dateline

If you fly south from the UK for ten hours, crossing the equator, and land in South Africa, you do not have to alter your watch. The season of the year will be reversed but time on the ground is the same. This is a great help when sporting events are televized in South Africa.

In contrast, take a short journey across the Channel to France and you move your watch forward one hour. The seven-hour flying time west to the USA, or twelve hours east to Hong Kong, mean major changes for your watch and can cause 'jet lag' for the traveller. As you move eastwards you appear to lose time, whilst gaining time as you move westwards. A particular problem could occur if you moved westwards at the same time as a friend moved eastwards. Suppose you met after twelve hours. You would appear to be 24 hours apart on your watches. To avoid this the International Dateline has been drawn on the map of the world. Either side of the line the date varies by one day. The line chosen is not a line of longitude but runs north to south across the earth avoiding inhabited islands.

Map projections

The earth is a sphere and most maps are flat. It is impossible to flatten out the spherical earth to make an exact map. Imagine trying to open out the skin of an orange. To overcome this problem, mapmakers have to agree which property of the earth they wish to keep and which they will allow to distort. For example, if they want a map where the areas on the map are scaled to be equal to those on the surface of the earth the shape of areas has to be distorted. All maps have to include some distortion.

The way the curved earth is transformed to a flat map is called a map projection. A glance in an atlas will show, in the very small print on the margin of the map, which map projection has been used. Computers allow rapid production of map projections using very complex mathematics. Whichever projection is used the choice represents the values and purpose of the mapmakers. Such purposes may be emotive or political.

A very famous early mapmaker was Gerard Mercator, a sixteenth-century mathematician. His famous Mercator Projection is useful for users who need to know correct shape, true angles and accurate bearings. However, to do this the map exaggerates the size of land masses nearer the pole. In contrast the projection produced by Gall in the nineteenth century, and revised recently by Peters, shows landmasses in their true proportions but distorts coastal shapes. In 1963 Robinson produced a projection which reconciled the problems of the Mercator and Peters Projections.

The Mercator Projection was popular with American and European users because it enlarged their part of the world at the expense of less developed regions in lower latitudes. The United Nations has used the Peters Projection so that the true size of countries is shown. During the 'Cold War' years the government of the USA used the Mercator Projection to exaggerate the size of the USSR and hence its threat. Today the Robinson Projection is more popular.

TASKS

1 If the longitude of New York is 75 degrees west, what is the time difference between it and London (GMT)?

2 Hong Kong is seven hours ahead of the UK. What is its approximate longitude?

3 Is jet lag worse when travelling east or west?

The impact of information technology

'The problem with revolutions is that they may be exciting but customers prefer evolution.' Computers have changed our lives dramatically. Some argue the changes are for the good, but when problems appear, the computer is blamed first. This page looks at the development of the personal computer and then the Internet. It concludes with a review of three projects currently under development.

Thirty years of personal computing: the story of how computing power became available to everyone

1971 Intel make the first computer chip.

1975 The MITS Altair 8800 (the name came from an episode of Star Trek) uses Microsoft BASIC. BASIC stands for 'Beginners all-purpose symbolic instruction code' a language which was written by a teenager Bill Gates and his friend Paul Allen.

1977 The Apple II, Commodore PET (Personal Electronic Transactor) and Tandy TRS-80 use Microsoft BASIC and tapes for programmes and data.

1980 Cambridge-based Sinclair Computers introduce the home-build kit for the MK14 for £39.95 plus VAT, then the Sinclair ZX80 using tape and a television set to allow computer games in the home.

1981 IBM, world leader in mainframe computers, decide to enter the PC market. This entry sets the standard for compatibility between machines. Prior to this Commodore, Apple, Acorn and Atari used different software and were not compatible.

1982 Another Cambridge company, Acorn, introduces BBC B to schools through government grants.

1984 The Apple Macintosh and IBM PC AT arrive.

1987 The computing industry adopts a horizontal structure, allowing systems to be built with components from several suppliers. Intel-style processors and Microsoft DOS can now be used in nearly all machines.

1990 Microsoft Windows 3 replaces DOS to allow a multi-tasking operating system that can interface with printers and scanners.

1999 Microsoft in the courts for illegal restrictions on competitors.

2000 50% of American homes have a computer. Now the PC comes under threat. In the office, terminals to a network may replace the PC workstation and out of the office the mobile phone with WAP is taking over much electronic communication.

Key dates in the development of the Internet

1962 American scientist J. C. R. Licklider envisaged computers connected globally. Another American scientist developed the theory of how computers might be linked.

1961–67 ARPANET the predecessor to Internet built with four western USA universities as nodes.

1972 First demonstration of email between the four universities. Pioneer designers from universities deliberately selected 'open architecture networking' which left the system open to other users. They agreed there would be no global control of the network.

1980–5 Explosion in the size of the network, with defence industries joining ARPANET.

1984 JANET established in the UK, and NSNET in USA, to link together all universities.

1990 ARPANET replaced by the Internet. Network expanded to include commercial users.

1994 Realization of the 'Information Superhighway'. In 8.5 years the Net had grown from 6 nodes running at 56 kbps to 21 nodes running at 45 Mbps. The Internet remains free, with open access matching the ideals of the first designers.

How secure is your email?

To use email, you need an Internet Service Provider (ISP). The software to link your computer to an ISP can be installed using a CD. Figure 19 shows the pathway for your message and highlights the ways in which surveillance takes place. Whilst most would accept such interception as part of national security, Internet use by organized crime or for industrial espionage causes concern.

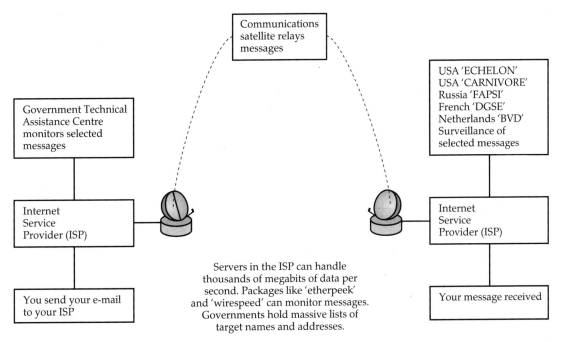

Figure 19 *The email pathway and possible surveillance*

E-commerce: the clear winner has been the consumer

Have you heard of B2C, business to consumer electronic commerce? In 1999 and 2000 newspapers covered the stories of the rise and rise of the dot.com companies. Investors put money into new sales companies run by young information technology graduates. Several of these companies never made a profit and collapsed. They had the Internet technology but lacked the purchasing and distribution expertise. This should be no surprise. Many small companies fail in their early years. However, their arrival has pushed many existing companies onto the Net. Big companies can now negotiate and purchase worldwide and even the corner shop can have its own website. With more sophisticated mobile phones and interactive television, this type of selling is here to stay.

Another issue concerns legal proceedings with Microsoft, the world's largest software producer. Critics suggest that Microsoft has used its power to eliminate competitors. US courts are investigating this complex problem.

E-science: the next winners will be the scientists

The World Wide Web (www.) will become of more use to scientists as 'middleware' – something between the hardware of the computer and software programs the computer can run. This next generation of technology will offer scientists over 100 times the power of the supercomputers available in 2000. It will allow them to handle the massive amounts of data produced by research. With middleware, scientists will set a computer a problem and it will pull together the data. Problems within the grasp of this new power will include data from atom smashing experiments, the human genome project and modelling the world's weather systems.

TASKS

1 Write a set of instructions for sending an email message. Try them out on someone learning the technique.

2 Download the 'Home' pages of at least one good and one poor website. Annotate the printouts to show good and poor features.

Biography and autobiography of important scientists

A wonderful way to learn about the contribution that an individual has made to their field is to read their autobiography or obituary, or one of the biographies written about them. Two great scientists are introduced on this page: Archimedes and Marie Curie. One male and one female, one ancient and one modern. Other pages refer to Sir Isaac Newton, Francis Crick, James Watson and Charles Darwin. There are many others you may wish to investigate, including Albert Einstein and Sigmund Freud. There are good biographies of all these scientists, or you can search for their names on the Internet.

It is difficult to talk of beginnings and progress in the arts. Artists and writers are certainly influenced by what has gone before but science is more a matter of progress and of each generation building upon earlier work.

Archimedes (287–212 BC)

Archimedes' screw, used for 'lifting' water

It is suggested by some that Archimedes was the first great scientist. This may be disputed by some who could cite the earlier Chinese anatomists. Archimedes certainly provided some of the early building blocks of science. He had the key belief in making detailed empirical measurements to support theory. Popular folklore remembers him for shouting 'Eureka' when, supposedly lying in the bath, he discovered the 'law of buoyancy'. Sometimes called 'Archimedes Principle'. However, he also:

- invented 'the Archimedes Screw' which is still used in irrigation and the mincing machine to move material along a tube
- made a model of planetary motion
- designed a siege gun to keep the Romans out of Syracuse
- worked on levers and weights for lifting heavy weights
- worked out how to calculate the areas and volumes of spheres and cylinders and found an approximate value for *pi*
- developed the idea of centre of gravity
- was one of the first 'scientists' to apply mathematics to the solution of problems
- demanded rigour in scientific experiments.

Some regard Archimedes as a lone genius, but it is more likely that he was part of a group of individuals searching for new knowledge. Roman soldiers killed Archimedes during the siege of Syracuse.

Marie Curie (1867–1934)

Marie Curie

Marie Curie was born in Poland, graduated first in her class, married and had two daughters. Her husband and close collaborator was tragically killed in a road traffic accident. Early stories of her life tell that she could memorize poems in one reading. Her great achievements were in the field of radioactivity and include:

- showing radioactivity to be an atomic property of uranium
- discovering and naming polonium and radium
- the award of two Nobel Prizes, one for Physics and the other for Chemistry
- organizing X-ray machines in the 1914–18 war to find shrapnel and bullets in soldiers.

Marie Curie died at the age of 67 as a result of years of exposure to radioactive materials. She believed that through learning and science people could overcome oppression. Marie Curie had faced male prejudice in her work as one of the first female scientists. Even today some critics suggest she was a very good scientist and hard working but not in the first league of scientists. Many others would disagree.

Any assessment of her work would have to take the following into the equation:

- she has been described as the 'mother' of the atomic bomb and nuclear power
- cancer treatment uses gamma rays to kill off damaged cells
- microbes that cause decay can be killed by low-dose radiation, so fruit and vegetables can be irradiated to stay fresh on the shelves longer

- syringes and surgical instruments can be sterilized using gamma rays
- carbon-14 dating can be used to find the age of anything that once lived
- potassium-40 can be used to date rocks
- engineers can use Geiger counters to find leaks in oil and gas pipes
- krypton-81 can be used to check people's lungs
- radiation is dangerous and accidents do occur
- disposal or the reprocessing of nuclear materials remains a problem.

TASKS

1 Identify one dead scientist. Prepare an obituary for them, which recognizes their contribution to science.

2 Carry out a search to identify those scientists who contributed to one of the following:

a organ transplantation
b manned flight to the moon
c personal computers
d global warming
d theory of numbers
e statistical testing.

5 Moral responsibility: the social, ethical and environmental implications of scientific discoveries and technological development

Definitions

Ethical	Issues and choices arising from a system of beliefs about right and wrong.
Extrapolation	Using existing facts, trends, theories and ideas to state what is likely to happen in the future.
Moral	Principles and values which determine what is believed to be right.
Organic	Outputs of agriculture using only plant and animal products as fertilizer, pesticides and fungicide.
Prediction	What is believed will happen in a particular way based upon experience and current knowledge.
Recycling	Reuse of materials that have been used once – for example, bottles, paper, steel.
Telecommunications	The technology of sending messages and information over long distances using electronic equipment.

Getting started

1 Is science destructive because it questions and uproots old certainties?
2 Is science so successful that it removes the old dependency on spiritual life?
3 Does science remove our sense of our unique selves?
4 Do the miracle cures of science remove ancient authority and tradition?
5 Does science tell us we are not special but just part of things?
6 Does science dull our appreciation of our own emotional inner life?
7 Will the cold logic of science eliminate music, art, literature and natural beauty?
8 How does science help us with the mystery of consciousness?
9 What are the ethical issues arising from recent developments in genetic engineering?
10 Do scientists understand the public, and do the public understand scientists?

Nuclear energy and fossil fuels

1 Has nuclear energy failed to deliver?
2 What is the legacy of fossil fuel extraction?
3 How will a world without petrol appear?
4 What contribution has nuclear energy made to life today?

Telecommunications

1 Are there worlds in our heads that science will never penetrate?
2 When all the leading firms in an industry have access to the same technology, where does the competitive edge come from?
3 How does the arrival of IT impact upon organizational structure and value added?
4 How do telecommunications and IT change the logistics and value of education?

5 Is the first quality revolution over and in future is quality in the relationship, not just the product?

6 How are telecommunications changing the way we use our banks?

7 Does the public have a right to know the benefits and otherwise of new developments in telecommunications?

Food supply and distribution

1 What is the difference between giving people a hand up and a hand out?

2 Should the EU and the government ban the dumping of food in landfill sites?

3 Should companies get tax breaks for giving surplus food to charities?

4 A recent report on GM foods did not conclude that they were safe, but that there was no evidence at all that they were harmful.

5 In England, only 100,000 cases of food poisoning are reported each year out of an estimated 4.5 million. Should eating places and food shops have to display a score out of ten awarded by local health authorities? What are the pitfalls?

Herbicides, pesticides and organic production

1 Does science reveal the 'dawn chorus' of birdsong for what it is?

2 Would you like to be a summer wwoofer? (willing worker on organic farms)

3 All male fish in the River Aire in Yorkshire showed signs of feminization. This is due to pollution from industrial detergents and natural hormones from sewage waste. The latter may be linked to the contraceptive pill. What a problem!

4 Which do you support: a bag of manure or a bag of inorganic fertilizer?

Waste disposal and recycling

1 Why are large holes in the ground so valuable?

2 What can we recycle to save money, air quality, materials and land?

3 Why are we buying our drinking water by the bottle?

4 Does packaging that you throw away convince you to buy?

Weapons and peacekeeping

1 Does science bring us nearer to the Orwellian world of *1984*?

2 What does science have to say to help us with the problems of death?

3 Under what circumstances should we agree to sell arms?

4 Are wars inevitable?

Outline

This section considers some of the serious moral questions that arise about science and the exploitation of scientific knowledge. It considers the questions raised when scientists discover new technologies and the ultimate responsibilities for any ills that follow. Consider, for example:

■ aerosol sprays damaging the ozone layer
■ exposure to sunlight, increasing the dangers of skin cancer
■ pollution and the possibilities of global warming
■ oils spillage and threats to beaches and birdlife
■ leaks from nuclear power stations
■ weapons of mass destruction.

Some parts of the media appear to suggest that every human disaster in the last 100 years was the fault of science. Newspapers dramatize and extrapolate the findings of science and raise terrifying prospects from the misuse of scientific findings. Early in the 21st century, findings from genetics fall into this category. Maybe some of the responsibility lies with those who mismanage the new technology or push the limits of safety for the sake of profit.

Nuclear energy and fossil fuels

Energy can be defined as the capacity for doing work. Energy can be found in heat, chemicals and the structure of the atom.

Nuclear energy

Nuclear energy is stored in uranium atoms, and is released as heat to create steam that drives steam turbines. The energy in a nuclear power station is created when neutrons strike uranium 235 in a process called nuclear fission. Nuclear energy was seen as the source of energy for the future. Accidents, such as those at Five-Mile Island, Pennsylvania in 1979 and at Chernobyl, in the Ukraine, in 1986, have caused many to question its use in the future. In the UK, nuclear stations were built on the coast, including ones at Hinckley in Devon, Sizewell in Suffolk, Hunterston near Glasgow, Dungeness in Kent, Dounreay in the north of Scotland and Wylfa on Anglesey. One problem for nuclear power stations is decommissioning them at the end of their lives.

France has few fossil fuel resources and despite its hydro-electricity capacity has turned to nuclear power. In the world there are about 500 nuclear reactors, producing nearly 20% of the energy supply.

Views are divided on the future for nuclear power. Technology has the ability to create almost unlimited cheap power with relatively low environmental risks. Those against nuclear power point to the accidents, dangers of military use, its inflexibility to meet peak demand and problems of nuclear waste disposal.

Fossil fuels

Fossil fuels include oil, natural gas and coal. They are limited resources that take a very long time to renew. Coal was a major source of energy and though resources are still considerable it has been replaced by oil in many places. It has fallen in popularity because:

- it scars the surface and causes spoil tips
- it is dangerous to extract
- burning coal causes environmental damage such as acid rain.

The decline in coal mining in the UK is partly related to environmental concerns, but is also a consequence of cheaper supplies from abroad and the activities of trade unions. The closure of coalmines has caused great distress to some coal mining communities. The UK government has provided special funds to regenerate these areas.

Oil is a major fuel in all countries. Oil produces fuel energy for heat or petroleum for transport. The principal production areas are in the Middle East of which Saudi Arabia is the largest. Norway and Mexico are also major exporters. The top importing nations are the USA, Japan, Germany, France and Italy. Oil has become a major political weapon, with producers rationing production to keep prices high and to make their resource last longer. Oil is relatively safe to extract, produces many by-products, including plastics, is easy to transport through pipelines or super tankers and is in great demand with expanding car ownership. The difficulties with oil include:

- unsightly extraction equipment and refinery buildings
- the need for large tanks for storage
- the heavy dependence on a continuous supply
- political aspects
- oil spillages, especially at sea
- the amount of longer-term reserves.

Natural gas is usually found near to oil fields. The UK produces natural gas from its fields in the North Sea. Natural gas is easily transported by pipeline and is cleaner than the coal gas it replaced. Natural gas is seen as a 'green' fuel. Known reserves of natural gas are mainly to be found in parts of the former Soviet Union. In the UK, natural gas has become a major source of fuel in power stations to produce electricity.

TASKS

1 What makes a good fuel? Suggest at least five criteria.

2 To what extent is the division of fuels into renewable and non-renewable groups blurred?

3 Name three products you use that are derived from oil.

4 Why are natural gas and oil usually found together?

5 Why are alternative sources of energy needed?

6 How can oil be used as a weapon?

7 How could you cut your consumption of fossil fuels?

Telecommunications

Telecommunications one hundred years ago

Before she set out on her Diamond Jubilee procession on the morning of June 22, 1897, Queen Victoria of England went to the telegraph room at Buckingham Palace … It was a few minutes after eleven o'clock. She pressed an electric button; an impulse was transmitted to the Central Telegraph Office in St Martin's le Grand; in a matter of seconds her message was on its way to every corner of the Empire. It was the largest Empire in the history of the world, comprising nearly a quarter of the landmass of the earth, and a quarter of its population … Within two minutes … the Queen's message had passed through Teheran on its way to the eastern dominions. By the time her carriage clattered down the Mall (say 20 minutes later) her thanks and blessings had reached Ottawa (in Canada), the Cape and the colonies of West Africa and the Caribbean.

Reproduced from *Pax Britannica* by Jan Morris (Copyright ©1979 J Morris) by permission of PFD on behalf of the Author.

Telecommunications today

- 'All information for all people, anytime, anywhere.'
- 'In the future, the refrigerator itself will directly trigger replenishment of missing items.'
  (Francis Lorentz, Chair of the E-commerce mission, France)

Radio, terrestrial, cable and satellite television, fax and teletext, hard-line, cordless and mobile telephone, smart and plastic credit cards, ID cards for access, computer and the Internet are the main ways in which we experience the telecommunications revolution. Within these main headings there are many sub-divisions.

The Net economy, as it is sometimes called, includes information technology and telecommunications equipment and materials. In many countries the telecommunications industry contributes up to 10% of the national GDP (France 5%, USA 8%) with a growth rate double other industrial averages. Technological advances and decreasing prices help to fuel these changes. Technological advances include XDSL, high-speed copper wire and fibre-optic transmission, allowing increased volumes of information per second and voice-data-image convergence.

Predictions for the future

In the next ten years, due to increased band width connections, over half of the population will live in houses where the Internet is always on, with each of us spending ten hours per week online. Interactive TV has begun for digital viewers and the videophone is here for a few but soon for the many.

Dialling the Internet in Europe: main providers in 1999/2000

Country	Operator	Internet division	Market share
Germany	Deutsche	Telekom T-Online	53%
Italy	Telecom Italia	Tin.it and Club-Net	41%
UK	Dixons	Freeserve	28%
Netherlands	KPN	PlanetInternet	32%
France	France Telecom	Wanadoo	32%
Sweden	Telia	Passagen	22%
Spain	Telefonica	Terra Networks	34%

Issues and trends for the telecommunications industry

- The mobile Internet through the use of WAP mobile phones.
- Mergers of Internet and entertainment industry companies such as AOL and Time Warner.
- Globalization of Internet companies led by launches in the USA and being followed by European providers.
- Higher speed provision and the battle between cable and satellite providers.
- High bids for licences to operate in some countries and increased legislative protection for smaller companies to deter global monopolies.
- Growth and collapse of dot.com companies (called 'barbarians' by more established companies, called the 'bricks and mortar' by the newer companies) where economic models of future growth attract investment in companies with little experience of market operation, who then collapse, often creating a crisis of confidence in other Internet stocks.
- Development of more secure intranets for particular professional and industrial groups – for example, automotive industries, retail distribution and energy industries.
- Concern that the Internet reinforces global

inequalities. In Africa (excluding South Africa) there are 1 million Internet users which is equal to the Internet population of Belgium!

- Even in the more economically developed world there are disparities, with 48% of homes in Finland connected, 41% in Sweden but only 10% in France.
- New cheaper access devices alongside the PC – for example, interactive TV, e-commerce terminals, personal digital assistants, mobile phones (currently 300 million users and 1 billion projected by 2003).
- Radical innovations in education, the treatment of disease and the promotion of health.
- Greater power to consumers, allowing global comparisons of prices and quality, and more information about suppliers, with the reverse auction as one innovative feature.

- Personalization by suppliers, individually tailored products, loyalty schemes and the use of purchase information to drive design, marketing and production (this is called developing the 'attention economy').
- Dangers of Internet fraud as suppliers proliferate without regulation or agreed codes of practice.
- The growing economic power of ISPs, search engines and other cyber-hosts, which could lead to the exclusion of small players by the larger ones.
- The worldwide shortage of skilled personnel. Attracting and training the best people is a top priority for many companies.
- E-commerce erases national boundaries where national currencies are a hindrance to trade and the dollar, pound and the euro are seen as vehicles for payment.

TASKS

1 Use the Internet to find information about the size, location and distribution of the telecommunications industry. Type in 'telecommunications' on your search engine. You will need a focus: try exploring a particular country, time period or form of communication

2 Send and receive email messages to and from a colleague with whom you are co-operating on a project.

3 Draw up a table of at least five different packages for owning and using a mobile phone. How does the best compare with the one you have?

Food supply and distribution

This page examines the constituents of a healthy diet, the sources of food and issues arising from the way in which that food is distributed.

Food, diet and nutrition

'I believed that no two people on the face of the earth were alike; no two people have the same fingerprints, lip prints, or voice prints. Because I felt that all people were different from one another, I did not think it logical that they should eat the same foods' (James D'Adamo).

Food and drink make up our diet. In a healthy diet we need:

- **energy foods** including carbohydrates and fats to provide fuel and heat. Carbohydrates are found in bread, potatoes, pasta and rice whilst fats are contained in cream, butter, margarine and oils
- **body-building foods** provide the chemicals for growth and body repair. The main body builders are proteins which are contained in meat, fish, milk, cheese and eggs. Vegetarians following a vegan diet obtain their proteins from combined vegetable sources but grains are incomplete protein and need to be combined – for example, nuts or pulses (for example, beans and lentils) with wheatgerm or soya or green vegetables
- **maintenance foods** to keep our bodies running well. Vitamins and minerals are the key foods here, including vitamin C in oranges and sodium in salt
- **water**, of which a minimum of 1 litre is vital but 2 litres per day are recommended
- **fibre** as roughage, including wholemeal bread, wholegrain rice, muesli, brown pasta, vegetables and fruit. They assist peristalsis, the movement of food through the gut.

Food supply

Increases in population have worried scientists for many decades. In 1798, Thomas Malthus predicted that the demand for food from an increasing population would outstrip food supply and famine would follow. This has not happened as technology has enabled farmers to increase their productivity. Boserup, a Danish economist, rejected Malthus in 1965 and suggested that 'necessity would be the mother of invention'. Thus more intensive farming methods would continue to increase food production.

Concern now focuses on the amount of food available. Scientists recommend a daily intake of between 2300 and 2600 kilocalories. The international Food and Agriculture Organization (FAO) believes that 75% of the world's population may be below these recommended figures. Malnutrition of this type reduces the quality of life for many people, and leads to diseases.

Food distribution

Jane lives on the street. Each day, she begs about £10 to spend on cigarettes, alcohol, bus fares and fast food. She has not eaten fresh fruit for three months.

Each day, the local supermarket disposes of about £500 of food that has passed its sell-by date yet is still edible, including meat, greens, potatoes, mushrooms, fish and milk. Hygiene laws prevent the store giving the food to Jane. Some of the supermarket food is redistributed by over 200 charities including one called Crisis. They say the current action is the 'tip of the iceberg' on waste food. Many food companies are now co-operating to donate.

The cases for and against distribution of excess food

For	Against
■ it feeds people in need ■ it reduces waste ■ companies try to reduce waste ■ boosts staff morale in donor companies ■ good publicity for companies	■ perpetuates poverty ■ puts off longer-term solutions ■ people become dependent on the food ■ self-help schemes would be better ■ charity replaces public welfare ■ government saves welfare money

TASKS

1 Talk to two or three people who are following a diet. Find out their reasons for the diet and the problems they find in following it.

2 Is alcohol good for you? How much is it safe to drink each week?

3 Food stores are increasing their range of organic foods. Visit a store and make a note of these products. Compare the prices of the organic brands with main brands. What conclusions can you draw?

4 Why are we purchasing bottles of water when there is plenty from the tap?

5 What is the current EU policy on fishing for member countries?

Herbicides, pesticides and organic production

Pesticides

Wild plants and animals have evolved to live alongside their natural predators and parasites. Cultivated crops have been developed to increase yields. This can mean that they have less resistance to local pests and parasites, especially if they are grown intensively. When whole fields are planted with one crop (monoculture) disease can affect large parts of the crop very quickly.

Pesticides are used to protect the crops from harmful organisms. They are substances manufactured to kill specific types of pest. Herbicides are used to kills weeds. Insecticides are used to kills insets and fungicides kill fungi. They have been very successful at protecting crops but have caused problems for the environment.

Herbicides

Yields fall if crops are in competition with weeds for space, light and nutrients. Herbicides were developed after the discovery of auxin (indoleactic acid or IAA). Related chemicals, such as dichlorophenoxyacetic acid and methylphenoxyacetic acid are selectively toxic to particular weeds without harming crops. They are systemic, which means they are taken in through the leaves of the plant and are carried to its roots.

They are very efficient but can cause harm if they drift into hedgerows, roadside verges and woodland. They threaten the diversity of species, remove wild flowers and harm wildlife.

Insecticides

Some plants produce their own insecticides. For example, the chrysanthemum produces pyrethrum which is a strong insecticide. Chemical control by humans developed when DDT (dichlorodiphenyltrichloroethane) was found. DDT poisons the nerves of insects and causes rapid death. Since only low concentrations are needed, the chemical stays active for a long time and as it was effective against a wide range of insects it was used widely. For example, it was used widely in the 1939–45 war to kill malarial mosquitoes. Unfortunately DDT remains in the fatty tissue of the dead animal and accumulates at each stage of the food chain. As a result, damage to many animal species, and in particular birds of prey, was found to be a consequence of DDT. As a result, DDT has been banned and replaced by biodegradable insecticides. These do not persist in the environment. Initially organophosphates were used but these are now thought to be harmful to humans. Today carbamates and pyrethroids, which are synthetic chemicals, have been developed. These are less toxic to mammals, and are biodegradable, but are lethal to fish.

Organic production

Since the 1960s, farmers in Britain have changed the way that they produce food. First came the move to higher production because:

- the market demanded higher yields so that food could be produced at economic prices
- increased applications of chemicals retained high yields and ensured the production of attractive crops for the supermarket shelves
- chemical fertilizers included nitrogen to aid protein production and encourage green leaves, phosphates to help roots and seedlings to grow, potash to make protein and increase resistance to frost and disease
- fertilizers were readily available from nearby agricultural merchants and easily applied to fields using machines.

However, problems began to appear as too much nitrogen causes toxicity, turns plants yellow and can leach into streams causing eutrophication (when excessive plant growth leads to water that contains little oxygen, which in turn kills fish and other animals). Soil erosion increased as hedgerows were removed to increase field size and streams began to silt up.

Then, for a minority, came the move to organic production, recognizing that:

- it was a return, in some ways, to older and less productive methods
- organic farming was a more sustainable way of using the land
- it produced more energy than it consumed, as well as protecting soil and water resources
- organic farming excludes the use of chemical fertilizers, herbicides and pesticides. Instead animal manure and compost is used
- that organic matter such as farmyard manure breaks down to release nitrogen, phosphorus and potassium
- manure reduces leaching
- organic fertilizers such as rock salt, fish and bone meal help the soil to retain moisture and yet have better drainage
- organic farmers still use the land intensively but rotate their crops and allow fallow years

■ with organic farming humus, earthworms and bacteria build up in the soil.

There are problems with organic farming. The Soil Association monitors the soil of organic farmers and it takes two years of lower yields before the soil is free of chemicals. Weeds can become a problem without herbicides, which means extra labour or covering the soil with a mulch or plastic. Organic farming works well if the farmer keeps a herd of cattle to provide manure.

Organic products are more expensive to buy in the supermarket and they are less attractive than the standardized, colourful and perfectly shaped crops produced with the help of chemicals.

TASKS

1 Visit an agricultural merchants' or a garden centre to examine the herbicides, pesticides and insecticides on sale. Include in your review the fertilizers available. Do any claim to be suitable for organic production?

2 Visit your local supermarket and compare fresh fruit and vegetables from the organic and non-organic shelves. Compare them in terms of price, size, shape, colour and regularity. Buy one item of produce and the same item from the organic shelves. Compare the tastes of the two and include your reaction in your survey. Prepare a report for your local newspaper, of up to 300 words, on the results of your survey.

Word-process your report in newspaper column style with an appropriate heading.

Waste disposal and recycling

Waste disposal

Start by thinking of all the waste output from your home every day. This could be solids such as paper, packaging, bottles, tins, food waste, ashes, clothing, shoes or liquids such as sewage and other dirty water, milk, alcohol, chemicals from painting, unwanted medicine and oils from car repairs. Industry and commerce will also add its waste products, but more than half of all waste is domestic. Lifestyles today generate more waste when our clothes, food and appliances are attractively packaged to entice purchasers. The more affluent we become, the more we appear to generate waste. New Yorkers produce 620 kg of waste per person per year.

Some of the waste is biodegradable and breaks down under the influence of bacteria – for example, paper, wool and food. Other waste is non-biodegradable and will lie in the ground for many years. The three main ways of disposing of solid waste are landfill, incineration and export.

Landfill

This is the most popular way for people in the UK to dispose of their solid waste. Eighty-four per cent of urban waste goes into holes in the ground. Twenty million tonnes are produced each year. The holes used are the product of the extractive industries. Gravel, sand, limestone, and road aggregates are extracted and then the holes sold to be filled with solid waste. In some cases hills of waste appear as a new landscape is formed.

Landfill sites have problems with contamination seeping into groundwater and some cities struggle to find suitable sites. Few people want to live near to a refuse tip with all its consequent pollution. Many of these sites include compaction facilities as well as recycling skips. Some separate the green waste and turn it into compost for resale.

Incineration

This is the usual way of dealing with solid waste in Japan and Denmark. In the UK there is a large incinerator in Stoke-on-Trent. The method does have its technical problems. If burning is not at the right temperature, harmful pollution can be released. Few people want an incinerator in their neighbourhood and they are usually located in poorer areas. However, incineration can have its benefits if the burning generates electricity.

Export

Some cities do not have the capacity to dispose of their solid waste and buy space in rural areas or abroad. Mexico earns valuable foreign currency by accepting waste from the USA.

Reducing waste and recycling

Non-renewable resources are being depleted and renewable ones exploited to the point where conservation is needed. The three main ways of reducing the amount of solid waste are reusing materials, recovering or recycling waste, and preventing waste.

Reusing materials

Curiously, in the UK milk bottles that are delivered to the door get reused 24 times. Supermarkets are paying customers and making donations to charity if their plastic carrier bags are used again. Public houses, hotels and restaurants return large numbers of empty bottles to the brewery each week. Motor car tyres are reused for lower speed activities.

Recycling or recovery

This approach is widespread in the UK and involves the collection of bottles, cans, newspaper, cardboard, plastics, clothing and shoes from a centrally located set of containers. Some local authorities arrange collections of newspapers on a monthly basis to help less mobile residents, but some authorities do little. Some industries are developing technologies to recycle their products after use. For example, a major supplier of plastics has recycled ladies tights to produce blocks of a wood-like material. Some car and computer makers are making their products easier to dismantle and reuse.

Industrial recycling has been part of production for a long time. Scrap metal collection makes an important contribution to production. There are predictions that resources for some metals will be exhausted in the near future (copper in 40 years, zinc in 60, lead in 20 and tin in 15). The problems are economic in terms of the costs of collection sorting and reprocessing.

Rates of recycling vary between countries, with Sweden, Austria and the Netherlands top of the league of European nations. In Berlin, factories and households have different bins for different types of waste. Now all members of the EU have recycling targets. Ideas for the future include tax incentives for those who reuse or recycle. Some countries are introducing deposit charges on plastic bottles in an effort to increase their reuse.

Despite these efforts, people in the UK throw away 10,000 million tins, worth several million pounds, every year.

Critics of recycling note that some recycling uses great amounts of energy and causes pollution. For example, an alternative to the high amounts of energy and chemicals needed to recycle paper encourages the farming of softwood forests.

Changing attitudes

In the future, many countries plan to change attitudes to waste production. They are looking to change the way we live so that less is consumed and smaller amounts of waste are produced.

TASKS

1 Carry out an audit of the waste material produced by your house each day (excluding sewage) for seven days. Try to classify the materials into metals, glass, paper, shoes, clothes, vegetable matter and miscellaneous. You could measure the amount in terms of number of items, volume and weight. How much of the material is recycled?

2 What happens to the material collected each week by your local refuse collector? What arrangements are made for recycling by your local authority?

3 Make proposals for the better management of waste disposal and recycling in your area.

Weapons and peacekeeping
The role of scientists

Some discoveries and inventions by scientists become the weapons of war. The atom and hydrogen bombs and chemical and germ warfare are examples. However, there are beneficial advances made under the stress of war. Developments in surgery and immunology are examples. Progress with plastic surgery to repair burned pilots was spectacular. Navigational radar, rocketry, jet engines and computers can be traced to World War II. Survival brings resources and focus to the activities of teams of scientists. After the war both the USA and USSR (as it was then) put enormous sums of money and hours of expertise into the 'space race'. Spin-offs from this research include teflon 'non-stick' saucepans, the miniaturization of computers, satellite telecommunications and the 'downsizing' of the workforce as automation took over. On this page the development of the atomic bomb is used as an example.

From gunpowder to atomic bombs

1775 – Antoine Lavoisier, an accountant, took over gunpowder production for the French government. Conditions were very unsettled in Europe and there was a need for the production of large quantities of high quality gunpowder. Accountant Lavoisier kept careful quality control records of the combination of the three ingredients: saltpetre, charcoal and sulphur. The results of his experiments revolutionized production of the best gunpowder in Europe.

1919 – Rutherford created oxygen from nitrogen and speculated on the existence of the neutron.

1932 – Chadwick discovered the neutron.

1938 – Fermi received the Nobel Prize for the fission of uranium.

1943 – The father of the atomic bomb is recognized as Robert Oppenheimer. He began bomb development at Los Alamos. Code-named 'the Manhattan Project', the scientists were very worried that the Germans were also developing the bomb. 'No one who saw it could forget it, a foul and awesome display' (I. I. Rabi, physicist).

1945 – Atomic bombs dropped on Hiroshima and Nagasaki.

1949 – First Soviet detonation.

1952 – First British detonation.

The atomic nations

The testing of atomic devices is recorded from 1945 when one explosion took place. In 1958 there were 116 tests and 178 in 1962. A Comprehensive Test Ban Treaty (CTBT) was signed in 1996. Signatories include the USA, the USSR, the UK, France and China.

Converts to non-proliferation

Algeria, Argentina, Brazil, Belarus, Kazakhstan, Ukraine and South Africa. These states had or were on the brink of having nuclear weapon capacity but renounced their power.

States giving proliferation concern

North Korea, Iran, Iraq, Libya, Israel, India and Pakistan. All of these states are under economic and political pressure to give up their nuclear weapons. India and Pakistan carried out tests in 1998 but have said that each will sign the CTBT if the other does.

One key role for scientists is monitoring observance of the treaty, which can be through geophones, microphones, magnetometers, pressure measuring cables, amplifiers, digital converters and optical disc computers.

Developing missile defence systems

The USA, aware of potential threat from communist and other countries, began the development of a space defence system (the National Missile Defence: NMD), nicknamed 'Star Wars'. The escalating cost, technical problems and the ending of the 'Cold War' caused a re-evaluation of this space missile system. Instead a boost-phase intercept system (BPI) is proposed. This would involve surface-based missiles, usually on ships, being fired to destroy incoming Intercontinental Ballistic Missiles (ICBMs). Satellites – which are already part of the Defence Support Program and detected every launch in the 'Gulf War' – would detect the launched missile and within 250 seconds a launch of an interceptor missile could take place from the ship.

The launch ships could be deployed according to current thinking on potential aggressors.

Such a system is cheaper, uses known technology, has none of the difficult cooling problems that have hindered 'Star Wars'. It is also difficult to hit with counter-measures.

Why not peacekeeping?

The United Nations and to a lesser extent NATO, has been involved for many years in peacekeeping. In early operations, the UN kept the peace in an area whilst waiting for a political settlement to be worked out. Today the UN is more active in demobilizing the combatants, collecting weapons, supervizing elections and monitoring the development of a locally based police force. Successes have been recorded in Namibia, Mozambique, El Salvador and Cambodia. The UN has been less successful in central Africa. The problems in Rwanda, Angola and Somalia are disappointing outcomes for the UN.

The UN recognizes the need to involve local political leaders and to have a sufficiently strong force in place to resolve the conflict.

NATO has also taken a leading role in central Europe in the regions of the former Yugoslavia. The problems in Kosovo were prominent in this action.

One of the dilemmas in peacekeeping is the decision to intervene in the internal affairs of a nation state. The lines between invasion, intrusion and intervention are fine and cause heated debate in the United Nation Assembly. There are always political aspects to any action by UN forces.

TASKS

1 Some of the reactions of scientists in the aftermath of the atomic bomb, first dropped in 1945:

'We had the means to end the war quickly, with great savings of human life. I believe it was the sensible thing to do, and I still do' (L. W. Alvarez).

'We were afraid that Hitler had the bomb first, and we made this bomb, which shortened the war and saved a lot of American and Japanese lives' (V. Weisskopf).

'If I had known that the Germans would not succeed in constructing the atom bomb, I would never have lifted a finger' (A. Einstein).

Compare the way in which the 1939–45 war ended against Germany with the way it ended against Japan. In view of your findings, do you support the dropping of the two atomic bombs?

2 For a peacekeeping operation that is currently in the news, examine the contribution made by the latest weaponry to the effective maintenance of peace.

⑥ The relationship between technology, science, culture and ideology

Definitions

Certainty   Lack of doubt about something happening.

Hazards   Floods, fog, avalanche, earthquakes, drought, volcanoes, storms.

Ideology   A set of beliefs and concepts used by individuals to simplify complex situations and choices.

Infinity   The number that is larger than any other numbers and cannot be counted.

Optimism   Hopeful about the future and believing that a course of action will be successful.

Pessimism   Belief that the worst scenario will occur and that success is ruled out.

Resources   Something becomes a resource when it becomes useful – for example, coal, water.

Sustainability   Actions to keep activities continuing in the long term.

Getting started

1 'The aim of science is not to open a door to infinite wisdom but to set a limit to infinite error' (Brecht).
2 'Science is more a way of asking questions than it is of giving answers' (Sir Robert May).
3 Does science have all the answers?
4 What is a polymath?
5 Can anything be absolutely certain in a field of rapid scientific and technological developments?
6 Is it easy for scientists to be self-righteous, after all they are not in power?

Resource exploitation

1 Are all non-renewable resources non-renewable?
2 Are all renewable resources renewable?
3 How can timber be farmed? What is the potential of a farmed coniferous forest for ecology, environment and amenity?
4 How can the demand for resources be slowed down?

Sustainability and stewardship

1 Have environmental protestors the right to pull up genetically modified maize?

2 Do people on national campaigns have the right to invade villages and farms?
3 Should those protesting about environmental damage break the law to attract media attention to their cause?
4 Are GM crops a good thing?
5 What tests could be carried out to check whether GM crops are safe?

Industry and ecology

1 Do you want to live organically and sustainably? Why not try an eco-village? Try www.gaia.org for a list of sites.
2 How can we live sustainably whilst making a decent living?
3 When it comes to environmental issues are the optimists or the pessimists right?
4 What happens with eco-tourism?

Intermediate technology and development

1 Why does Western technology fail to deliver in some countries?
2 Have bicycles and cycle routes started to appear in your area?
3 Is small beautiful?
4 Is intermediate technology a way of keeping some areas dependent?

Natural hazards and disasters

1 Which hazards are predictable?
2 Which hazards affect the UK?
3 What is the difference between cyclones, hurricanes and tornadoes?
4 Which disaster have you worried about in recent weeks?

Outline

This section uses five topics to explore the relationship between technology and science on the one hand and culture and ideology on the other. Technology and science are part of society where patterns of behaviour are set in cultural systems including traditions, ideas and values. Thus, technology and science are both reactions to and creators of cultural patterns.

Technology and science have had a bad press in recent years. There is much public criticism of the negative effects for some of the innovations brought by scientific research. The problem lies in the unforeseen outcomes of some innovations. Drugs research led to damaged babies, and changes in animal feed to human illness. The findings of genetic research and the potential for animal and crop modification challenge society. The popular mobile telephone, overhead electricity supply cables, nuclear processing plants and computer screens have all been named as potential hazards. The problem is that we could become a 'nanny' state with all the dangers that follow. On the other hand, scientific issues are technically complex and difficult for non-experts to understand. The issue is made more difficult by commercial and political considerations. One suggested way to move forward is to establish public meetings at a local scale where interested people can be briefed on new developments.

Resource exploitation

When people need something from the earth, it becomes a resource. Until people started using petroleum and uranium they were not resources. People make things become resources because they want to use them. Just as materials become resources so the process is reversible as materials are replaced by better ones. The canal narrow boat was replaced as the main form of transport for heavy goods by the railway, which was in turn replaced by the lorry.

The earth receives 17×10^{13} kW of energy from the sun per day. The earth is made up of 5.98×10^{21} tons of matter. Despite this vast abundance much of these resources are not accessible to people. Much of it is not available – for example, the minerals in the earth's molten core. Resources can be divided up in a number of ways:

- **natural resources** include minerals, climate, and soils
- **human resources** include people and their capital
- **renewable resources** are part of the flow of nature and can be used again
- **non-renewable resources** are finite and can be exhausted.

Energy resources

Coal, oil and natural gas account for the majority of the energy consumed on the earth and they are all non-renewable. They have been easy to exploit and cheap to use but their use pollutes the environment. Nuclear energy uses uranium and is classified as non-renewable.

Renewable energy resources cause less environmental damage and include hydro-electric power, waves, tides, the sun, geothermal energy, crops, timber and biogas. Of these, only hydro-electricity makes a significant contribution to energy supplies. Critics of hydro-electricity point to the environmental damage caused by dam construction and the subsequent flooding of land. Schemes in China, Turkey, Brazil and Ghana have been criticized in these respects.

Forests are an interesting example of a renewable resource. Recent trends have been for forests to be replanted as they yield their crop of timber. This is particularly the case in Europe and North America. However, in Latin America and Africa the practice is not widespread. Nearly all European forests are commercially managed for a long-term sustainable future, but in the tropical forests deforestation exceeds reforestation by up to 20 times.

Reserves of resources

Reserves of a resource are the known quantities of a resource that can be realized given current knowledge of methods of extraction. New methods of extraction or refining could increase the amount of reserves. For example, oil reserves can be explored using geological surveys, geophysical methods and trial drill holes. The decision to exploit an oilfield will depend upon:

- the quality of the oil, its chemical composition and freedom from impurities
- the size of the reserve and the capital needed to develop it
- access and location of refineries and geological depth
- world demand and price levels
- political conditions and security in the area.

The growing demand for resources

Increasing population and changing lifestyles that demand more resources continue to increase the pressure on the earth's reserves. In the last 100 years more resources have been used up than in all the previous centuries combined. The factors in the resource equation are:

- will the population of the earth continue its exponential rise?
- will consumption per person continue to rise as less economically developed areas adopt Western lifestyles?
- will alternative energy resources deliver power in time?
- how much longer can oil last (Estimates suggest 40 years)
- will cities become more compact?

TASKS

1 To promote development of the country and remote rural areas, the Turkish government is proposing to build a large dam. This will supply electricity and irrigation water to a large area. However, there are environmental dangers. You are taking part in a debate on the motion:

'This house supports the development of the dam building scheme in Turkey.'

Prepare notes for a five-minute speech for or against the scheme. Include in your notes your main points and try to anticipate and refute those of the opposition.

2 Describe a day in your life if supplies of oil had been exhausted five years ago.

Sustainability and stewardship

Sustainability refers to development that meets the needs of the present generation, without compromizing the ability of future generations to meet their needs. Consider your lifestyle and the way you consume resources. As we take on the latest innovations, such as the mobile phone and the Internet, we consume more energy than earlier generations. We also tend to travel more, thereby increasing the consumption of fuel and requiring new roads and airports to be built.

In 1999, the population of the world reached 6 billion. Forecasts suggest that it will reach 9 billion and then begin to decline. The future is uncertain as some of the high population growth areas begin to adopt birth control, change their customs and women become more emancipated.

The earth can provide enough food for all these people but the differences in the location of production and hungry populations as well as gaps in wealth make sustaining all these people a problem. Overpopulation and some modern developments threaten the environment.

In 1992, the United Nations recognized the problem of sustaining the earth and, working with member countries, produced Agenda 21.

Key points of Agenda 21

1   Sustainable development is a local and a global matter, involving local people and national governments.
2   As part of their stewardship role, local and national governments should study how they:
   ■ consume resources
   ■ plan sustainable changes in their area
   ■ plan for a sustainable future.

Agenda 21 can be summarized by the slogan 'think globally and act locally'.

Seven key concepts of sustainable development

1   Interdependence
      People, the economy and the natural environment are interdependent at a range of scales from the local to global.
2   Citizenship and stewardship
      People have rights and responsibilities including participation and co-operation.
3   The future
      Responsibility extends to protecting the needs and rights of future generations.
4   Diversity
      Recognition and respect for the cultural, social, economic and biological diversity of our environment.
5   Equity
      Acknowledgement and respect for quality of life, equity and justice for all people.
6   Sustainable change
      Plan and monitor change to ensure sustainability of developments and carrying capacity.
7   Uncertainty
      Understanding of the uncertainty of outcome and taking appropriate precautions.

Examples of sustainable development

1 Commercial fishing

We need to balance the need for food with the need to sustain fish stocks. Around Britain and the rest of Europe the amount of commercial fishing has been so great that fish stocks have fallen. The European Union has therefore imposed quotas, regulations on net size, closed seasons and exclusion zones to conserve stock. This has proved a tough policy for politicians, fishermen and consumers. However, it is vital if fishing is to continue over the long term.

2 Forests

Forestry provides a valuable source of income for some countries. It also provides employment for large numbers of people. It is very difficult to stop forest clearance and deny land to poor landless peasants who live near to forests. Their governments may need the foreign exchange to improve agriculture or education and there is worldwide demand for their hardwood timber. Sustainable forestry allows some mature trees to be removed from the forest without decreasing its biodiversity. The trees are cut and removed with care from the forest and new trees are planted. However this model is hard to supervize in some of the more remote forests.

3 Building on brownfield land

The UK faces a demand for more houses as well as space for commerce and industry. Recently local authorities have been encouraged to develop on sites that have become derelict in urban areas. Former manufacturing sites, coal yards, railway sidings, gas works and military sites have become the focus for development. This brownfield land may not be ideal. The site may need cleaning of dangerous chemicals and fumes, access is not always easy and the environment not all that desirable. Demand from developers and house buyer is for housing on the edge of cities on greenfield sites. However, building inside the city can regenerate the area, cut the demand for fuel to travel, reduce the need for new roads, preserve agricultural land and allow urban communities to grow again.

TASKS

1 The UK government recognizes the need to build at least 4 million new houses in the next few years. The question that has to be answered is where to put them.

  a What are NIMBYs and DINKYs?

  b What is the difference between brownfield and greenfield land?

  c Population surveys suggest that the number of elderly people will increase as will the number of single-parent households. What do these changes mean for housing design?

  d People want to move out of urban centres to areas on the rural fringe. Suggest reasons for the authorities wishing to keep people in urban areas. What policies could they implement to help people stay in, or move into, urban areas?

  e Some housing authorities are considering the building of new towns, some selecting villages as growth poles and others are infilling existing villages. Apply each of these policies to a rural area near to you and list advantages and disadvantages of each policy.

2 Some smaller market towns are implementing Local Agenda 21 by allowing a Farmers' Market in their market squares. Many of these towns had lost their regular market many years ago. How does this change help to implement Agenda 21?

3 Find out to what extent Local Agenda 21 is affecting your local area and the people living there. What actions could you take?

Industry and ecology

Rotherham, in the heart of the Yorkshire coalfield, has become the first urban authority in the UK to select 'green electricity'. Its power will be generated from wind turbines, coppiced willow and agricultural waste. This will replace power produced from coal, gas and nuclear power. Initial costs will be higher but running the system will eventually be cheaper.

Industry: its development and structure

The Industrial Revolution

This began in the middle of the eighteenth century, as the UK became a manufacturing nation. It was fostered by a series of brilliant inventions and innovations, including:

- Brindley building canals to move heavy loads via horse-drawn barges
- Telford building cast iron bridges for canals and roads
- Kay, Hargreaves and Cartwright inventing the flying shuttle, spinning jenny and power loom to revolutionize the textile industry
- Priestley discovering oxygen
- Wedgwood producing high quality pottery
- Watt devising the steam engine, for use in the industry of Birmingham, and Trevithick turning it into a high-pressure engine.

These inventions led to manufacturing industry and the migration of people from the depressed countryside to the towns for jobs in the new factories.

Industry: primary, secondary, and tertiary

- Primary industries extract natural resources directly from the land and sea. They include coal mining, oil drilling, farming, fishing and forestry.
- Secondary industries, or manufacturing industries, process natural raw materials to make products. These may be finished products or the materials for further manufacture. They include steel production, car assembly and food processing.
- Tertiary industries provide a service. These are now the largest employers in the UK and include teachers, doctors, entertainers, plumbers and shop assistants.

Industry: inputs, processes and outputs

A useful way of looking at industrial activity is through a systems viewpoint. An economic system has three main components:

- inputs – what goes into the industry
- processes – what takes place inside the industry
- outputs – what is produced by the industry.

Inputs include labour, raw materials, energy, management knowledge, research, finance and machinery. Processes could include assembly, shaping, making, pressing, moulding, welding, packaging and distribution. Outputs include the goods for sale, waste products and profit.

Ecology

Ecologists study ecosystems where habitat and populations living together (called communities) combine. In woodland, the trees, decaying vegetation, the plants and animals living there and the soil make up the ecosystem. Ecosystems are linked as birds and insects move between them.

Interactions in ecosystems: food chains and pyramids

Plants produce their own food through photosynthesis. All other living things feed directly or indirectly on plants. Plants are producers and the rest consumers. For example, grass seed is a source of food for mice which are, in turn, eaten by predators such as the owl. This is called a food chain. In food chains herbivores eat only plants, carnivores eat only meat and omnivores eat both plants and animals. As you pass along a food chain the number and mass of members decreases. This is called the food or biomass pyramid. The size of the biomass is determined by the ability of the plants at the bottom of the pyramid to produce food.

A great deal of energy is lost at each stage of the food chain. Thus humans get more energy from eating vegetables directly than from eating the animals that consume the vegetables.

Communities that are well adapted to their habitat grow in numbers along the well-known S-shaped curve (see page 41). Food and water supplies, space, waste products, disease, climate and light condition their numbers.

Food production and the ecosystem

This often means careful management of the ecosystem. In fact when farming takes place an artificial ecosystem is produced. Inorganic fertilizers, pesticides and insecticides disturb the fragile ecosystem. Farming tends to intensify the use of the land for productive purposes and speeds up the regenerative cycle.

Threats to bio-diversity

Many plants and animals are at risk due to the destruction of wildlife habitats – for example, tropical rainforests through timber extraction, land clearance for ranching and the mineral extraction, wetlands being drained for agriculture, and coral reef damage from tourism. One hundred and sixty countries signed the Bio-diversity Convention in Rio in 1992 to protect rare plants and animals. Despite this the pharmaceutical companies still search the rainforest for plants and animals with medicinal qualities.

Industry and eco-villages

Eco-villages are intended to provide a good life without taking more out of the earth than they are giving back. Eco-villages are rural, and urban dwellers find them tough to live in. Quite a number come to try, but few are able to stay. The characteristics of eco-villages include:

- woodland, providing timber for construction and fuel
- spring water supply
- reed beds for water purification
- reuse of domestic water on gardens
- use of manure as fertilizer
- gardens for vegetables
- eco-tourism as a form of income

- residents with sources of income or the ability to work from the Internet
- animals to produce butter and cheese, and bees for honey
- craft industries such as basket making, pottery, painting
- hostile neighbours and too many curious journalists
- eco-friendly building materials such as straw, sawdust and wool.

Industry and ecology in conflict

All types of industry produce the wealth upon which we depend to buy homes and food, pay taxes to provide health and education services and spend upon clothes, leisure and pleasure. During the wealth creation process by industry there is a danger that some industrialists lose sight of the environmental damage they might be causing. They can produce air, land, water, noise and visual pollution. The challenge is to get the right balance between the production of wealth and environmental damage. Both sides of the balance are important for each other.

TASKS

Read pages 133–4 and prepare for yourself ten short-answer questions. Put the questions away in an envelope. Prepare two postcard size sets of revision notes, one for industry and the other for ecology. After about one week,

read your two postcards and then try to answer your ten questions. How well did you do? Which part of the page do you need to revisit? You could use this postcard system for all revision, but remember to label the cards.

Intermediate technology and development

Since 1945, many of the more economically developed countries (MEDCs) have given loans or aid for the development of poorer nations. This has been partly driven by humanitarian concerns but also by the desire to form trade relationships and expand markets.

Alternatives to the notion of Western aided development have been developed by a number of leaders including Gandhi, Nyerere and Schumacher.

Mahatma Gandhi (1869–1948)

Gandhi encouraged rural development in India as a basis for development. Before Gandhi, the British had encouraged industrialization based upon the cities. The policy advocated by Gandhi (called Satyagraha) encouraged craft and cottage industries so that every village became self-sufficient. This balanced rural and urban development. After Gandhi, Indian governments have tended to favour capital-intensive industry in urban areas and rural deprivation and poverty persist.

Julius Nyerere and the Ujamaa

In Tanzania, between 1967 and 1980, Nyerere had the strategy of Ujamaa (familyhood) with the return of land to collective ownership, traditional ways of life, community responsibility and village co-operatives. Alongside this ideal, healthcare, housing, rural crafts and co-operative agriculture were developed. Nyerere did not see Western development as the way forward for his country. He believed in self-reliance and during the scheme, Tanzania had one of the best health services in Africa.

Dr E. F. Schumacher

Schumacher developed the concept of Intermediate Technology in the 1960s, and published his ideas in the famous book *Small is Beautiful* (1973).

The main characteristics of Intermediate Technology Projects are:
- technology that is appropriate for the circumstances found in the LEDC
- labour-intensive projects, since people are unemployed or underemployed
- local tools, techniques and resources used in a sustainable way
- planned as local, small-scale, low-cost

schemes that can be managed, controlled and funded locally
- harmony with the local environment and customs.

Examples of Intermediate Technology projects include:
- providing villages with simple bamboo water pumps rather than sophisticated electrical ones
- providing bicycles for farmers to deliver produce rather than a single lorry to collect produce
- using small local streams to generate electricity, this reduces deforestation to provide fuel (for example, in Nepal)
- building clay stoves (Jiko in Kenya or Chiminea in Mexico) to provide a more efficient use of fuel
- placing lines of stones along the contours of hill-sides to slow down run-off of water
- building large clay pots (Thai pots) to collect rainwater from roofs during the rainier seasons
- providing cement and chicken wire to reinforce walls and roofs (for example, for the Maasai in Kenya).

Advanced and inappropriate technology

Some development projects introduced to LEDCs from MEDCs have been based on the technology of the developed country. This has not always been successful because, when the MEDC withdraws at the end of the project, the people in the LEDC are unable to maintain the technology. This may be because they lack the finance or skill. Another disadvantage is that the products of this sophisticated technology are designed and destined for the MEDC, to the disadvantage of local people. Sophisticated telecommunications, machinery and transport are not needed and production does not serve local markets.

Criticism of Intermediate Technology

Some critics of Intermediate Technology suggest that:
- it hinders the development of a country
- people become locked into their traditional ways and do not receive the advantages of progress
- new telecommunications and health provisions reach people anyway and disturb traditional ways of life and make Intermediate Technology inappropriate.

TASKS

1 Quotes linked to Dr Schumacher about Intermediate Technology include:

'If you want to go places start from where you are. If you are poor start with something cheap. If you are uneducated start with something relatively simple.'

'The best aid to give is intellectual aid, a gift of useful knowledge … The gift of material goods makes people dependent, but the gift of knowledge makes them free – provided it is the right kind of knowledge.'

'A project that does not fit, educationally and organizationally, into the environment will be an economic failure and cause disruption.'

'Give a man a fish and you feed him for a day; teach him how to fish and he can feed himself for life. Teach him to make his own fishing tackle and you have helped him to become not only self-supporting but also self-reliant and independent.'

Select one or more of these quotations and explain its meaning. How might it be applied to someone living in a rural area of a less economically developed country?

2 Prepare the case against the use of Intermediate Technology for development and outline an alternative strategy for a named place.

Natural hazards and disasters

Few days pass without news of another natural disaster. Some of these disasters are the product of natural forces. They include earthquakes, volcanic eruptions, tropical storms, flooding, drought, fire, fog, ice, avalanches and landslides. Some of these have been affected by the activities of people. All of them have effects upon people.

These natural hazards may affect only a small area or a very large one. The effects may be short-lived, for example, ice on the roads on winter mornings, or may change a place completely, for example, after a volcanic eruption. Some cause death and involve massive financial damage. Others are merely inconvenient.

The public respond quickly and generously to help the victims of yet another disaster. This is particularly the case when poor countries are hit and do not have the resources to protect their inhabitants.

Describing a hazard

The following headings can be used to describe or classify a hazard.

1 Natural or human-made causes.
2 Severity – this can range from a few dead or injured with damage over a small area, to many dead or injured and widespread massive damage.
3 Frequency – some hazards occur regularly in some areas, for example, avalanches in the Alps, tornadoes and hurricanes in the USA.
4 Duration – this may be only a matter of seconds in the case of an earthquake, whilst a drought may persist for several years.
5 Location – floods occur in many parts of the world, volcanoes are linked to fault lines in the earth's crust, especially around the Pacific Ocean, whilst tornadoes are linked with the mid-west of the USA.
6 Predictability – some weather hazards can be predicted using satellites and other equipment but earthquakes can still be a surprise.

The table below summarizes these effects for six natural hazards.

Accounts of two natural hazards and their effects

Earthquakes

In 1995, a major earthquake hit the Japanese town of Kobe. The earthquake measured 7.2 on the Richter Scale (major earthquake) and lasted 20 seconds. In total, 5500 people were killed and 310,000 made homeless. The ground moved 18 cm horizontally and 12 cm vertically. The core of the earthquake, the epicentre, was close to the surface and caused major devastation in three large cities. Transport was severely disrupted as bridges collapsed. The hospital building and shopping centre collapsed. The earthquake occurred because two of the earth's crustal plates, the Pacific and Philippine plates, slipped along the Nojima fault. Other earthquakes have occurred in California, Afghanistan and Papua New Guinea.

Cyclones

In April 2000, cyclone Hudah hit the island of Madagascar and then moved on to Mozambique on mainland Africa. One hundred thousand people had to leave their homes because of flooding. Gusts up to 200 mph wrecked the town of Antalaha in Madagascar that was caught in the eye of the storm. Hudah was the third cyclone to hit the area in two months. United Nations' observers estimated that 200 people had been killed and 130,000 affected by previous storm. The greatest danger came from flash flooding of the River Zambezi where people were trapped in the trees and had to be rescued by helicopter. It is very difficult to predict the path and impact of these cyclones. Disasters of this type can destabilize a country politically and economically.

Type	*Predictability*	*Scale of potential effects**				
		Area	Loss of life	Economic loss	Long-term effects	Total impact
Avalanche	Very unpredictable	1	3	2	1	7
Drought	Predictable	5	5	5	5	20
Earthquake	Quite predictable	5	4	5	4	18
Flood	Predictable	4	5	5	4	18
Hurricane	Very predictable	4	4	4	4	16
Volcanic eruption	Quite predictable	2	4	4	5	15

*Note: effects graded: 1 (smaller) to 5 (larger)
Predictability and effects of hazards

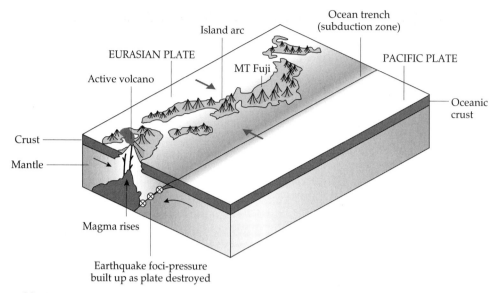

Figure 20   *Earthquakes occur along fault lines where the earth's plates meet*

TASKS

1 Figure 20 shows the way in which an earthquake occurs. Find and explain another diagram showing the formation of a cyclone.

2 Describe and account for a natural hazard or natural disaster that has recently occurred in the UK.

Further study suggestions and example questions

Further reading

Barber, P. and Board, C. (1993) *Tales from the Map Room: Fact and Fiction About Maps and Their Makers*, BBC Books, London.

Bolles, E. B. (1997) *Galileo's Commandment: An Anthology of Great Science Writing*, Abacus, London.

Bragg, M. (1998) *On Giants' Shoulders: Great Scientists and Their Discoveries*, Sceptre, London.

Dunbar, R. (1995) *The Trouble With Science*, Faber and Faber, London.

Kahney, H. (1993) *Problem Solving*, Open University Press, Buckingham.

Sobel, D. (1995) *Longitude: The True Story of a Lone Genius Who Solved the Greatest Scientific Problem of his Time*, Fourth Estate, London.

Trefil, J. (1996) *101 Things You Don't Know About Science*, Cassell, London.

Websites and videos

An excellent website for the story of the atomic bomb is www.atomicarchive.com. Videos linked to this section include the films *Gandhi* and *Twister*.

Questions

1 Why should Thomas Paine, a man who died in 1809, be adopted as patron saint of the Internet? Try starting with www.tompainelewes.org.uk.

2 How can scientific research and the introduction of new technologies be done in such a way that has public support and involvement?

3 'Science is too important to be left to scientist. When science raises profound ethical and social issues, the whole of society needs to take part in the debate.' How do you think this could be realized?

4 Is there any other way of knowing than through experiments?

5 Differentiate between 'knowing how' and 'knowing that'.

6 Give examples where accurate prediction helps with intervention and control.

7 Does science dull our appreciation of our emotional lives with its cold logic?

8 For an issue or problem of concern to you, give optimistic and pessimistic viewpoints.

9 Define sustainability and suggest how your school or college could adopt sustainable policies.

10 A number of people, including senior politicians, writers and scientists, refuse to own a mobile phone. Suggest reasons for their position.

11 How could taxes be used to reduce the amount of waste produced by the average household?

12 Since famine still exists, should GM crops be introduced into countries where there is hunger?

13 Should owners of vehicles found to be over legal limits for pollution creation face fines and even imprisonment?

14 Do natural weather disasters still exist?

4 Religious experience and its alternatives

Definitions

Conviction   A strong belief.

Doctrine   A principle or belief that is taught.

Hedonism   A philosophy emphasizing happiness.

Humanism   A system that puts human interests and the mind of human beings first. A rejection of the supernatural.

Materialism   Making bodily or physical wants your priority.

Nationalism   A favouring of one's own nation, sometimes to the point of desiring domination over others.

Principle   A fundamental truth on which others are founded.

Religion   A belief in a higher controlling power or powers. A system of beliefs or worship.

Tenet   An opinion or principle or doctrine that a person believes to be true.

Getting started

1 'Religion is the opium of the masses' (Marx).
2 Should the religion of the state get involved in politics?
3 'Blessed are the peacemakers ...' (Sermon on the Mount). Religion causes more conflict than any other issue. Why?
4 We do not need a church, temple or mosque to worship our God or Gods. Is this true?
5 Should religious faiths be involved in secular life – for example, the industrial and economic life of a country?
6 Is it any wonder people are moving towards substitutes for religion when they see all the suffering and evil in the world.
7 Too many people belong to a religious faith out of fear. Do you agree?
8 Why don't young people go to church? Why are congregations decreasing in number?
9 Fundamentalism, in any religion, is dangerous. Is this true?
10 Should religions move with the times?
11 'Imagine there's no heaven ...' (John Lennon).
12 How can a place be considered holy?
13 Why do people make pilgrimages?
14 There is a tendency to want religion for our rites of passage. Is this acceptable?
15 Should non-church-goers be allowed to marry in church?
16 'If we didn't have religion we wouldn't have national holidays!'

Outline

For this part of the unit you will need to analyse and evaluate both religious and non-religious views of life. Although you are only required to focus on one religion in detail, it will be desirable for you to have some knowledge of other religions. This will enable you to make comparisons. For the religion that you choose to focus on you will be required to show knowledge and understanding of its central tenets and how these are translated into day-to-day living.

You will also need to consider the various substitutes there are for religion, the principles on which they are formed and their practical implications for everyday life. These are:

■ humanism
■ nationalism
■ materialism
■ hedonism.

Rite of passage: Jewish faith

Central tenets of any one religion and how they are translated into day-to-day living

The six major world religions are:
- Buddhism
- Christianity
- Hinduism
- Islam
- Judaism
- Sikhism.

There are other religions, but these six are generally accepted as the major world religions. We will take each one in turn, remembering that this information is intended only as a starting point, and you will need to do further research to fill in the gaps. It may also be worth making links between these religions, looking at the principles of faith and moral codes that they have in common. How many of the principles of faith, or 'commandments' are general enough to be believed by members of other religions? How much is placed on an individual's interpretation when they are translated into day-to-day living? You should explore these questions.

Different religions have different priorities or concerns. But there is something in the code of each that can be interpreted to give guidance on how members should live. The major issues that are influenced by religion are listed below, but you could consider this further and perhaps add your own.
- Family life, marriage and divorce
- Sexuality and sexual ethics
- Prejudice, discrimination and equality
- The world of work
- Crime and punishment
- Human rights
- Suffering
- The sanctity of life.

What follows is a brief summary of the central tenets of each religion.

Buddhism

The basis of the teachings of the Buddha are to be found in his first teachings. These are 'The Four Noble Truths' and 'The Eightfold Path'. Buddhists believe that full understanding of these truths will lead to peace, happiness and enlightenment. 'He who by his good deeds, transforms his evil acts is like the moon freed from the clouds' (Dhammapada).

A statue of Buddha

The Four Noble Truths
- Life is suffering.
- The cause of suffering is desire or craving.
- Suffering will cease when desire is abandoned.
- The path to cessation of desire is to be practised.

The Eightfold Path

Right views	knowing the difference between what is good and what is bad
Right thoughts	thinking that is free from selfish desires, thinking that leads to actions that are not done for selfish aims
Right speech	speaking without causing harm or offence to others
Right action	acting in a socially considerate way to others
Right livelihood	not earning a living in a way that causes others to suffer
Right effort	making your priority your spiritual path
Right mindfulness	being aware of your thoughts so that you live in harmony
Right concentration	practising meditation

Christianity

Fra Angelico's painting of the Sermon on the Mount

Christianity takes its central tenets from two main sources: the Ten Commandments and the Nicene Creed. Read the Ten Commandments in the Bible and compare them with those of Judaism. The Nicene or Apostle's Creed sets out the beliefs of Christians as:

> I believe in God, the father Almighty, creator of Heaven and Earth.
> I believe in Jesus Christ his only Son, our Lord.
> He was conceived by the power of the Holy Spirit and born of the Virgin Mary.
> He suffered under Pontius Pilate, was crucified, died, and was buried.
> He descended to the dead.
> On the third day he rose again.
> He ascended into heaven, and is seated at the right hand of the Father.
> He will come again to judge the living and the dead.
> I believe in the Holy Spirit,
> the holy Catholic Church, the communion of saints, the forgiveness of sins,
> the resurrection of the body and the life everlasting.

Within Christianity there are many different denominations or branches. They each stress different things about Christian beliefs and therefore have different attitudes to certain issues. An example of this is contraception, where the Roman Catholic Church teaches that it is wrong to use artificial contraception whilst other denominations accept it.

Hinduism

Hinduism is a way of life, governing social, moral and political behaviour. This faith began over 3500 years ago. Hindus worship one God, but this one God has many different names and manifestations. Hindus believe in reincarnation.

Hindu moral law, moral duty or responsibility varies from person to person according to their situation (gender, age, social position, education and profession). The general code of behaviour stresses truth, non-violence, honesty and respect for all living things.

A Hindu's life is divided into four stages:
- the student, or pupil, stage
- the married or householder stage
- the retirement stage
- the stage of release.

It is every Hindu's duty or sacred law to do what is correct, what is required according to stage of life, caste, education and so on. This moral duty extends to self, family and the world.

To study Hinduism further, you will need to research these three important terms:

Dharma   Satya   Ahimsa

Islam

Muslims believe in one God. It is traditional to call God 'He' and Muslims use the name Allah rather than God. Muslims believe that Allah cannot be compared to the human race.

Muslims follow the teachings of the Qur'an – revelations given to the prophet Muhammad. Muslims aim to live out the will of Allah as described in the Qur'an.

You will need to research the following terms for yourself:

Taqiva   Shariah   Jihad

However, what follows is a brief insight into Muslim beliefs on some issues.

- All human beings are the creation of Allah and are loved by him. Human life is sacred. Men and woman are equal.
- Muslims are to be charitable at all times.
- Muslims believe that Allah handed over the planet into the protection of human beings. They are responsible for caring for and not abusing its resources.
- Muslims strive to live a life of devotion, self-sacrifice, love and compassion.

The law of Islam influences many areas of everyday life. To take your studies further you could investigate the teachings in these areas:

- marriage, divorce and the family
- the sanctity of life
- women's rights
- relationships
- alcohol, drugs and tobacco
- justice, crime and punishment.

(This activity could also be applied to the other five religions.)

Judaism

Jews believe that moral guidelines come from God and that they are set down in their holy book – the Torah. These guidelines are expressed as commandments. However, Judaism teaches that morality isn't just a matter of sticking to the rules. Morality has to come from within; living by the commandments is a way of developing morality.

The Torah tells of the Ten Commandments given to Moses on Mount Sinai, but then details more than 600 other mitzvot (commandments) that Moses was instructed to pass on to the people.

The Thirteen Principles

Judaism is based on thirteen principles of faith. They were defined in the twelfth century.

Research the Thirteen Principles, which begin:

1 God, does, and will create everything.
2 God …

The full list can be found in texts from the RE department of your school or college.

Sikhism

Sikh Guru: Teacher

This is the youngest of the six major world religions, beginning almost 500 years ago in India. Sikhs base their religion on the teachings revealed by God to ten Gurus or teachers.

The key teachings of Sikhism are:
- God is one
- God is the only eternal reality
- God is present in creation and in each human being and therefore all human beings must be respected equally.

There are no priests in the Sikh religion because if there were it would deny the teaching that all people are equal. In the gurdwara, the Sikh place of worship, everyone sits at the same level on the floor.

One of the fundamental practices of Sikhism is that of meditation. Daily meditation and sharing this with others develops a relationship with God. There is an emphasis on caring and that those in need must be protected. However, religion must not simply be a way of saving one's soul.

To study Sikhism further you need to find out what the following mean:

Guru   Haumai   Sikh   Seva

You could also research Sikh attitudes towards:
- the family
- relationships
- peace and war.

(This activity could also be applied to the other five religions.)

Knowledge, truth or belief?

When considering religious belief and faith it isn't easy to distinguish between knowledge, truth and belief. If you analyse the ways in which religious beliefs originate then you may well have to accept one of the following:
- that religious belief is indeed an acceptance of propositions on the grounds of authority or evidence – for example, the authority of the Pope or the documentary evidence of miracles
- that religious belief is simply a form of opinion and that it rests on grounds insufficient for a complete demonstration
- that religion is an intellectual perception of fact or truth and therefore it can be described as knowledge rather than belief.

TASKS

1 Take just one aspect of everyday life – for example, equality – and trace each religion's attitude to, or rulings on, the issue. You may be surprised at the outcome. It is also interesting to look at the overlap between religions in terms of rules, commandments and beliefs. Again there are many aspects that religions share.

2 What response would you make to a person who suggests that it is impossible to prove the existence of a Supreme Being?

Substitutes for religion

Those who follow a belief that is agnostic or atheist do not accept belief in a god as a source of authority. They believe in the importance or significance of something else. You need to ask yourself whether following an 'authority' that is not a god or a Supreme Being is more or less likely to make the follower moral. If there isn't a god, why be good?

Humanism

What follows is a summary of the philosophy of humanism. To take your thoughts further you should read the works of:
- John Stuart Mill (1806–73)
- Bertrand Russell (1872–1970)
- Julian Huxley (1887–1975).

Humanists believe that this is the only life we have and therefore it should be lived well. Good actions, those that are right and moral, are those which promote happiness. Wrong actions are those which produce the reverse. Humanists regard human reason as the guiding force on life; they do not believe in a spiritual world. Knowledge comes through the senses: we can only believe what we can see, touch, hear, taste or feel. In that way humanists are materialists for they believe in 'matter'.

Humanist morality is a code of human conduct followed for the benefit of human beings. The aim is the greatest happiness for the greatest number.

Materialism

A materialist is a person who believes that whatever exists is either matter itself or is dependent on matter for its existence. Materialism and humanism are linked. Both believe that people should have faith in themselves rather than a belief in a god, and complete involvement in this life instead of concern for the next.

To take your understanding of this further you could read works by Karl Marx (1818–83) and Feuerbach (1804–72), where links are made with materialism, humanism and the question of the existence of a Supreme Being.

Hedonism

What picture comes into your mind when you think of a hedonist? The word has come to be associated with pleasure seekers, only interested in gratifying their own selfish needs without thought or concern for others. This popular use of the word is somewhat misleading.

Hedonism is a branch of philosophical thought concerned with the question of right or wrong, and has strong links with both materialism and humanism. The word comes from the Greek *hedone*, meaning pleasure or happiness and hence the link with the notion of a selfish pleasure seeker.

Hedonists, however, find themselves in one of two groups:
1 those who emphasize their own happiness (egoists)
2 those who emphasize the happiness of others (altruists).

Nationalism: nation – right or wrong

The concept of nationalism is complex. Is it really an alternative or substitute for religion? Judaism and Islam are very much linked to nation and national identity. In the UK the Church and State are linked.

The New Age

This is seen as the birth of a new consciousness. The beliefs of New-Age people are very diverse but include some key concepts:
- the individual contains God and the universe within
- existence has a spiritual element
- the fundamental essence of the universe is unity.

TASKS

1 Humanists believe in the 'greatest happiness for the greatest number'. On what occasions would this be an acceptable position? Are there examples recent from history that would qualify?

2 Which of the Ten Commandments of Judaism or Christianity would the altruist accept?

3 Consider the Eightfold Path of Buddhism. Where would there be agreement with a humanist?

4 What does history teach us about the consequences of nationalism? Consider the rise of extreme nationalist organizations. Suggest reasons for their emergence and the long-term consequences they might have.

5 What links can you see between New-Age beliefs and the more traditional religions and philosophies already considered?

5 Creativity and innovation

Definitions

Art   A work of creative imagination. Application of skill to the production of beauty.

Artist   One who has the qualities of imagination and taste required in art.

Create   To bring into being, to make out of nothing.

Innovation   To renew. To introduce as something new. To make changes.

Technique   Method of performance. The mechanical part of artistic performance.

Getting started

1 Oscar Wilde said, 'All art is quite useless.' Is it?
2 'A labourer works with his hands, a craftsman works with his hands and mind, an artist works with his hands, mind and heart.' What is your response to this?
3 'Art doesn't create; it copies or imitates.'
4 Should art reflect society?
5 Why should a painting cost more than transplant surgery?
6 'Keep music live!' Why?
7 Is it possible to describe a building as 'ugly'?
8 Are artists motivated by financial reward?
9 Do prizes and awards such as Oscars reward 'art'?
10 Architects should be more aware of practical considerations when they design buildings.
11 Most great art is based on a religious theme.

Outline

You should be able to show knowledge of two of the following eight art forms.

Visual arts: painting, photography, sculpture

Visual art goes back to the cave dwelling people and their scratchings on walls. These may have been to decorate or to inform. Even today, bodies are painted to threaten or attract. Visual art may still include a purpose that is both functional and decorative.

Performance arts: the stage, the screen, music

These art forms also have their roots in ancient rituals and ceremonies from all cultures. Music in body percussion, dance in stamping rhythms and drama in storytelling and news broadcasting.

Architecture

Dwellings were a symbol of the dweller's importance or wealth. Corporate buildings reflect the image of the organization. The size of a building often represents its value to society.

Fashion

What we wear is often seen as an insight into our own self-image. Fashion can also represent or reflect the values of the age.

Representative of what?

Fashion

Messages conveyed by clothing

When you meet someone do you ever make judgements about him or her because of what they are wearing?

It has been argued that clothing can reveal a lot about the wearer in terms of:

- age
- social class
- occupation/education/income
- personality
- opinions
- taste
- political leanings
- current mood!

All this information may be registered unconsciously and judgements are often made. Is this why certain organizations insist that employers follow a dress code – ties and jackets for men and tailored skirts and blouses for women? Corporate dress codes do not normally include denim jeans, polo shirts, trainers, leggings or T-shirts. And what about the golf club that insists members do not wear tracksuits or sportswear in the lounge bar?

Fashion is here today and gone tomorrow

Consider Laver's Law from his book *In Taste and Fashion* (1945, Harrap). He proposed a timetable to explain attitudes towards fashion.

When someone wears a fashion that is:	People say it is:
10 years before its time	Indecent
5 years before its time	Shameless
1 year before its time	Daring
current	Smart
1 year after its time	Dowdy
10 years after its time	Hideous
20 years after its time	Ridiculous
30 years after its time	Amusing
50 years after its time	Quaint
70 years after its time	Charming
100 years after its time	Romantic
150 years after its time	Beautiful

(Alison Lurie, *The Language of Clothes*, Bloombury, 2000)

The fashion industry

The fashion industry is a multi-billion pound (or dollar) industry, and no self-respecting fashion victim would be seen without the 'designer label' items in their wardrobe.

Fashion ranges from exclusive garments produced by couturier houses to mass-produced, low-quality, disposable clothing. The amazing garments of the fashion house catwalks become the concepts for millions of items of clothing the following season. No one is quite sure how we come to like and desire the next fashion but the clothes are ready for us when our taste changes.

TASKS

1 What judgements do you instinctively make about the people in these illustrations? Use the list at the top of this page. Consider each aspect on the list and apply it to the illustrations. How easy is it? Check your response against that of someone else. Do you both agree?

2 Apply Laver's Law to the following:
 i) kaftans of the 1960s
 ii) flairs of the 1970s
 iii) punk fashion of the 1980s
 iv) the gothic look of the 1990s
 v) one of today's fashions.
 vi) a daring fashion from last year.

3 a Find the names and fashions associated with particular designers and fashion houses over the past four or five decades. How many designers from the 1960s are still designing and selling in the new millennium?

 b Look at the designs paraded on the catwalk of any Paris/London/Rome fashion show. How many make it to the High Street shops? What influence do they have on ready-to-wear clothing?.

Painting, photography and sculpture

These are often known as the visual arts as they produce works of creative imagination that appeal to the eye. It is, of course, possible to suggest that sculpture appeals to the sense of touch as well. Each is considered separately although it isn't possible to divorce entirely one from another.

Painting

In order to write with authority on this particular art form, you will need to have some knowledge about various periods and movements. You will have to refer to particular works and artists. The focus of your comments will, of course, depend on the question. Consider the following:

'Justify the criteria you would use to judge great works of art. You should illustrate your answer by reference to at least one of the following: painting …'

You cannot possibly answer this or similar questions competently without reference to specific examples.

What follows is an introductory list of the main periods and movements in painting. It is not exhaustive, there are other schools of art or art movements.

Renaissance	1400 – late 1500s
Baroque	1600
Realism	1700
Romanticism	late 1700s – mid 1800s
Impressionism	1870 onwards
Abstract	1900 onwards
Surrealism	1920 onwards
Pop Art/Modernism	1920

When looking at paintings, think about the following.

- Could you give informed comment on the inspiration for the painting?
- Is it making any social statement?
- Could you justify its inclusion in a gallery claiming to contain great works of art?

Photography

Photography can be seen as the science and art of using a camera. It has been described as both creative and functional as it requires a combination of technology and artistic flair. The person using the camera is responsible for the balance between the two.

When the French painter Delaroche saw his first photograph in 1839, he predicted 'from today painting is dead'. We all know this wasn't the case! Photography became a respected art form in its own right; perhaps a more immediate art form than painting.

It is accepted additionally that photography has a functional role. You should be able to add to the list of uses for photography. These include:

- photojournalism and 'freezing' history
- eyewitness records
- state occasions
- family weddings and similar occasions
- personal and domestic records, for example, holiday 'snaps'
- the school photograph
- forensic photography
- and what about the Pirelli Calendar?

But the photographer is also an artist. The photographer is as creative as the painter. Photographers need to see in a perceptive way in order to create pictures. They too are concerned with changing light and shade, surface textures, colours and shapes and how these can be used to create particular effects. They are concerned with subject, composition and perspective. Just as with painting, photography has gone through an evolution of style. What follows is a list of the major movements in photography. Notice how there is a similarity with the movements associated with painting.

Pictorialism
 – the impressionist approach
 – the naturalistic approach

Straight photography
 – the new realism
 – the documentary approach

Dynamism

Structuralism, Abstract, Surrealism

High art photography
Research your own examples

Sculpture

The word sculpture comes from the Latin *sculpere* meaning to cut or carve out. A traditional definition of sculpture is the representation of a form or idea by cutting, carving or shaping, in some way, solid matter. Today, sculpture includes installations, plays and assembly of artefacts, sound and movement.

   Until the turn of the twentieth century, most sculpture was more or less life-like. However, just as many types of art experimented with the possibilities of abstract or symbolic form sculpture was no exception. There are examples of such sculpture in the street furniture of our shopping malls.

   Sculpture draws its inspiration from many things including great people, great events, mythology and legend, classic forms, religion, celebrations and commemorations.

Greek classic form

TASKS

1 Give an example of a painter and work for each of the major periods in painting.

2 Match the following works with their major period in painting:

'Virgin of the rocks'	by Leonardo da Vinci
'Summer's day'	by Willem De Kooning
'Persistence of memory'	by Salvador Dali
'Self portrait'	by Rembrandt
'Whistlejacket'	by George Stubbs
'Red disaster'	by Andy Warhol
'Odalisque'	by Ingres

3 Write an account of the work of a major photographer. Include photocopies of some major pieces of their work.

4 Is anything that is three-dimensional a sculpture? Can the pile of bricks or car tyres exhibited in exhibitions be sculpture? What about the sheep in formaldehyde or the unmade bed?

5 Research examples of works of sculpture. Discover the name of their maker, their purpose, location and other works. Where does 'The Angel of the North' (see page 145) fit in the different types of sculpture?

6 With a small number of other students, begin discussions about the inclusion of particular works of visual art for exhibition in a gallery. The gallery could be given a particular theme – for example, colour, myths and legends, faces and so on. Decide on ten pieces to include and justify your choices in a presentation.

Architecture

Is architecture a science or an art? When primitive cave dwellers built a crude hut as a shelter from the elements, using mud and with tree branches for support, they became both scientist (realizing the technology needed) and artist (as architect designing the building). Clearly, creativity and design are used as well as principles of mathematics and civil engineering. Architects have to consider the materials at their disposal, the space available, the function of the building and the budget set. At the same time architects work in a cultural context, they may be part of a current fashion trend and they recognize contemporary popularity for certain tastes.

Styles in architecture

Examples of ancient architecture are still with us today. The pyramids, temples and sphinxes of Ancient Egypt; the curricula, temples and amphitheatres of Ancient Greece; the aqueducts, baths, temples and arena of Ancient Rome are fine examples of ancient architecture. These are all reminders of a long cultural interest with buildings.

Modern architecture — the Lloyd's building in London

A number of architectural periods can be identified, including:

Romanesque	Dignified churches, palaces, massive castles. Round arches, thick stone walls, small windows. Examples include the Tower of London, Caernarfon Castle.
Gothic	Lofty windows, stained glass, buttresses, pointed arches. Examples include Notre Dame, Paris and Lincoln Cathedral.
Renaissance	Sumptuous palaces, chateaux, churches. For example, St Paul's Cathedral in London.
Palladian	Fine English Georgian houses, symmetry, porticoes. For example, Harewood House
Modern architecture	Steel, concrete and glass with a functional design and an atrium. Buildings designed individually for their purpose such as the ground-saving skyscraper. For example, Canary Wharf.

This is a brief outline of specific movements. Old movements still inspire today. Modern buildings are often required to fit in with surroundings and this gives today's architect the challenge of ensuring this happens. They need to be concerned with the relationship of one building to another. This is where the architect and the town planner overlap.

Taste

As with all forms of art, architecture is often a matter of taste. Read the following passage. It is adapted from a much longer article by Jonathan Glancey, first published in *The Independent* in 1989. The Prince of Wales has long been 'a potent critic of modern architecture'. Here Max Hutchinson, the President of the Royal Institute of British Architects at the time the article was written, counters some of the Prince's complaints about his profession.

There are many ironies in the battle between the Prince of Wales, champion of traditional architecture, and Maxwell Hutchinson, the new President of the Royal Institute of British Architects, who are squaring up for a fresh skirmish this autumn with the publication of two books – Prince Charles's *A Vision of Britain*, published by Doubleday, and Hutchinson's *An Architect Replies*, published by Faber and Faber.

Prince Charles is a pessimist; he has little respect for modern architecture and even less for what passes for 'progress'. In this respect he is well in tune with the majority of the British people. Hutchinson, on the other hand, is an optimist, a believer in progress, computer-generated architecture, new technologies, new building materials, and new ways of living and working. He is on the same side as the architect most disapproved of by Prince Charles – the urbane Richard Rogers, designer of the Lloyd's headquarters in the City of London (a masterpiece according to Max, an oil refinery in all but purpose to the Prince of Wales).

Much has happened since the Prince of Wales raised his banner at Hampton Court at the 150th anniversary celebration of the RIBA in 1984. Rather than make sweeping statements, Prince Charles attacked specific schemes. The new extension to the National Gallery in Trafalgar Square – designed by architects Ahrends Burton and Koralek – was likened by the Prince to 'a monstrous carbuncle on the face of a much loved and elegant friend'.

There was a rush to support the Prince. Developers, architects and town planners backed his bravery. Terry Farrell, architect of Post-Modern developments in central London and chairman of the Urban Design Group, announced in 1986 that 'there is a very strong consensus behind the ideas of the Prince of Wales'. Francis Tibbalds, then President of the Royal Town Planning Institute, offered the Prince 'unreserved backing'. Alice Coleman, the Department of the Environment's adviser on the use of design in housing estates to prevent crime, claimed the Prince 'was better placed than most to see a wide cross-section of problems in Britain'.

Popular support for the Prince of Wales stems largely from a deep mistrust of architects.

Working-class housing designed by patronizing middle-class architects in the Sixties and city centres destroyed, as the Prince has pointed out, by greed, short-sightedness, architectural dogma and bad design, have both helped to discredit the architectural profession.

But, as Hutchinson stresses, the majority of today's architects have had nothing to do with these sins. Young architects have been designing for the retail revolution. Since the collapse of the public sector in the Seventies, the best of them have been busy on shops, flat conversions, restaurants and bars. Their work ranges over any number of styles, yet receives far less publicity than the new buildings of 20 and 30 years ago. These young architects – and few of them are Classicists in the traditional sense – do not support the Prince. They admire such ultra-modern buildings as the Hong Kong Shanghai Bank designed by Norman Foster. The Prince should also like this building. After all, what recent construction could be more old-fashioned in spirit than Foster's masterpiece? Like a medieval cathedral or a Victorian railway station, Foster's building pretends to be no more than what it is, a dramatic conception stretching new materials and engineering to their limits. It employed the best modern craftsmen, who are inheritors of a long tradition linking architecture and engineering.

Max Hutchinson says that 'the intervention of the Prince of Wales has made honourable that which would have been considered cowardly half a century ago: the renunciation of the new in favour of the old'.

Many architects say that if only the Prince would look a little more closely at new architectural talent and would think a little more closely about a building's structural integrity rather than its appearance, then he might win over the profession he maligns.

The Independent Magazine, 2 September 1989

TASKS

1 Select a site in an urban settlement you know well. Identify the styles that have been the stimulus of the buildings around you.

2 Consider the article by Jonathan Glancey, where many issues are raised. How does Maxwell Hutchinson counter the Prince's views? Do you think Prince Charles reflects popular views?

3 There are other issues implied by the article. Architects have to consider issues other than the aesthetic appeal, such as:
- energy efficiency
- accessibility (particularly for the disabled)
- health and user safety
- convenience
- security.

Make an assessment of a modern building using these criteria.

The stage, the screen and all kinds of music

Stage

What is meant by 'stage'? What activities are being referred to? Performances on a stage include:

- plays
- musicals
- musical hall
- variety
- opera
- ballet
- pantomime.

All of these are usually performed on a 'stage', but the key point is that we are not talking about that physical area where performances take place. The concept of stage is wider and includes drama, action, performance, atmosphere, entertainment and make-believe. A play can be performed in a church, on a hillside, in the market place, the school drama studio, or a village hall.

'All the world's a stage …' (Shakespeare).

Background

Staged performances began at various times in different parts of the world, but in some parts never really developed, whereas in others they became very much part of the culture. In some public performances women were not allowed to be a part of the team of players. In its early days, the performers would act, sing and dance because everything went together. Much later in Western culture performances were separated into singing drama (opera) and dancing drama (ballet or dance). Today the musical is very popular and has come full circle with Bernstein, Rice and Lloyd Webber, Rogers and Hammerstein.

Where did performance all begin?

It may have been part of the ritual and superstition of the early hunter-gatherers. Did the hunter act out the killing of the bull in order to help his hunting to succeed? Did he dress in bull's hide with horns and mask? Later festivals grew up around the seasons. When the harvest was gathered there was rejoicing. Thanks was given for a good harvest and ceremonies were devised to ensure the success of the next crop. These were all very early 'performances' and they involved the community.

Screen

In December 1895, the very first commercial film show was opened in Paris by the Lumière brothers, and in 1896 they put a show on in Regent Street, London. This was the first public showing of moving pictures in Great Britain. Flickering images across a screen – the 'movies' had arrived. A sound track was added in 1927. Since then, technical developments within the industry have been rapid. Compare the special effects of the early James Bond films with those of later films. How impressed were you by the last animation or science fiction film you saw? The screen is, in many ways, more versatile than the stage but is it more exciting? As the notion of 'screen' is particularly complex it's probably easier to look at all its facets using our old friend the spider diagram.

Each leg of this 14-legged spider represents an impact of the screen and movies.

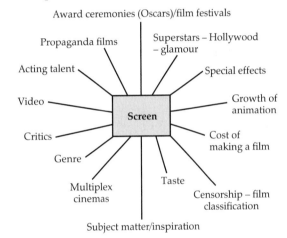

Figure 21   Aspects of the cinema and film-making

Screens come in a range of sizes from huge ones at sporting events to the miniature hand-held television. The multi-screen cinema has arrived to revive movies as a way of spending an evening.

There are many types of film, including musicals, historical drama, documentary, comedy, sci-fi, romance, cartoons and biopics. We all have our favourite film and recognize the power of the screen to draw us into the action. Films draw upon our emotions, they make us laugh, cry, sing and fall in love. In the hands of the great film directors, films become classics that are watched by many generations.

All kinds of music

Music   Art of expression in sound.
Musical Pleasing to the ear, melodious.

Music is usually associated with an instrument – whether it is a stick hitting a surface or a beautiful voice, the latest synthesizers or a penny whistle. A General Studies examination question is unlikely to ask you for in depth knowledge of the history of the orchestra or the development of music to the present day. But it is likely to want your ideas or opinions on the nature or value of music, its place within the performing arts, and how its functions have developed or changed. You may be required to place certain types of music into historical or cultural contexts, make links with fashion trends or explain the popularity or enduring nature of some music.

Music forms part of our earliest memories. The sound of 'Happy Birthday to You', mobile chimes or nursery rhymes evoke childhood. It is also part of our daily adult lives and forms a background to much human activity. The music industry is a multi-million pound industry supporting not only composers and musicians but also technicians, entrepreneurs, marketing experts and the media.

Functions of music

Why do musicians make music? Here are some reasons.

To express a cause
> protest songs – Joan Baez, Ralph McTell

To keep traditions alive
> for example, the didgereedoo of the Australian aborigine

To enhance ceremonies
> coronations
> festivals
> weddings

For religious purposes
> hymns
> plainsong
> chants

In war
> to frighten the enemy – bagpipes, drums
> to raise morale – Vera Lynn, Glen Miller

To create an atmosphere
> for example, music before football matches

Story-telling
> folk music
> ballads

TASKS

1 The following are different types of performance.
- Mumming plays
- Ancient Greek tragedies
- Roman and medieval drama
- Mystery plays
- Morality plays
- The Elizabethan Theatre of Shakespeare
- Restoration drama
- Realism
- Symbolism.

a Name an example of each of these. Try to refer to particular authors.

b What effect did each type have on the development of the stage?

c What is the function of each?

d Did they reflect an aspect of the society or era in which they flourished?

e Were they simply to entertain an audience?

2 Many cinemas closed in the 1960s and 1970s. Can you explain why the cinema appears to have made a comeback in recent time?

3 Films involving animation have been box-office hits. Why do you think they have become so popular?

4 Select one of the following and prepare a written answer. Allow only 30 minutes for your writing.

- The Royal Opera House should never have attracted lottery money.
- Why are different cultures identified by particular rhythms, melodies or sounds – e.g. reggae?
- Music was one of the three disciplines that the Ancient Greeks studied; the other two were sport and mathematics. Should the study of music be on the National Curriculum?
- Why are musicians so popular?
- Is music 'the food of love'?
- Why are open-air concerts usually sell-outs?

5 Select one of the issues raised in the stage, screen or music sections. Invite three or four people to join you to discuss the topic.

6 Two colleagues were naming the person who had made the greatest contribution to popular music in the last 50 years. One of them said he was clear Jimi Hendrix was the one. The other colleague disagreed and wanted to nominate John Lennon.

How would you distinguish between opinions that are paraded as fact, and opinion? How do we demonstrate the 'rightness' of an opinion?

Try presenting a reasoned argument to support your opinion.

⑥ Aesthetic evaluation

Definitions

Aesthetic   Relating to possessing – or pretending to – a sense of beauty.

Aesthetics   The principles of taste and arts. Philosophy of the arts.

Evaluate   To determine the value of. To decide worth.

Philistine   A person of material outlook: indifferent to culture.

Taste   Intuitive feeling for what is aesthetically right.

Getting started

1 Should art reflect reality?
2 Can you justify art for art's sake?
3 Is art, in all its forms, accessible only to the wealthy?
4 Is beauty in the eye of the beholder?
5 Is there an element of 'The emperor's new clothes' in our attitude to some art forms – for example, opera?
6 'There's no such thing as good taste – only taste.'
7 Is it possible to compare:
   ▪ Wren with Spence
   ▪ Constable with Lowry
   ▪ Da Vinci with Picasso
   ▪ Quant with Versace
   ▪ Rodin with Moore
   ▪ Tchaikovsky with Lloyd Webber or Bernstein
   ▪ Pollock with Warhol?
8 Why does some art endure?
9 If you could own one piece of visual art, what would it be?

Cheap seats: £30?

Outline

You should be able to consider the art forms previously outlined (on page 145) in terms of:
▪ their appeal to individuals and their wider appeal
▪ the effect of such art on the individual and society
▪ the value of art
▪ the way art reflects reality: the use of subject matter
▪ whether or not art has or should have practical applications
▪ your personal views.

Some knowledge of the terms describing different aspects of the above art forms, and specific artists within disciplines, is desirable. An understanding of techniques is also expected.

'Mona Lisa' by Da Vinci

Aesthetic evaluation

The course requires you to show an informed personal response to:

- architecture
- fashion
- painting, photography, sculpture
- the stage, screen and all kinds of music.

These have to be considered bearing in mind the following aspects:

- the quality and extent of its appeal to the individual and in a wider sphere
- its effect on the individual and on society
- whether it is sufficient in itself or has a message or practical application
- its relationship with, and treatment of, reality – its subject matter.

However, in considering aesthetic appreciation it is difficult to separate the concept into compartments. They overlap, interconnect and interrelate. You can't consider one aspect without referring to or commenting on aspects of the others. In the following four pages you must be looking to make some of the links yourself.

The quality and extent of the appeal to the individual

The American composer Aaron Copland suggested that when you first come into contact with a piece of 'art' you have a sensuous response, that is, you decide quite subjectively whether you like it or not. For example, what is your response to each of the pieces of art shown on these pages? Your response might cover three stages:

Stage 1 Do you like it? Does it appeal to your visual senses?

Stage 2 A more expressive response would be, 'I like it because …' or, 'I don't like it because …'. Continue the sentence in terms of the examples.

Stage 3 Now you can be more analytical. You can analyse the techniques used by the artist, compare the work with similar works or contrast it with those that are completely different.

Our personal response to the visual and performing arts is often referred to as taste. When considering the quality or appeal of art, however, it is possible to apply criteria and assess art within the terms of these criteria. You can make this personal assessment of a work of art in a national gallery, a film nominated for an Oscar, a painting by a ten year old, or the design of a new public library.

'Water Lilies' by Claude Monet

Some criteria to apply to a work of art:

- relevance
- talent, genius, skill and technique
- subject matter
- impact and message
- context.

As well as your personal response, the world of art includes many 'Guardians of Taste'. The list that follows suggests some. You could add to the list.

- Art critics
- Theatre and film critics
- Gallery owners
- Those who commission works
- Patrons
- Arts Councils
- Funding bodies
- National opera, theatre and ballet.

All of these have an interest in taste or appreciation of the arts. There is, however, an economic perspective for each of them. Critics make their living out of passing judgements (whether sensuous, expressive or analytical). Gallery owners must attract buyers. Patrons want value for money and theatre and cinema owners need full auditoria.

Art, both visual and performing, can also be the subject of competition. Examples include the Eurovision Song Contest and the Oscar ceremonies. If the first response is sensuous, how can it be possible for a committee to agree on the best? Who judges the judges?

The effect on the individual and society

The individual

It has been said that art has a civilizing effect – 'music hath charms …'. Consider how many public places, both in and out of doors, are 'decorated' by forms of art. They include hospitals, schools, churches, corporate offices, hotels and railway stations. Next time you are in such a place be aware of the use of art. Three-dimensional structures are also to be seen in the atrium, the City Square, the shopping precinct, on the village green, by the harbour or sea front. Murals have become popular in the subway as a way of recording contemporary life or historical events.

Individuals are said to respond to their surroundings. Attractive colourful surroundings are less likely to be abused or damaged and town centres have been redesigned with this in mind. The idea behind adding background music in large shopping centres is that it adds atmosphere to a busy and stressful place. Buskers and pavement artists are encouraged to add colour and life to public places. All of these provide the individual with an aesthetic experience as they go about their daily lives.

Society

Quite small communities have their community arts programme. In the UK, local authorities give grants for such projects, from the embroidering of a village map to the funds for an artist in residence. Any new village or town community centre is usually designed to allow for the staging of performances and often contains examples of the work of local artists.

Societies use art to commemorate, celebrate and protest, and much art has a historical or social context. The following pieces of art are examples of the way art and design are used in public buildings and places.

- The village or town war memorial
- Listed buildings
- Coventry Cathedral
- The Millennium Dome
- Crystal Palace
- 'Guernica' – Picasso
- 'The Match' – Lowry
- The pyramids at Giza
- Nelson's Column
- Shaftesbury Memorial Foundation
- Religious statues and icons.

You can add further examples from the area in which you live.

Village war memorials are examples of public art

Is art sufficient in itself or does it have to have a message or practical application?

What good is a painting, film, sculpture, play, or concerto? Does it contribute to our daily lives?

What purpose does it serve? Is it intended only to produce that first sensuous response, and is that sufficient?

Most artists would argue that art serves a wider purpose. For example:

- an image, painting or sculpture, can outlast what it represents
- art can produce a relic of the past that informs the present
- beautiful buildings can also be functional
- art informs design
- art communicates
- art is a vehicle for the sharing of events
- art has commercial value
- art provides an outlet for self-expression
- art education teaches perception, analysis, self-expression and communication. It is a vehicle for learning
- artists' creations and appreciation allows us to respond to a complex world.

Consider the following, written by the conductor Sir Simon Rattle in 1998. His comments focus particularly on the performing arts but it can be argued that they are relevant for the studying, practising and appreciation of all art forms.

'Art education shifts the emphasis from observing to doing and the learning is in the doing. The arts teach not just facts but the interpretation of those facts … I am deeply disturbed by the cold-shouldering of the non-commercial arts by politicians of all stripes. Here is a source of mystery to me – why do our politicians treat the arts as if they are some kind of luxury add-on to people's lives? In all their many forms they have proved to be a factor which has enabled so many people to move off the runway and fly.'

Art's relationship with and treatment of reality – its subject matter

It could be argued that photography is the only visual art form that has a firm relationship with reality. Look at the photograph below. What is it? With the use of angle and close-up photography the photographer has been able to produce an image that is abstract. If you look closely enough you might see what it is!

Is art able to replace reality? This question is complex. Do Michelangelo's cherubs on the ceiling of the Sistine Chapel, or the painting of Psyche by Fragonard represent reality? You need to separate these two concepts before you can begin to consider the links between subject reality and realism. Is the question:

a Does the work of art reflect real life?
or
b Does it look like that which it is said to represent?

Let's take these questions one at a time.

Does the work of art reflect real life?

Here you will need to undertake further research in order to provide yourself with an answer.

What follows is simply a starting-off point. Realism as an art movement that began in the late 1840s. It was a movement designed to represent people in everyday situations rather than gods, classical heroes or religious figures. It emphasized contemporary modern life and included its more unattractive aspects. Make a list of Realist artists and their works. Compare their work with that of earlier styles, including those that dealt with classical or formal themes.

Does it look like that which it is said to represent?

Look at some of the modern, contemporary works by painters and sculptors, or even the Impressionist paintings of the late 1800s, and decide for yourself.

Consider the work by Patrick Heron. Can you see a link with the title?

'Sequoia roots' by Ansel Adams

'Portrait of T.S. Eliot' (1949) by Patrick Heron

When a piece of art does not look like that which it is supposed to represent it is said to be abstract art. In this style of art, form and colour are more important than representational qualities. The work of art is often considered to be a simplification or modification of some real object. In making a simplification the artist is trying to emphasize some aspect or distil some essence.

A consideration of most concepts related to the arts will ensure that you will have to interpret and evaluate opinions. Your friend says that the painting of Sir Thomas More by Holbein is more impressive than 'The Laughing Cavalier' by Frans Hals. You apply the criteria on page 154 and find that you disagree. Both are judgements. Is your reasoning any more sound because you have applied those criteria? Is yours a deceptive argument because you're basing your judgement on what could be considered to be unsound reasoning?

TASKS

1 Apply the criteria for assessing a work of art (as given on page 154) to a range of examples from both the performing arts and visual arts with which you are familiar.

2 Consider your own local community. Make a list of the opportunities available for people to either appreciate art or practice it.

3 Does all art have to be symbolic? Are some works of art metaphors for society?

4 Consider the following extract from a newspaper article concerning the vacant plinth in Trafalgar Square. What is the article suggesting about society's attitude to art? Is it something just to fill an empty space?

> The debate over how to fill the vacant plinth in Trafalgar Square has concentrated largely on the hole rather than what the hole sits on. On the face of it the problem looks like one of absence – the three other pedestals already hold statues, so the emptiness of the one in the north-west corner is an obvious anomaly. And it is a peculiarly vexatious hole, for at least 155 years nobody has quite been able to agree about its shape – is it shaped like a politician or a pop star or a soldier? Is it Diana-shaped or Mandela-shaped or even, as one man proposed, shaped like a giant pigeon?

> In the absence of any consensus, the Royal Society of Arts, have turned to that most dependable form of Polyfilla, contemporary sculpture.
>
> from 'Private View – Some day my plinth will come' by Thomas Sutcliffe, *The Independent*, 26 January 2000

5 Study the quote by Sir Simon Rattle and answer the following.
   a Write an argument that counters the notion that non-commercial art has value.
   b Explain the final metaphor.
   c Think 'synoptically'. Is Rattle making a link between art, economics and science?
   d Argue the case for the inclusion of performing arts or visual arts in the school curriculum.

6 Research some of the work of Jackson Pollock or Mark Rothko. Apply the criteria suggested on page 154 and be prepared to go beyond the sensuous into the expressive and analytical as you comment on their work.

7 Choose an art style or movement and produce a piece of continuous prose that describes the development of the movement, its influences and characteristics. Include in the essay any comment on the social context that is relevant. The essay must include examples and images.

Further study suggestions and example questions

Further reading

Berger, J. (1972) *Ways of Seeing*, Penguin, Harmondsworth.
Cole, W. O. (ed.) (1991) *Moral Issues in Six Religions*, Heinemann Educational, Oxford.
Gombrich, E. H. (1989) *The Story of Art*, Phaedon Press, London.
Lurie, A. (1992) *Language of Clothes*, Bloomsbury, London.
Smith, L. (1991) *A Beginner's Guide to Ideas*, Lion, Oxford.
Young, D. (1987) *Bats in the Belfry*, David and Charles, Newton Abbot.

Video

What is Art? (2000) RITE.

Preparing for exams

As suggested on pages 141–4 you will need to consider further research into one religion as detailed knowledge of one religion is required by the OCR specification. However, it is useful in an answer to be able to compare aspects of the different religions in order to make a point. It will be to your advantage to have knowledge of more than one religion.

Example questions

1 Account for the fact that some music has an enduring appeal while the appeal of other music is short-lived. [50]

To answer this effectively you will need to:
■ identify which music has lasted and refer to specific examples
■ consider why the music has lasted.
■ explore examples of short-lived music to find what they have in common?

2 'It is only possible to lead a good life by following a particular faith or religious teaching.' Consider the arguments both for and against this viewpoint. [50]

A good answer must consider a range of arguments for both sides of the viewpoint. It must also recognize that either position can be clearly held and that a humanist stance is legitimate. Start with a definition or explanation of the concept of 'a good life' and consider the behaviour and values associated with it.

3 If you could own two works from the visual arts (painting, photography, sculpture) what would you choose and why? [50]

In order to answer this question, you need to have some detailed knowledge of two works of art. You would be expected to comment on such areas as:
■ the social or historical content
■ the inspiration for the piece
■ the artist's technique

■ your personal reasons for selecting the piece
■ if there is time, mention one or two pieces that were on your shortlist.
And of course – why you like them!

NB: A word of warning. It may be legitimate to comment on the monetary value of the piece you have chosen and that owning it might considerably add to your wealth! But you must at all times be aware of the content of the specification. This unit requires an informed response in terms of aesthetic evaluation and any answer must be based on this concept.

4 'We define and describe ourselves by the clothes we choose.' Discuss the accuracy of this statement with reference to current fashion. [50]

To answer this question you will need to have knowledge of current fashion, its various styles, 'looks' and trends. You will have to decide whether or not you agree totally with the statement or whether you find that the statement has some truth but cannot always be applied.

More about synopticity

To take you further into synopticity consider the following tasks or discussion issues. Identify the domains of knowledge being linked here.

1 'Scientific research proves that there is no Supreme Being or Creator.' What scientific discoveries or technical developments might a non-believer use to support this statement?

2 The law allows peaceful demonstrations and yet at times the right to protest or march is denied or limited to minority groups. Is this acceptable in a democratic society?

3 Fundamentalism has been known to fight against technological advancement. Does this suggest that scientists have done more harm than good to humanity and human morals?

4 Ideologies and values

Definitions

Beliefs   Acceptance of a thing, or things as true. Things that individuals, or groups, think are true but which they may not be able to prove.

Ideologies   System of connected ideas, usually reflecting beliefs and values, with the capacity to influence large numbers of people. A network of beliefs and values drawn together to produce a measure of political coherence. A set of beliefs and values which may be defended passionately, even violently. Dogma that is rigidly adhered to (according to opponents).

Values   What individuals or groups think something is worth. The worth of something as determined by individuals or groups, but not necessarily expressed in monetary terms.

Getting started

1 In a liberal democracy does real freedom have to somehow balance 'freedom from …' with 'freedom to …'?
2 How do political parties change with the passage of time? Has Conservatism moved from changing slowly and conserving what was good, to support of the free market and incentives for individuals?
3 Was Old Labour a party of clear principles when New Labour is just opportunism manipulated by spin-doctors?
4 'There is no such thing as society. There are individual men and women, and there are families.'
5 'Feminists may have made some converts but they also made a lot of enemies.'
6 'Save the pound and you'll save the English way of life. That's what patriotism is about.'
7 'Fundamentally racist? I suppose most of us are, really.'
8 'They're not just football hooligans; the worst of them are caught up in ideologies they don't understand.'

Outline

This section begins with a review of some important political ideologies, how they may influence the values held by individuals and groups in the community and the ways in which different ideologies might be promoted by different groups in the community.

It moves on to consider some important current social, economic and political issues and the way in which these are influenced by different views and values.

Finally, it examines life in different communities and how it might reflect, and be influenced by, ideologies and values.

No politics, we're British

The Guardian, 15 February 2000

Important political ideologies and how they may influence values

From ideologies to real life

Usually, students are rather wary of ideologies because they are seen as abstract and difficult. They often ask for ideologies to be presented in simple terms. It's not an easy task. Books on political theory often tax the comprehension of specialists in the subject. Ideologies do influence our lives although, in the stereotypes we sometimes construct, the English tend to be seen as rather more reserved than the images we are sometimes presented with of, say, the French or Italians. Ideologies are not just abstract concepts for a few very clever people. Their meanings have a practical relevance, although they do change over time – a sort of 'ideological evolution', or even 'revolution' – so some changes are quite subtle while others are rather more fundamental.

- **Liberalism** was originally seen as progress and development through the exercise of individual talent and initiative within an open-minded and tolerant framework.
- **Conservatism** used to be leadership by an élite with regard for tradition, private property and enterprise, and recognition of the importance of the nation. 'New Conservatism' stands for the free market with a more limited role of the state, together with greater individual freedom and the defence of the nation, its symbols and constitution.
- **Socialism** sought for the abolition of the capitalist system in favour of common ownership of the means of production (land, labour and capital). In its most extreme form, as Communism, this revolutionary ideology became prevalent in most parts of Eastern Europe. In the UK, the Labour Party adopted a rather different interpretation with the regulation of the free market through state intervention and the government acting to promote greater equality and providing a range of social services. This socialist approach was particularly associated with the 'Old' Labour, reformist, view. 'New Labour' is sometimes described as 'the Third Way' that seeks to combine what is called 'market socialism' with a greater sense of citizenship, personal responsibility, community and wider participation.
- **Nationalism** may suggest a country with a distinctive culture, which operates either independently or with considerable self-autonomy, placing a strong emphasis on the country's sovereignty.
- **Fascism** is sometimes seen as an extreme form of nationalism and often associated with Germany in Hitler's days. It may be seen as the creation of a united nation, under a charismatic leader, with the aim of eliminating certain groups, beliefs and races. Critics see it as authoritarian ultra-nationalism.
- **Feminism** is an example of how an ideology need not be a party political set of beliefs. It is a good example of the claim that politics need not be about political parties. Many beliefs are not directly political but they enter a wide political arena in the search for supporters, power, influence and resources. Feminist writing can be found at the end of the eighteenth century. The suffragettes, who fought for votes for women in the early 1900s, can be seen as feminists. As a wider movement, which sought to challenge the political, social and economic inequality that favours men and disadvantages women, we look to the 1960s. The women who inspired the movement were seeking to improve their legal, social, economic and political status – but there were several strands of feminism.

Conflict within ideologies

Ideologies seem to offer a common purpose but they rarely unite their followers. The nature of beliefs and values tends to mean that, though we may seek consensus, we also have to find ways to manage conflicts within the supporters of our ideology.

TASKS

1 It is often said that politicians in the UK have abandoned ideology and that they change their policies according to the popular mood rather than ideological conviction. How far do you agree?

2 Tabulate the main differences in ideology between a republican in the USA and a communist in Russia.

3 Select a famous reforming leader such as Gandhi or Mandela, and outline the main thrust of their ideology.

Important social, economic and political issues: racism

Race is a sensitive subject. The murder of a black teenager, Stephen Lawrence, and the failure of the Metropolitan Police to find his killers has highlighted the racism that lurks within the fabric of British society. Some of the most senior police officers have talked about the 'institutionalized racism' within their forces, yet it would be unfair to single out only the police for such an accusation.

A headline from *The Sun* newspaper (19 April 2000) focuses on the issue of racism:

William Hague is dead right

The subject was 'asylum seekers' (referred to in an earlier section of this book – see page 103). The editorial went on to say that 'every time the Tories speak out, there is a rush to brand the party "racist". *The Sun* thinks that view is nonsense.' It claimed that 'tackling asylum seekers head on is NOT racist. It is REALIST'. A headline in *The Daily Mail* on 20 March 2000 proclaimed:

Still at large here, 126,000 asylum cheats

A black trade union leader wrote an article in *The Independent* on 14 April 2000. The headline to his article read:

The racism that lies at the heart of this Government

He referred to a Home Office minister, who had said that his own department was 'institutionally racist'. He went on to criticize the government's policy towards asylum seekers. For him 'the mood music is playing a hostile tune for black Britons' and 'the Home Office, and indeed the ministers … are playing their part in the orchestra'. He reminded the Home Secretary that, on the day the Macpherson Report was severely critical of the Metropolitan Police, it was he who had said that: 'In terms of race equality, let us make Britain a beacon to the world.'

This is clearly not a new problem. In the quotes below, the word 'steamers' is the only clue that these comments do not belong to the modern age:

> 'Few people realize the magnitude of England's alien problem. Eleven steamers arrive with immigrants from Eastern Europe every week in the Thames alone.'
>
> *Illustrated London News*, 30 April 1904

Seven years later, on 11 January 1911, it said:

> 'There is so much talk at the moment of the alien population of the Metropolis that many seem to forget that our laws dealing with the foreign would-be immigrant to this country are strict, even if, according to some, they are not strict enough.'

Austin, *The Guardian*, 16 February 2001

TASKS

1 Find out about the main legislation that is intended to reduce racial discrimination.

2 Give examples of racist attitudes and behaviour that you have observed.

3 Should schools do more to promote anti-racist behaviour? If so, how?

Important current social, economic and political issues: the protection of individuals and groups from abuse

People are presented with many different views and values through television, radio, the newspapers and promotional mail. By law, news reporting on television has to be 'balanced'. The BBC and Independent Television often attract the criticism of politicians because of perceived 'bias' against one party or another. The press also operates under the law that helps to protect individuals and groups. Minority groups and private individuals are vulnerable to attack and exposure through the media. The time-honoured question of whether the press determines, or reflects, public opinion remains unanswered.

Consider these figures relating to people described by a *Guardian* headline of 30 March 2000 as moving 'from refugees to political footballs'.

Cutting off our nose to spite a race

Britain faces a skills shortage. A Home Office report finds most successful asylum-seekers are highly skilled but racism stops them working.

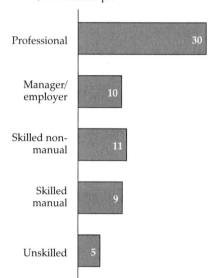

Jobs they came from
% of total sample

Professional	30
Manager/employer	10
Skilled non-manual	11
Skilled manual	9
Unskilled	5

Source: Home Office

The Guardian, 30 March 2000

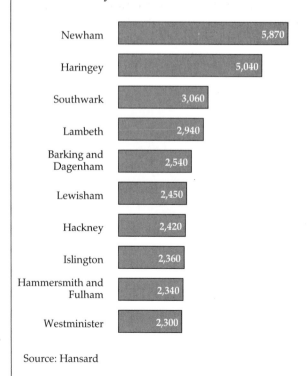

Top 10 London boroughs supporting asylum seekers

Borough	
Newham	5,870
Haringey	5,040
Southwark	3,060
Lambeth	2,940
Barking and Dagenham	2,540
Lewisham	2,450
Hackney	2,420
Islington	2,360
Hammersmith and Fulham	2,340
Westminister	2,300

Source: Hansard

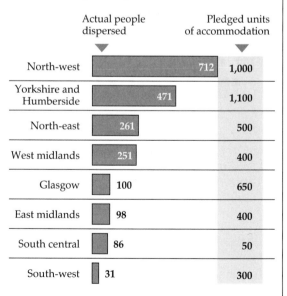

Local authorities voluntary scheme to disperse asylum seekers

	Actual people dispersed	Pledged units of accommodation
North-west	712	1,000
Yorkshire and Humberside	471	1,100
North-east	261	500
West midlands	251	400
Glasgow	100	650
East midlands	98	400
South central	86	50
South-west	31	300

The Guardian, 30 March 2000

Immigration and Asylum Act 1999

Key measures

● Most cases to be decided within six months by April 2001
● Vouchers worth £35 a week for an adult to replace welfare benefits. No change given
● Accommodation provided on no-choice basis around UK
● Fines of £2,000 per illegal passenger on lorry drivers coming to Britain
● Regulation of immigration advisers
● Increase in airline liaison officers abroad to curb numbers travelling to Britain on forged papers
● New legal framework for detention of asylum seekers
● Crackdown on marriage for immigration purposes

The Guardian, 30 March 2000

The Kosovo war contributed to the record number of asylum applications to the UK in 1999

TASKS

1 Form a discussion group to consider ways in which the media can abuse individuals and minority groups. During the group discussion try to focus particularly upon the role of the media now that information and communications technology has increased the speed of news gathering.

2 Suggest ways in which these groups could be protected, within the law, from abuse. Include in the discussion the problems raised by the increased number of asylum seekers and the apparent racial intolerance in the community.

Life in different communities: the influence of ideologies and values

Being British: nationalism and 'Britishness'

One of the most potent, some might say 'volatile', of ideologies is nationalism. England, Wales, Scotland and Northern Ireland form a nation, the United Kingdom (without Northern Ireland, they become Great Britain). The people holding passports for this area are British. They occupy, relatively speaking, a small geographical area but it would be a mistake to view the country and its people as homogeneous. For example, there are great variations in wealth. Even in England, life in our poorest areas (which may range from deprived inner cities to parts of a county such as Cornwall) is very different from life in comparatively wealthy areas like many parts of Surrey.

Nationalism can lead to dangers. Nationalism can easily shade into patriotism (a strong belief in one's country usually associated with a willingness to defend it in times of emergency). Xenophobia (a much narrower view, 'my country right or wrong', accompanied by a hostility to foreigners) may not be far away for those who believe strongly in nationalism. Wars in many parts of the world can be attributed, to a greater or lesser extent, to nationalism. Even pacifist sympathizers faced a huge moral dilemma when asked to defend the interests of their nation against the extreme nationalism, the fascism, of Hitler's Germany in 1939.

Whilst nationalism can lead to wars that change history it can also manifest itself in smaller short-term events. When Leeds United Football Club, from England, met Galatasaray Football Club, from Turkey, in the semi-finals of the UEFA Cup in 2000, two Leeds supporters were stabbed to death prior to the game in Istanbul. Feelings of nationalism and racism erupted. West Yorkshire Police mounted the biggest security operation every seen in the UK when the return game was played in Leeds. Galatasaray supporters were banned from attending the return match and Turks who had lived in Leeds for years had to seek police protection. Then, as in the past, football provided a superscreen for those who wished to foment violence and race discrimination.

Nationalism, and patriotism, can be a potent force as far as voters are concerned (see the article opposite entitled 'Bulldog spirit').

Tony Blair... claimed Labour is 'the true patriotic party'

Bulldog spirit
How Blair has attempted to redefine patriotism

● "The New Britain" was a Labour slogan in the 1960s as the party, led by Harold Wilson, focused on the need for social and economic change. As the economic climate worsened, the catchphrase "'I'm Backing Britain" was coined, to encourage shoppers to buy British goods.

● 1986 Neil Kinnock claimed patriotism as one of Labour's principal values, telling the Scottish Labour conference that his patriotism was the "confident and generous patriotism of freedom and fairness".

● 1992 The patriotic theme rebounded against Kinnock at a rally in Sheffield, when against a backdrop of union and national flags he whipped Labour supporters into a fist-clenching frenzy before leading the shadow cabinet in a chorus of Jerusalem.

● 1995 Tony Blair attacked Tories for waving the union flag at the close of their conference when they "have spent 16 years tearing apart the fabric of our nation". He called on voters to help turn Britain into a nation reborn. "One Britain. That is the patriotism for the future."

● 1997 Election campaign mastermind Peter Mandelson introduced the bulldog, in a party political broadcast, as a symbol of New Labour, saying: "Some may be surprised that we use the bulldog. But New Labour is the party of one nation and the bulldog is a way of saying this. It is an animal with a strong sense of history and tradition."

● 1997 In his party conference speech later that year Tony Blair used the word "Britain" 53 times, "country" 31 times, and "nation" 19 times.

Mandelson and bulldog in 1997

Sally James, *The Guardian*, 28 March 2000

Devolution and the emergence of the nationalist challenge

One of the pledges of the incoming Labour government in 1997 was that Wales and Scotland should have a referendum, so that 'the people' could decide on whether or not the two countries should have some form of devolved government. Both are countries with their own symbols and tradition. The Welsh have long been associated with leeks, daffodils, St David's Day, the red dragon, choirs and their own language – now taught in all primary schools. For the Scots, it is the thistle, kilts, clans, St Andrew's Day, and their own legal, educational and, to some extent, monetary system (in the form of Scottish banknotes). Both have their own national political parties (the Scottish National Party and Plaid Cymru, the nationalist party of Wales). In the referendum in Scotland there was a clear majority in favour of a Scottish Parliament with limited tax-raising powers. In Wales, the situation was less clear cut. Those who voted were divided with only just over 50% favouring a Welsh Assembly with more limited powers.

When they have power, do politicians ever give some away?

Politicians rarely like to concede power once they have it – but that is precisely what devolution involves. The Welsh Assembly has proved a constant problem for the Labour government. The Labour Party got more seats than any others in the subsequent elections but it did not get the majority anticipated. Criticisms of the methods used to elect its Welsh leader, Alun Michael, were widespread. He eventually resigned to be replaced by the original contender favoured by many Welsh voters, Rhodri Morgan. When the Assembly voted not to implement the controversial scheme for performance-related pay for teachers, which had been introduced in England, the Assembly was told it lacked the powers to take this action. Nationalism is based on factors like 'identity' and 'spirit' – the intuitive parts of politics where emotions battle with our sense of reason.

The Irish Question

Northern Ireland provides another, if more long-standing, example of the problems associated with nationalism. The 'problem' (trying to secure harmonious relations between two communities divided by religion) has gone on for centuries. The majority in Northern Ireland is Protestant whilst the minority is Roman Catholic. The political parties are different from those in Great Britain and are divided mainly on religious lines. Most MPs elected to Westminster are Unionists (Protestants who support the union with England, Wales and Scotland). A much smaller number tend to represent the Catholic community. Two, members of Sinn Fein, who represent the Catholic community and are looking for a united Ireland, were elected to the parliament at Westminster in 1997. They have not taken their seats at Westminster because of arguments over whether or not their party has direct links with the IRA.

Just across the Northern Ireland border is the predominantly Catholic and independent Irish Republic (Eire). Northern Ireland has had its own parliament (Stormont) but, in the late 1960s, violence between Catholics and Protestants erupted once again. In 1972, Stormont was placed under direct rule from Westminster. With the devolution of at least some powers to Scotland and Wales, the government in London worked hard to produce an Assembly for Northern Ireland, bringing together representatives from all groups in the community. The problem lies in different groups in Northern Ireland wishing to belong to different nations.

TASKS

1 What do you understand by the term 'being British'? Define the term as the passport authorities use it. What characteristics are usually associated with the British, by people in Great Britain and those from other countries?

2 Why are many Welsh, Scottish and Irish people passionate defenders of their country?

3 Do people in the UK really see themselves as Europeans?

4 Why is it so difficult to secure peace in Northern Ireland?

5 Explanation and evaluation of human behaviour

Definitions

Analysis A detailed study in order to increase understanding and explanation, involving taking something apart in order to find causal factors.

Community All the people who live together in a particular area or who have agreed to work or co-operate together. A group where everyone knows all the other members.

Evaluation Making a decision on the worth, value or significance of something, usually involving identification of good and bad features.

Poverty A state of being extremely poor, with only the most basic essentials for living.

Psychology The scientific study of the human and human behaviour, attempting to understand how people think, including statistical and non-numerical methods of investigation.

Rationality Thinking clearly to make judgements based on reason rather than on emotion.

Getting started

1 How reliable are the findings we get from psychologists and sociologists?
2 Is there any such thing as society and community?
3 How do people form their views on large national issues and smaller local problems?
4 Should we always take the long-term view?
5 Where do you stand on the environment and how did you get there?
6 Do you always act in a rational way?
7 How do you waste your time?
8 To which community do you belong? Who is the leader of your community and what is your relationship with the leader? Who do you wish to include and exclude from your community?

Outline

This section begins with an examination of the research methods used in the social sciences and their reliability and how different views are formed and expressed. Parallels and differences will be identified between these methods and those of other scientists.

The section then looks at the influences on human behaviour and how far people are influenced by their background, thinking, personal circumstances, environment and the views of others. From the influences on human behaviour the section moves on to consider the behaviour itself in a range of contexts, including in social, political and economic life and concludes with a consideration of how people can influence social, political and economic issues.

Closing our post offices will destroy village life

UP TO 5,000 rural post offices are facing closure if the Government goes ahead with plans to pay benefits direclty into bank accounts.

Last week a petition signed by three million people was handed in to Number 10 protesting at the plans.

The Sun, 19 April 2000

Research methods in the social sciences and their reliability

Pioneers of research methods in the social sciences

Michael Young and Peter Willmott did much pioneering work in the social sciences during the 1950s and 1960s. In a touching obituary following Willmott's death, Michael Young provided an unusually clear insight into the research methods of social scientists. Young wrote:

Peter could talk to anyone and get him or her to talk to him. This belonged to the anthropological side of the institute in its community studies (the other side was statistical). We considered the qualitative method essential; indeed, it was one way to touch on the individual experience.

But surveys of random samples were (and are) needed too. The individual's experience has to be put into a context to show how far anyone's experience is, in some way, typical or not. Without random samples one cannot normally generalize about anything; but without picking out the individuals, the results of the random sampling can be lifeless. The third feature of our method was that it had to be readable. Since Peter, all members of 'Bethnal Green School' have to tried to avoid the jargon which is the curse of sociology.

The Guardian, 9 April 2000

Objectivity

Social scientists try to be objective. They try to suspend their own view of the world and see it as others see it. Good social scientists are people with thinking and analytical skills. Social scientists need to acquire knowledge of a subject and they must seek to distinguish between belief (something that people think is true) and truth (philosophers usually argue that something is true if it corresponds to the way the world is). Social scientists must certainly be able, in their analysis, to recognize a fallacy (a bad argument that can easily be mistaken for a good argument). They will copy the great detectives of fact and fiction in the use of deduction (if the premises on which an argument is based are true, and the argument is a good one, the conclusion must be true). They will also use induction (a type of argument in which even if the premises are true and the argument is good, the conclusion is still only more or less probable).

Can it be measured?

Willmott was able to blend the qualitative (listening to people talk, reading their accounts of events, watching them at work and play, encouraging their reminiscences) with the quantitative (the 'number crunching' side) to form a view of the social groups he was studying. The work was influential because many people read the books and reports, and identified with the conditions being described.

Social science research is going on around us all the time. A few examples include:

- psephologists who measure and attempt to explain voting trends
- psychologists who advise the larger shopping chains on colour to encourage people into shops
- sociologists who study life in the inner city in order to make recommendations to government
- educationalists who have designed 'performance indicators' and 'benchmarks' to allow schools to measure how well they are doing
- criminologists such as David Anderson, a leading American economist who devised a complex algebraic formulae in an attempt to assess the annual cost of crime in Britain. His four-year study concluded that the cost was £60 billion.

Are the findings of social scientists reliable?

Usually, the research methods of social scientists are reliable. The problem is usually in the interpretation of their findings. Sometimes, because of the mass of figures used, or the specialist language involved, the social scientist may not be very clear. The media can distort their findings in an effort to attract more customers through the use of sensational headlines.

TASKS

1 If a General Election took place tomorrow, how would you vote? Aim to measure the voting intentions of, say, as post-16 group. Discuss/list the reasons why your measurements might not be reliable if used to predict wider voting trends among young people.

2 Using information published annually in education performance tables (the 'league tables' which cover issues such as the proportion of students getting five or more Grade C and above GCSEs, and the average student points score at A level), aim to measure the performance of your school/college over a five-year period. On the basis of your findings, what judgements about the quality of the education offered can you make? Discuss the ways in which the information might be incomplete, thus leading to judgements that are nor wholly reliable.

Influences on human behaviour

People are influenced in their behaviour by many factors including their background, personal circumstances, environment and the views of others. The plight of people caught in the poverty trap provides one interesting context for the study of these influences.

The poverty trap

There are many influences on human behaviour – psychological, physiological, sociological, environmental and many more. Research into patterns of human behaviour is abundant but specialists even in the same field of research, though they may use similar methods, do not always agree on how their findings might be interpreted.

People can be divided into many groups, of which the better off and the poor are two. The better off, however they may be defined, usually have a voice. They are often educated and articulate. They understand the complex world of communications. They can 'network' using people similar to themselves. They are often more confident and they understand organizations. The poor, who are said to be 'always with us', have no such advantages. They may have been born into poverty or reached a position, through circumstances that may or may not be of their own making, where they have little or no money. Most of us know the hymn 'All Things Bright and Beautiful'. Those were the days when the rich man was in his castle and the poor man was at the gate.

Poverty is very difficult to define but even in Victorian times there were vast pieces of social science research carried out by the likes of Henry Mayhew, Charles Booth and Seebohm Rowntree. Agreement on a definition of absolute poverty is not easy to achieve. Relative poverty tries another route. It is very difficult to balance income and expenditure, to differentiate between needs and wants and to take into account what the poorest people in UK could expect to have.

The welfare state in the UK was designed, in part, as a 'safety net' so that no one would starve, but when the welfare state was established, in the second part of the 1940s, the television was a luxury confined to the rich. Now, it is seen as a 'necessity'. Perhaps the same will eventually apply to personal computers and mobile phones.

The extent of poverty has been studied through research by the Organization for Economic Co-operation and Development (OECD). This indicates that poverty affected 20% of the UK population a year, on average, between 1991 and 1996. During the six years of the study, it was revealed that 38% of the population spent at least one year below the official 'poverty line'. The UK did not come out well when compared with other industrial countries, both on a short-term and long-term basis (see the bar chart below).

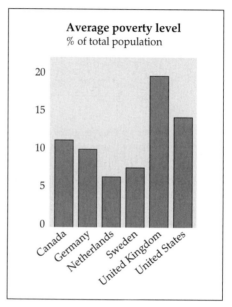

'Tories legacy of poverty' by Charlotte Denny, *The Guardian*, 12 January 2000

Begging became a common sight on Britain's streets during the 1990s

The table 'The bottom line' shows which groups are most likely to be poor when poverty is defined as having an income that is 50% below the national average income after housing costs. The articles on this page indicate how difficult it is to find effective ways of measuring and tackling poverty in different areas.

The bottom line

People in poverty by personal, economic and family status. 1996–7, UK

	Total number	Proportion poor	Number in poverty
Adult women	22.2m	24%	5.3m
Children	13.0m	35%	4.5m
Adult men	21.1m	20%	4.2m
Elderly	9.8m	31%	3.0m
Lone parent family	4.3m	63%	2.9m
Unemployed	4.6m	78%	2.3m
All	2.9m	25%	14.1m

Note: Poverty defined as below 50% average income after housing costs

Source: Department of Social Security, 1998

The Guardian, 3 April 2000

The socially excluded

Using the Department of the Environment's index of local deprivation (which covers England's 354 local authorities) the ten most deprived boroughs in England in 2000 were:

1 Tower Hamlets (London)
2 Hackney (London)
3 Newham (London)
4 Easington (north-east England)
5 Liverpool
6 Knowsley (north-west England)
7 Manchester
8 Islington (London)
9 Southwark (London)
10 Hartlepool (north-east England)

The Guardian, 3 April 2000

Not everyone who lives in those areas is poor. In response to the continued existence of poverty in the UK the government set up what it has called the Social Exclusion Unit. This unit aims to reduce poverty and to strengthen community links. It has targeted groups who are usually poor and are almost always the most vulnerable in society. They are recognized as the people with no voice. There are plenty of potential members: those on low incomes, single-parent families, truants, those caught up in a life of drug addiction and petty crime, refugees, pregnant teenagers and the homeless are just some examples.

Cities lose out in poverty league table

Many deprived communities stand to lose hundreds of millions of pounds of government funding under a new nationwide poverty league table which classes some of the poorest inner-city areas as better off than rural districts.

A leaked document from the Department of Environment has revealed dramatic shifts in the rankings of England's 354 local authorities under the index of local deprivation.

Some local authorities accused the government of manipulating the statistics to shift funding away from London and other major cities to other parts of England.

The biggest losers include Leeds, which moves from 56 to 146, and Sheffield, which falls from 25 to 90. The biggest beneficiary is Easington, once a thriving Durham mining community which moves up from 52 to four.

Many London boroughs have also seen a dramatic shift. Under the old index compiled in 1998, 13 London boroughs were ranked

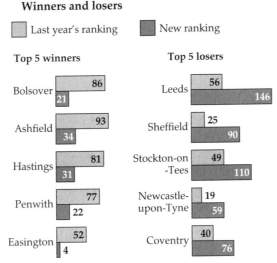

Winners and losers

☐ Last year's ranking   ■ New ranking

Top 5 winners

Bolsover 86 / 21
Ashfield 93 / 34
Hastings 81 / 31
Penwith 77 / 22
Easington 52 / 4

Top 5 losers

Leeds 56 / 146
Sheffield 25 / 90
Stockton-on-Tees 49 / 110
Newcastle-upon-Tyne 19 / 59
Coventry 40 / 76

among the top 20 most deprived areas in the country, with 19 among the crucial top 65.

Under the new rankings, only six London boroughs are in the top 20 and only 13 rank among the top 65, which together receive 80% of all single regeneration budget funding which was worth a total of £16bn over the past four years.

Five inner London boroughs — Hackney, Islington, Newham, Southwark and Tower Hamlets — remain in the top 10.

Local authorities benefiting from the new rankings include many shire districts and forming mining communities. Among them are Sedgefield, Durham, (up 68 places), Hull (up 13), Hartlepool (up 27) and Blackburn (up 16), the constituencies of, respectively, the prime minister Tony Blair, Mr Prescott, Northern Ireland secretary Peter Mandelson, and home secretary Jack Straw.

The new index was compiled by academics at Oxford University using six indicators — income, work, health, education, housing and geographical access to services and transport — rather than the 12 used in the previous index. London authorities and metropolitan council argue that the new index fails to recognise that cities have a mixed pattern of affluent areas and small pockets of severe deprivation.

The new index also underplays factors such as crime and ethnic minorities among whom English is often second language, while giving undue weight to factors such as access to public transport.

Julia Hartley-Brewer, *The Guardian*, 3 April 2000

Towards the end of 1999, the Social Exclusion Unit made the following recommendations:

- **truancy:** cut time lost by a third by 2002
- **rough sleepers:** cut by two-thirds by 2002
- **neighbourhoods:** national strategy embracing jobs, crime, health, housing and 'dynamic local leaders' for the worst estates
- **teenage pregnancy:** better co-ordination, advice, childcare, support packages, Child Support Agency targeting of fathers
- **teenage training:** create a new advice and support service to steer deprived 13–19 year olds through the system.

TASKS

1 Find examples of wealth and poverty in your community. How did you identify the examples? What criteria did you use? What other information would you have liked to have had to help you make your decision?

2 Find current examples of poverty in the national or local press. What could be done to help alleviate such problems?

3 On a map of England, locate and label the ten most deprived boroughs. Comment on their distribution. What factors make some areas poorer than others?

4 Find out about the work of the government's Social Exclusion Unit. To what extent do you consider its recommendations realistic?

5 What is life like for the 'socially excluded' who live below the 'poverty line'?

Human behaviour and how it is reflected in social, political and economic life: living in impoverished environments

Tackling the problem of impoverished environments

Successive governments have tried to tackle the problem of impoverished environments. Ministers are planning a complex system of poverty monitoring linked to what are seen as 'national efficiency guidelines'. They will need to persuade the Treasury to approve a multi-billion-pound urban regeneration programme, much of which will focus on England's 3000 poorest neighbourhoods. Equally deprived areas are to be found in Wales, Scotland and Northern Ireland. Some would say that, welcome though improved physical conditions would be, the root of change needs to be planted close to things that help to change human behaviour.

Grimethorpe, a former pit village in South Yorkshire

London as a special case

Half of the ten most deprived local authority areas are in London, yet the capital city remains attractive to those seeking their fortune. Areas like the 'West End' and the 'City' are international magnets for theatre, cinema and club-goers. London draws more the 14 million visitors a year from abroad. It is the seat of government and Buckingham Palace is the grandest of the royal residences. As a community, a bringing together of streets, areas, groups, common interests – however one might seek to define 'a community' – there are more than 50 distinct ethnic communities. Some are associated with particular areas: Bangladeshis in Brick Lane, the Chinese in Gerrard Street, Caribbeans in Brixton, and the Jews in Golders Green.

The Canary Wharf experience

Living in any part of London is expensive but some parts are more expensive than others, even when the distance between them may be short. Canary Wharf is part of the modern, high-tech, re-packaged Britain of 'Cool Britannia'. It is served by new transport schemes such as the Docklands Light Railway and the Jubilee Line extension. However, Canary Wharf is, despite its glittering wealth, part of Tower Hamlets – previously identified as the poorest local authority area in the country. At Canary Wharf there is 5.8 million square feet of office space with a further 3.2 million under construction. Eventually, there will be 11 million square feet. The working population has risen from 8000 in 1994, to 27,000. The eventual target may be 100,000. The Canary Wharf Group plc is valued at between £2.6 and £2.9 billion. Yet in other parts of the borough, unemployment is four times that of the London average and there are some of the highest rates of mental illness, heart disease, alcoholism and drug dependence in the country.

Despite its glittering wealth, Canary Wharf is situated within the poorest borough in England

The gap between these people in Tower Hamlets may, at times, appear like a chasm, but there are opportunities. This is how Robert John, a company director, puts it:

> 'Paul Reichman [Chairman of Canary Wharf Group plc] said to me right at the beginning that we must always remember that we are new members of an old community.'

In order to persuade more local people to work in the complex, Robert John's company has invested in a skills-match programme and liased closely with local schools. It may have paid dividends. A survey showed that the number of workers at Canary Wharf who live in Tower Hamlets rose from 4.5% in 1997 to 8.45% in 1999. John Everely, a social scientist at London University's Queen Mary and Westfield College makes some comparisons with great philanthropic Victorians – the Cadburys in Birmingham and the Rowntrees of York – who invested heavily in facilities for their workers, but the resources available are dwarfed by the sheer scale of the problem. He reminds us of the gap.

'If it is bridgeable, it's only by the longest bridge in the history of the world.'

Regeneration money has been forthcoming. The London Docklands Development Corporation spent £3.9 billion of public money before it was wound up in 1998. Another £9 billion was added by the private sector. Recently, John Eversley's team undertook some research for Tower Hamlets Council as part of a further bid for £50 million of government regeneration funding. It found that:

- 51% of households live on under £10,000 per year
- only 25% of adults were in full-time work
- 84% of households were on some kind of state benefit
- 36% suffer from health problems
- 44% of households contain someone suffering from a long-term illness or disability.

Views of people living and working in London

The eco-activist:
'Since 1994, I've turned up at more than 50 "Critical Masses" and 2 "Reclaim the Streets" demonstrations. I just want an improvement in London; it doesn't matter what the ideology is really. Not any more.'

The socialite:
'The shop was originally going to be on Chelsea Green, behind Fulham Road, but we didn't think that road was going to be fashionable enough. We decided on Matcomb Street because Jimmy Choo is here and it is a bit more exclusive.'

The policeman:
'One example of our relationship with the community is Operation Malachite, which concentrates on brothels and prostitution. These girls are our community and are entitled to as much protection as anyone.'

The bus driver:
'I love London. I live in Tottenham … I have looked at other garages like Peckham, Catford, Woolwich and I don't like them. I have always been here and everyone knows me. Why go somewhere where you're not known?'

The night-working noise abatement officer:
'I like being called out to Old Compton Street because it is always lively. It is a convergence for a lot of cultures. There is the Italian thing, the gay thing, the Chinese thing, the club thing, and the showbiz thing. Purely on a people-watching basis it is an interesting place.'

Observer Magazine, 23 April 2000

TASKS

1 Write a similar set of comments to those given by people living and working in London, but for your own community.

2 How would you define 'community'? In what ways do communities differ?

3 How, if necessary, can anyone influence a local community and help to change the way that people behave?

6 The relationship between law, culture and ethics

Definitions

Culture Prevalent tastes at a particular time. Prevalent tastes at a particular time established by a dominant class/group. Prevalent, but different, tastes established by many groups.

Dissent Showing disagreement with a particular law/policy.

Ethics Actions that are in accordance with the accepted norms of society. A moral code or a set of moral principles.

Law enforcement Actions taken by the police to enforce the laws. Actions taken by the courts to determine innocence or guilt and to decide on the type and length of punishment for those found guilty of breaking the law.

Laws Bills given the consent of both Houses of Parliament (the Commons and the Lords) and which have been signed by the Queen to give the royal assent, making them Acts of Parliament.

Pressure groups Organizations that represent a particular cause or the interests of a particular group and which may seek to influence parliament/government/local authorities.

Getting started

1 'The police are fighting a losing battle to maintain the law. They must be given more resources.'

2 'Too often the law is concerned with the rights of the offender. We should think more about those of the victim.'

3 'Famous people should be entitled to more privacy.'

4 'Part of the problem with government in this country is that the interesting bits are shrouded in secrecy.'

5 'There is never likely to be a law that permits euthanasia.'

6 'The rights of animals are just as important as those of humans and need to be defended.'

7 'The best way to get something out of politics is to join a pressure group.'

8 'Sometimes, the only way to change a law is by breaking it.'

Outline

This section begins with an examination of crime and law enforcement, including examples of:
- a legal dilemma
- morality and the law
- the difficulties of law enforcement.

There is a section on the law and important ethical and cultural dilemmas such as:
- the 'lawful excuse'
- equal rights
- discrimination against groups, races or individuals
- euthanasia
- animal rights.

The section concludes with a consideration of the issues surrounding obedience to the law:
- the operation of pressure groups
- legal and illegal activities
- different forms of dissent and protest.

Crime and law enforcement

Is an Englishman's home his castle?

This section considers a case of law enforcement where ethical issues were raised. It concerns the right of a house owner to defend his home against thieves. So was this Englishman's home his castle? That is what many people believe, but what does it actually mean? In many ways it is connected with security and the rights of the citizen. Our private property, if we own our own home, is our castle. We can rightfully raise the drawbridge against almost anyone who wishes to enter our property unless they have permission from the courts to do so (usually in the form of a search warrant executed by a police officer).

The case of Tony Martin

Tony Martin lived in a near-derelict farmhouse in a rural part of Norfolk. He was an ideal target for burglars. When two of them tried to break into Tony Martin's property, he shot them with an illegally held shotgun. One was wounded and the other, a sixteen year old, died. The jury of twelve people, chosen at random from the electoral roll, had to decide whether Tony Martin was guilty of murder of whether there might be a less grave offence based on self-defence and the right to defend his property. He was found guilty of murder and jailed for life.

What the papers said
A *Guardian* editorial of 20 April 2000 warned us:

Do not make him a hero.

What Tony Martin did cannot be condoned.

It claimed that: 'He broke a fundamental rule of civilized society: rejection of the use of unnecessary and undue force.'

On 21 April, its letter column carried the headline:

This murder was justified

Here are two contrasting views of *Guardian* readers:

When are we going to realize that burglary is not a property crime. It is a crime against people and is the worst thing you can do to someone without physically attacking them. It ruins lives, particularly in the case of elderly people and whose who live alone. In this proper context, the actions of Tony Martin do not seem so unreasonable or excessive. It was not his property he was defending, but his right to security and peace of mind, without which our lives are worthless. What other protection is there for those in his position? They are on their own. Do not be surprised when someone goes too far.
Tony Wilcox
Northwich, Cheshire

I regard the conviction as both right and justified. What signal would it have sent out if he had been acquitted: that anybody can take the law into their own hands? The last thing this country needs is go down the route of America, where people are largely responsible for their own security. Do we want the mob rule and vigilante groups? We pay taxes to fund the police force and however slow they may or may not react to burglaries, it is their job to deal with crime not the public's. It is all too easy to take the populist Daily Mail view of ``he got what he deserved'' (the victim), but in this case it is the farmer who got what he deserved, however wrong the actions of the victim were.
Tim Harvey
Northwich, Cheshire

The Guardian, 21 April 2000

Reasonable force?

The media reported claims that some members of the jury had been 'intimidated'. The policing of rural areas was widely criticized. Coverage was said to be patchy and response rates slow. The Chief Constable of Norfolk revealed the extent to which his force was under strength. Had the police 'failed' Tony Martin because they did not have the resources to do otherwise? In defending themselves, on their property, people are entitled to use 'reasonable force' but what does that mean?

The *News of the World* (24 April 2000), the biggest circulation Sunday newspaper, conducted a poll involving 1001 of its readers. Only 24% agreed that Tony Martin's life sentence was the right punishment. It reported that *The Sun*, another News International paper, had used phone-in lines so that readers could say whether they agreed or disagreed with Tony Martin's punishment. 134,066 said 'no' and 4139 said 'yes'. What we must remember is that this does not necessarily mean that the majority – even when it seems to be overwhelming – is necessary 'right'. As the *Guardian* reader asked (21 April 2000): 'What signal would it have sent out if Tony Martin had been acquitted: that anybody can take the law into their own hands?'

TASKS

1 Find out more about the Tony Martin case. List the arguments for and against his actions. Which do you favour?

2 What recommendations would you make in the light of this case?

Crime and law enforcement: difficulties in law enforcement

Newspaper reports show some of the difficulties encountered when operating the law. The problem is that the law is a product of government together with many years of experience in practising its execution. Politicians have to make difficult decisions about what the law should be and the lawyers and judges have to enforce it.

The moral maze of enforcing the law

Politicians are often accused of trying to occupy what is called 'the high moral ground', which some people interpret as 'telling us what to do and how to behave'. There is certainly a case to be argued for some 'absolute' moral standards – there are very few people who do not believe that murder is wrong. Essentially, morality is about what is 'right' and what is 'wrong'. The law tells us what is right, because it is legal, and what is wrong, because it is illegal. In that sense, the law of the land is usually clearer than either morality or religion.

However, some difficulties emerge. Whether or not you agree with a particular law is irrelevant. If you break it, and are found out, you risk some form of punishment as set out by the relevant Act of Parliament.

The position for politicians

Politicians have the power to change the law but sometimes, like a potent medicine, this has undesirable side effects. Recently a number of politicians have been challenged about the legality of some of their activities. They have been caught doing something rather sleazy, have occupied the front pages and led the evening news. Here are three well-known politicians who stepped into this moral maze.

Prime Ministers who stepped into the moral maze

'It's time to get back to basics: to self-discipline and respect for the law, to consideration for others, to accepting responsibility for yourself and your family, and not shuffling it off on the state.'  **John Major** in speech to Conservative Party Conference in 1993 calling for a return to traditional family values. The policy backfired when a series of ministers were caught in sexual scandals	**'There is no such things as society. There are individual men and women, and there are families.'**  **Margaret Thatcher** interview in Woman's Own, October 1987. Widely interpreted as an attack on the future of the welfare state and the health service, Thatcher's remarks were condemned by members of her own party at the time and finally disowned by William Hague last year	**'This party is a moral crusade or it is nothing.'**  **Harold Wilson** in speech to Labour Party Conference, October 1962. The words came back to haunt him when his Government became mired in allegations of financial sleaze

The Observer, 5 September 1999

TASKS

Reflect on the following statements and consider the issues they raise.

a   We live in a society with very diverse beliefs and values. Not everyone will accept the same moral code.

b   People tend to have a sort of 'hierarchy' of law. Hardly anyone murders someone else but almost everybody commits traffic offences.

c   Politicians find it difficult to resist 'moral crusades' because they feel that these will appeal to 'right-thinking people' in the electorate. The difficulty is the old adage that advises people to 'practise what they preach'.

The law and important ethical and cultural dilemmas

Case 1: GM crops and the law

Greenpeace is one of Europe's best known pressure groups. Genetically modified crops are the subject of some controversy. Growers argue that their use can lead to major advances in the world's food supply. Environmentalists argue that this is simply a cover for rapid commercialization and practices that will damage the environment.

On one such site, 28 Greenpeace protestors pulled up £750 worth of GM maize at a Norfolk farm. The protest group even filmed the event. They were arrested and charged with theft and causing criminal damage, in the first case of its kind. When it came to court, a jury cleared the 28 of stealing and was unable to reach a verdict on whether or not they were guilty of criminal damage. Their defence was that they had a 'lawful excuse' to do what they did because they were acting to protect other maize crops and the environment from allegedly contaminated GM maize pollen.

Case 2: The schoolgirl's trousers and the law

School uniforms are not widely seen in Europe and the USA. In the UK they survive, usually in the form of 'dress codes'. The legal position regarding what schools can and cannot enforce in the way of uniform is reasonably clear.

The need for equality between the sexes adds a rather different dimension. The law does not allow sexual discrimination. In one school, girls were not allowed to wear trousers. Backed by the Equal Opportunities Commission, one 14-year-old schoolgirl decided to take her school to court in 1999. The girl did not challenge the right of the school to have a uniform policy. What she did claim was that the school's refusal to allow girls to wear trousers amounted to unlawful sexual discrimination. Conscious of possible legal costs and publicity, the school did not go to court and the girl concerned may now wear trousers.

Case 3: Child curfews

Antisocial behaviour – noise, graffiti, vandalism and worse – is something that affects the lives of many people.

Stereotypically, the young are bored, adventurous, inconsiderate, insensitive, lively and – that most elusive quality – 'cool'. Whatever the reality behind the stereotypes, the problem is real enough. Parents are accused of not being able to control their children who, influenced by undesirable media images, often apparently fuelled-up on drugs, roam the streets, estates and the centre of villages behaving in an antisocial way that is intensely annoying. 'Something must be done – but what?' Ideally, policy should target causes, but that is expensive. The Labour government has introduced curfews and antisocial behaviour orders. Local authorities and the police have the unenviable job of enforcing them.

Who wears the trousers?

What the employers say

British Airways
No option to wear trousers at present. "We've done extensive research into what cabin crew feel comfortable in and market research has suggested that female staff prefer to wear skirts." But any women working on ramps or in loading areas can wear trousers, as can pilots.

Nationwide Building Society
Has offered women employees option to wear trousers since 1994. There are two sanctioned styles of trousers – summer and winter – and three lengths of skirt. "But from our figures it looks like 10:3 in favour of skirts."

Liffe Futures and Options Exchange
"All traders are asked to dress smartly in business attire. Smart trouser suits would certainly be acceptable."

Marks & Spencer
Trousers have always been available as part of uniform. "Trouser wearing is increasingly more popular amongst staff, especially in the food halls."

Tesco
Has allowed female staff to wear trousers since 1992. Trousers come in a choice of two styles.

Association of Female Barristers
Option to wear trousers introduced by lord chief justice in 1996. "It's a non-issue for professionals, and it's not really our job to be concerned with dress."

Dudley Group Hospitals Trust
No trousers at the moment, except in specialist areas, but policy is being reviewed. "By the end of this year anyone who wants to wear trousers will be able to."

Sally James, *The Guardian*, 1 September 1999

TASKS

1 The protestors who pulled up the GM crop were acquitted. Is this a blow for freedom or a dangerous precedent?

2 Examine the case for and against a school uniform.

3 Responsibility – but whose? How might you define 'responsibility' and how would you try to deal with the problem of antisocial behaviour?

Case 4: Smoking

The Great Dilemma: life or death?
Don't bother about the smokers – it's their own fault.

Smoking is one of those so-called 'forbidden pleasures' as far as many young people are concerned. Plenty of boys and girls (increasingly the latter) break the law by buying cigarettes when they are not legally old enough to do so. Packets carry a health warning and the links between smoking and serious illnesses such as cancer and heart disease are well known. For young people, a cigarette represents part of the 'grown-up' world supposedly inhabited by adults. 'Minor' law breaking may offer a 'buzz'.

Smoking is addictive and it endangers health, yet, for many years, groups that claimed to protect the rights of smokers challenged these claims. Now times are changing. Cigarette advertising is strictly controlled and many firms, aware of the dangers of 'passive' smoking, no longer allow smoking in the workplace. Once, non-smoking areas were relatively uncommon on trains. Now, the rail company First Great Western has removed its single smoking carriage on expresses. In the USA, Philip Morris, the largest cigarette manufacturer in the world, has at last admitted, on a corporate website, the dangers of smoking. Both individual smokers and states have launched civil legal actions against the tobacco companies.

How tobacco shaped the world we live in

● Tobacco began growing in the Americas about 6,000BC. By 1BC, native Americans had begun to use tobacco to dress wounds and as a painkiller

● On October 15 1492 Christopher Columbus was offered dried tobacco leaves as a gift from the native Americans he encountered. Sailors brought tobacco back and the plant was soon being grown all over Europe.

● Tobacco was used as currency. It served as collateral for French loans during the American War of Independence

● In 1847 Phillip Morris was established, selling hand-rolled cigarettes. Cigarettes became popular when soldiers saw them being smoked by Turkish and Russian soldiers and brought them back to England

● In 1953 Dr Ernst L Wynders found that putting cigarette tar on the backs of mice caused tumours

● In 1964 the US surgeon general issued a report called Smoking and Health which led to the first act of government regulation in sales and advertising. A year later Britain banned cigarette advertising on television, followed by the first health warnings on cigarette packets. Tobacco companies began to diversify into other areas

● Tobacco consumption fell in the 80s in the developed world but increased in the developing world, where half the adult male population are now smokers. Consumption is now increasing in the developing world by about 3.4% a year

● By 2020, smoking is expected to kill 10m people annually worldwide – about one in three adult

deaths. That is more than the total death toll from malaria, maternal and major childhood illnesses and tuberculosis combined.

● Of these deaths, more than 70% will be in the developing world.

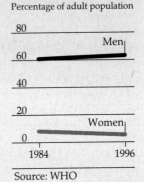

UK smokers
Percentage of adult population

Chinese smokers
Percentage of adult population

Source: ASH

Source: WHO

The Guardian, 14 October 1999

TASKS

1 Are smokers to be pitied or punished?

2 Do smokers have rights?

3 What are the responsibilities of the tobacco companies?

4 Tobacco brings considerable funds to the Exchequer, but should doctors have the right to refuse treatment to those suffering from smoke related illnesses?

5 How could the anti-smoking message be made more effective?

Case 5: Euthanasia

In 1997, Dr Philip Nitschke was the only doctor in the world who had legally helped patients to die. He worked in the Northern Territory of Australia where, for eight months, euthanasia was legal, until the Federal government outlawed it. Since then, the American State of Oregon has legalized euthanasia – but that action is also subject to challenge by the Federal government. Holland changed it's laws in 2001.

> Executioner or criminal? Legal or back-street euthanasia? Right or wrong? It's the kind of thing that we should be debating here because – like it or not – euthanasia is a subject whose time has come. In the USA and Australia it is seen as the great moral question of our time and has replaced abortion in terms of ethical talking points … In Britain there is little informed discussion.

'Dr Death asks some painful questions' by Ann Treneman, *The Independent*, 3 November 1997

Dr Nitschke, operating entirely within the law as it then stood, earned the nickname 'Dr Death' – as did an American doctor who was sent to prison for practising euthanasia illegally. In 1999, a British jury took only just over an hour to dismiss a murder charge against a British doctor who openly advocated giving help to terminally ill, elderly patients who wished to die with dignity. Though acquitted of the charge, the 52-year-old doctor retired early because of the stress brought on by the case. The case came after a *Sunday Times* article in July 1997, when another GP and campaigner for euthanasia was reported to have 'helped' at least 50 of his patients die.

Opponents argue that euthanasia is a potentially dangerous practice and that the main responsibility of doctors is to sustain life. The extent of 'unofficial' euthanasia is unknown and a group of bereaved relatives have formed a pressure group called SOS-NHS Patients in Distress. It plans to take legal action under the Human Rights Act, which came into force towards the end of 2000. The ethical dilemma for doctors seeking to act in 'the best interests' of their patients, using guidelines set out by the British Medical Association, is probably the most difficult they are likely to face.

Euthanasia and doctor assisted suicide around the world

Britain

Euthanasia is unlawful, whatever the circumstances.

A doctor may administer drugs which hasten a patient's death, as long as the intention is to ease suffering or distress. If the intention is to shorten the patient's life, even by hours or minutes, this amounts to murder, which carries an automatic life sentence.

To prove murder, however, the prosecution has to show the drugs, rather than the illness, caused the patient's death. Otherwise, the crime is attempted murder.

Doctor-assisted suicide – where a doctor gives a patient the wherewithal to commit suicide – is also illegal.

Aiding, abetting, counselling or procuring suicide carries a maximum prison sentence of 14 years.

Surveys show that most doctors favour legalising euthanasia or doctor-assisted suicide. But the British Medical Association, which is holding a special conference on assisted suicide later this year, is opposed.

A House of Lords committee has come out against legalisation, and the government has firmly ruled out a change in the law.

United States

Dr Jack Kevorkian, known as "Dr Death", who filmed himself giving a lethal injection to a dying man, was recently convicted of second degree murder. Doctor-assisted suicide has also been legal in one US state, Oregon, since 1997. Legislation is in the pipeline in California. In all other states it is illegal.

The Netherlands

Voluntary euthanasia — mercy-killing at the patient's request — is technically illegal but has been "decriminalised" since 1984.

If strict rules are complied with, and mercy killing is carried out at the patient's "explicit request" and when there is "intolerable suffering without prospect of improvement", a doctor will not be prosecuted.

However, a study published earlier this year showed that doctors were repeatedly breaching rules and that the safeguards were inadequate.

Campaigners against euthanasia claimed the study showed that euthanasia could never be safely regulated.

The Dutch parliament is considering legislation to legalise euthanasia. About 3,000 people a year die in the Netherlands as a result of voluntary euthanasia, according to latest figures.

Australia

Euthanasia was legalised in the Northern Territory in 1995, but the law was overturned by the supreme court in 1997. Attempts to reinstate it have been unsuccessful. In all other states it is illegal.

Switzerland

Doctor-assisted suicide has been legal since the late 1970s.

Claire Dyer and Sally James, *The Guardian*, 12 May 1999

TASKS

1 Find out more about the main terms of the Human Rights Act.

2 Are there any circumstances in which euthanasia can be justified?

Case 6: Animal rights

To be or not to be? Hunting with animals

Few subjects have generated more passion and emotion, in recent years, than hunting with animals. A private member's bill won overwhelming support in the House of Commons but finally fell in mid-1999 because of lack of time – a fate common to backbencher MPs who bring forward controversial proposals that do not command total government support. In 2001, another anti-hunting bill only reached the House of Lords.

Opposed to a hunting ban is the Countryside Alliance, an umbrella group claiming to represent wider rural interests. The Alliance grew out of a 'Countryside March' which drew an estimated 250,000 supporters to central London in March 1998. A bigger march planned for March 2001 was postponed because of foot and mouth disease restrictions.

Placards belonging to some of the 250,000 people who took part in a 'Countryside March' through London

The Countryside Alliance claims that a ban on hunting will lead to the loss of 16,000 jobs in rural areas. Opponents claim that the methods used to calculate job losses were so flawed that only one-tenth of that figure will actually be lost.

Country people are angry. Increasingly, government is a big-city, even international, thing. Over the last 20 years, local councils have lost many of their powers. The loss of green fields for housing development, a crisis in agriculture, the closure of village amenities, the absence of regular policing, high petrol costs and a lack of public transport threaten rural life. A government inquiry chaired by Lord Burns has reported on the possible effects that a ban on hunting might have on the rural community.

Anti-hunt protestors at the Essex Farmers and Union Hunt in Maldon, Essex

The changing countryside

Now, however, less than 2% of Britain's jobs are on the land although, each day, 300 people move to the countryside and about 20% of England's population live in the countryside. Both the cities, and their people, are moving outwards. Politicians talk the language of 'change' and 'modernization'. Traditional country pursuits are threatened although David Beskine of the Ramblers Association (a pressure group which was recently successful in its battle for 'the right to roam') claims that all is not quite as it seems. According to him:

> 'People's emotions are being manipulated. The Countryside Alliance is really made up of field sport enthusiasts and a small band of rich landowners and shotgun manufacturers with vested interests. Something stinks about the whole bunch of them.'

The article 'Countryside concerns' (page 180) gives some different views.

Case 7: More animal rights

The savage arena

Animal welfare is big business. It exists in an arena of cruelty and violence. The RSPCA, one of the country's oldest pressure groups, has been criticized because of the graphic nature of some of its advertisements. As an organization, it relies to some extent on legacies from elderly people yet its Special Operations Unit operates in an underworld of crime and amorality. It is a world where there is still cock fighting and dog fighting (both illegal since 1835, and the latter particularly difficult after the Dangerous Dogs Act of 1991). It is a world of blood lust, betting and drugs. Videotapes of the dogfights are also made. No one should be under any illusions. Changing the law, which may affect hunting with animals, is difficult enough with so many conflicting interests involved. Enforcing the law is often where the real problems start.

COUNTRYSIDE CONCERNS

THE concerns of those who live in rural areas are varied. Five of those who were closely involved with the Molland march spoke passionately yesterday of their hopes and fears for the countryside.

Paul Beazley, 48, is the headkeeper at the Molland shoot, which is owned by the St James's gunsmiths, Holland & Holland. He believes that the countryside's only hope is tolerance, from both sides.

Last month he raised £6,000 for the Devon Air Ambulance with a one-day charity shoot. "We've got to let people know what we are about," he said. "I've no problem with the minority who have a genuine moral objection, but most of the antis really know absolutely nothing about the sport they are trying to ban."

Kate Stevens, tenant farmer with 850 acres, a large part of it moorland, supports a right to roam but would prefer it to be a voluntary. She said: "People should be allowed to enjoy the countryside but they must behave responsibly and follow the country code."

Howard Reeves, 53, former policeman and water bailiff, resents being told he cannot kill the badgers or birds of prey that attack his game birds. "I think I am going to have to move to Scotland because it is the last real wilderness left," he said.

John Howarth, 53, a lorry driver, moved to Molland from Lancashire a year ago. He is a "shooting man" who pays £600 a year to be part of a 12-gun syndicate that rents its own shoot.

He said: "We get ten days' shooting a season; it's my money and I should be allowed to spend it how I like. I enjoy training gun-dogs and I get a lot of satisfaction from it. Once they've got rid of fox hunting they are not going to stop there because they've got the blood lust."

David Filmer, 44, honorary Mollandonian, who is married to a local woman, lives in a council "box" in Horsham, West Sussex. "The farm labourers' cottages I grew up in Kent now sell for £150,000 to people who commute to London everyday," he said. "Real country people like me can't afford to live there anymore."

The Times, 2 March 1998

TASKS

1 Compare the photographs of pro- and anti-hunt campaigners. Why might such evidence be both reliable and unreliable?

2 For a rural area known to you:
  a Consider the ways in which life is changing.
  b How are people from urban areas influencing the changes in rural life?

3 To what extent do you consider each of the differing views of the countryside to be justified? As an opponent of the views, what arguments might you use against them?

4 Find out about the work of the RSPCA and the problems it is facing.

Obeying the law
Protest within the law

In a democracy, opportunities should always exist for protest and dissent. BMW's sale and break-up of Rover cars will cost 10,000 jobs in the Birmingham area. The workers, their families and trade unions have made their feelings known by organizing huge but peaceful protest marches in the city.

> Everyone there was equally worried about the situation. People spoke and reflected on the damage done to Rover in the area and how BMW handled their affairs. There was a very sombre but determined atmosphere and at one point everyone sang 'You'll Never Walk Alone'.
>
> *Sutton Coldfield Observer*, 7 April 2000

Protesting to save jobs at Rover's Longbridge car plant

Dissent and breaking the law

The Animal Liberation Front is a pressure group that takes a different view. Its members have frequently broken the law in an effort to protect the rights of animals. ALF literature takes an uncompromising tone:
'Since its formation the ALF has saved thousands of animals from death and suffering. Its actions have also played an important part in the closing down of many animal abuse establishments through the tactic of economic sabotage. The price paid by activists has been high. Some have been sent to prison for many years, and the average sentence is increasing. The prisoners are imprisoned for selfless acts of compassion, born of the frustration of waiting for the rest of society to respect animals. They are not "terrorists" or "misguided"; their activities are an important part of the struggle for animal liberation, perhaps the most important part.'

> Police are investigating after a letter bomb was sent to a pet supplier yesterday.
>
> Northumbria police said it was too early to link the incident, in which no one was injured, with similar parcels sent to firms dealing in agriculture and livestock elsewhere in the country.
>
> However, detectives are liaising with their counterparts in North Yorkshire.
>
> *The Guardian,* 23 January 2001

Following a similar incident in North Wales, an animal rights supporter was arrested by police.

Protest and taking the law to the limit

The protests organized by farmers and road hauliers against high petrol and motoring costs, which first surfaced in September 2000, had a devastating effect on the nation's life and economy.

Road rage: police restraining a protestor outside a petrol depot

TASKS

1 Under what circumstances would breaking the law be justified?

2 Is there any difference between a politician, a lawyer, a judge, a schoolteacher and someone under the age of 16 when they break the law?

3 When did you last break the law?

Further study suggestions and example questions

Further reading

Barker, R. (1994) *Politics, People and Government*, St Martin's Press, London

Claxton, G. (1992) *Live and Learn*, Open University, Milton Keynes.

Kumar, R. (1996) *Research Methodology: A Step by Step Guide for Beginners*, Sage. New York.

Nuttall, J. (1995) *Moral Questions*, Polity, London.

Simpson, D. (1999) *Pressure Groups*, Hodder & Stoughton, London

Thompson, M. (1994) *Teach Yourself Ethics*, Hodder & Stoughton, London.

Types of question

Questions for this unit cover aspects of society, politics and economics (ideologies and values, exploration and evaluation of human behaviour; the relationship between law, culture and ethics).

Questions where material is provided

A typical (but shortened) extract might be similar to this one, written by Alexander McCall Smith (*The Guardian*, 23 September 2000) when the most senior judges in the UK were asked to decide whether or not an operation should take place to separate Siamese twins.

It has been an epic legal battle. Two parents came to Britain to have their babies. Conjoined twins were delivered and it was discovered that surgery to separate them would result in the death of one, although possibly saving the life of the other. The parents declared that they did not want this for religious reasons, and the Catholic Church supported them in their opposition. But the twins have been born into a society in which there is sufficient attachment to the principle that the welfare of children is generally more important than the wishes of the parents, and the view has been taken that the operation should go ahead.

Now, after a thorough and at times charged hearing, the Court of Appeal has confirmed this result. The judges have not found it easy, and who can blame them? It is unusual to hear judges commenting publicly on the difficulties of deciding a particular case, but in this instance they seem to have been engaged in a bout of public agonizing over their decision about what is the right thing to do.

Of course, the opponents of the decision will say that adults should not be allowed to decide that a child will die and that adults (the judges) have condemned the weaker twin to death. But this is simply wrong. If the operation goes ahead and the weaker twin dies (as seems inevitable) her death will not have been caused by the surgeons, it will have been caused by the impossible condition with which she was born. That is a result of biology, not of human intervention.

Additional extracts might then lead to a question about the inter-relationship of law, ethics and morality. In this case, the focus might be on what is considered 'right' and 'wrong'.

Essay questions

1 It is often claimed that the second half of the twentieth century brought far greater equality between the sexes. Evaluate the arguments for and against the claim that there is now greater equality of opportunity and achievement between men and women.

2 In 2000, a popular Sunday newspaper ran a 'name and shame' campaign that it claimed was designed to inform the public about alleged paedophiles living near them. Many of these people were attacked and driven from their homes. Some were innocent of any crime. Public opinion was divided about the actions of the newspaper. Compare and contrast the arguments of those who claimed the newspaper was right with those who claimed it was wrong.

Endpiece

There is a danger that we will always think that every problem that is connected with people, and the way they operate in the political and economic systems, can be solved. In reality, finding a solution is likely to prove impossible. This does not mean that the process of analysing a problem, gathering evidence (from the many sources available) and putting forward ways in which a particular problem might be addressed (hypotheses) is a waste of time. Both the process and outcome are important for all students because the skills involved should be transferable to other studies and to ways of working beyond the world of schools and colleges.

Approaches to A2 internal assessment

The internal assessment option

Coursework has been renamed as internal assessment because it is completed under conditions set by your school or college. The A2 section of the OCR General Studies specification offers you a choice. You can either take a written paper or you can choose to take the coursework option instead. For those wishing to take the coursework option, one assignment will be set in advance by OCR. In each examination session a topic within the social domain will be specified. The aim of each assignment will be to pose a problem set in the context of a wider issue. You will be asked to complete a report of not more than 3000 words and this may include features such as drawing, diagrams, computer-generated images and statistical analysis. An important feature of the assignment is that it provides opportunities for the generation of evidence of all six Key Skills.

Approaching coursework and being successful

Start early

Start the planning process as soon as the assignment material is made available. You will be under a lot pressure to organize your studies and to be successful. An early start, and an outline 'plan of action' is better than a last-minute panic and trying to complete the assignment without having left sufficient time to do it properly. Examiners are very good at recognizing the amount of time that students have spent on preparation and research activities.

Understand the assessment process

Assessment criteria are probably not uppermost in the minds of most students, but knowledge of them can pay substantial dividends. There are 90 marks for the assignment and they are distributed according to six assessment criteria which you need to satisfy.

Satisfying the criteria

The assessment criteria are:
- selecting, interpreting and evaluating sources and evidence [15 marks]
- understanding the concepts involved [15 marks]
- communicating in a clear, reasoned and effective way [15 marks]
- demonstrating the relationship and limitations between different types of knowledge [15 marks]
- using problem-solving skills for complex activities [15 marks]
- drawing and justifying relevant conclusions [15 marks].

Finding more information

More detailed information can be found in the General Studies specification booklet – your teacher/tutor will have a copy. Knowing what the examiners are looking for is particularly important for a coursework assignment. What you must do is meet all the criteria. For example, good evidence, well evaluated and well communicated, is necessary for success, but it will not be sufficient if maximum marks are gained for that and few are awarded for the other four criteria because these were neglected.

What to aim for

Look for possible solutions to the problem by using a range of critically evaluated sources that show you understand both the concepts and how different forms of knowledge can be applied, using clear and reasoned communication techniques that will lead you to a logical conclusion in no more than 3000 words.
- Keep to the word limit. It doesn't have to be exactly 3000. It could be less but it should not be more.
- Address the problem that forms the assignment. Don't write generally around the theme or lose sight of the problem partway through.
- Your work must be your own, but it is often helpful, and it is part of the Key Skills process, to discuss aspects of the problem with others.
- Vary your approach when you compile your report and present it in an interesting and informative way, using different types of evidence.
- Always keep the six assessment criteria in mind.

Telling it like it really is – an example of a typical coursework assignment

This is the sort of problem that may be presented to you for your coursework assignment for the OCR General Studies specification.

Problem outlined

Vandalism is a growing and complex problem in a community known to you. The vandalism has caused conflict between groups. It has made many parts of the area unsightly. The outcomes of vandalism are costly to remedy and the police have been criticized for inactivity. Among those involved in trying to solve the problem are councillors, the police, young people, residents, business people and local groups.

Assignment

Illustrate the main issues involved. Analyse their cause and identify two of the likely solutions to the problem of vandalism. Which solution would you prefer? What reasons can you give for this choice? How would you work towards the chosen solution?

The sources used for your assignment must be listed in detail at the end of your submitted work.

Approaching the assignment

- Always try to focus on key command words in the question such as: 'illustrate', 'analyse', 'two likely solutions', 'which solution', 'reasons', 'how'.
- Gather the evidence from different sources. Don't just try to download from the Internet or rely too much on replies to letters.
- Be selective in your approach. Don't hide key points of analysis in a mass of descriptive detail.
- If you can, use different research techniques. Primary research can be a valuable experience but it is time-consuming and it is unlikely that you will have time to construct a sample that is large enough to produce firm conclusions.
- Don't use graphics just for the sake of it. Use graphics, diagrams or photographic evidence to illustrate a point.
- Avoid sweeping statements and generalization. Don't be afraid to use arguments just because they are 'different', but make sure that they are reasoned and logical.
- Acknowledge sources at all times. Don't copy large chunks of someone else's material or ideas. Use sources selectively to make a point or to illustrate an argument.
- List sources at the end of the assignment but don't try to impress by seeking to give the impression that you have used far more sources than is actually the case.
- On completion, read carefully through your assignment, making any corrections that might be necessary. This can help you to avoid unnecessary mistakes.
- Make sure you meet all deadlines for the completion and submission of your work.

Synoptic case studies

Synoptic case study 1: Human achievement

Knowledge is very seldom discrete, and developments in one area of human existence usually impact on others. Synopticity requires you to identify the different kinds of knowledge and make links between the three domains.

Imagine you have been invited to take someone on a physical and intellectual Tour of Human Achievement. You have to ensure that on their journey they visit the following six areas of achievement:

- technological and scientific achievement
- achievements in the field of medicine
- events or individuals that have had a positive impact on values or morality
- improvements in social and world conditions
- achievements in contributing to the arts and culture
- contributions to human knowledge.

Where would you take them? Who would you introduce them to? What would you have them witness? As their 'tour guide', what would be your commentary at each stop?

Your commentary is expected to analyse the wider impact of each person or event on human existence and development. Here are some suggestions. You will need to do further research into each to make your commentary full and give your fellow traveller insight.

Technological and scientific achievement

- Moon Walk 1969. Meet Armstrong, Aldrin, Ford.
- Witness Concorde's maiden flight in 1970. Meet Brian Trubshaw.
- The wheel. Meet a caveman!
- 1814. Be a passenger on 'The Rocket' and meet Stephenson.
- Meet Babbage in 1823 and discuss the possibilities of his 'computer'.
- Meet Bill Gates in 1999.

'One small step for man ...'

Achievements in the field of medicine

- 1922. Meet Fleming and discuss the future of antibiotics.
- 1967. Meet Dr Christian Barnard at Groot Schoor Hospital in Cape Town after his first heart transplant operation.
- 1628. Find out about the circulation of the blood from William Harvey.
- 1978. Be at the birth of Louise Brown, the first test-tube baby.
- Visit Cambridge today and witness ongoing research into the human genome.

Events or individuals that have had a positive impact on values or morality

- Listen to the Sermon on the Mount – circa AD 30.
- Attend the 'Live Aid' event in 1985.
- 400 BC Ancient Greece. Meet and talk to Socrates, Plato and Aristotle. Discuss with them their philosophies on belief and knowledge.
- Listen to Martin Luther King's 'I have a dream …' speech in August 1963.
- Meet Nelson Mandela on the day he is released from prison in 1990.
- Listen to Michael Buerk's report from famine-torn Ethiopia in 1985.

Meet Nelson Mandela on the day he was released, after 27 years' imprisonment

Improvements in social and world conditions

- Travel to Calcutta in the 1980s. Visit Mother Theresa.
- Witness the first meeting of the United Nations in 1945.
- Witness the trial of John Brown in 1859.
- Meet Gandhi in 1924 when he was elected President of the Indian Congress Party.
- Be present at the first meeting of the International Red Cross in Geneva in 1945.
- Read the Beveridge Report in 1945.
- The World Health Organization and its aim to eradication of smallpox. Attend the 1974 launch of its expanded project for immunization.
- Visit Marie Stopes in 1918.

Achievements in contributing to the arts and culture

- Visit 14th century Renaissance Italy and meet Leonardo da Vinci. Discuss the plans he drew up for air travel and ask him about his model for 'Mona Lisa'.
- Watch Laurence Olivier filming *Wuthering Heights* in 1939.
- Visit the Cavern Club in the early 1960s and listen to the Beatles.
- Meet Shakespeare in 1612 and ask him about his inspiration and the sources of his plays.

Contribution to human knowledge

- 1476. See Caxton demonstrate the printing press he introduced to England.
- Meet Stephen Hawkings and discuss how he pushed the boundaries of our understanding of our universe in 1974.
- 1859. Read Darwin's newly published *Origin of the Species*.
- 3000 BC. Babylon. Witness how the Sumerian's invention of writing shaped their civilization.
- 1953. Learn about the structure of DNA from Watson and Crick.

There are others of course and some of your ideas may not be represented here. What follows is an example of the type of commentary that would not only place the achievement in context but would analyse its wider impact on humanity.

Sample answer – the invention of the printing press

We're taking a trip to 1476, to Westminster, to witness William Caxton producing books from the printing press he had brought with him from Cologne. We're watching the first books to be printed in England by means of moveable type. Caxton will go on to produce service books for the clergy, and tales of romance and chivalry, many his own translation. Because of his involvement in writing, translating and printing he will be seen as one of the founders of literary English and will have an influence on the form of the language. Caxton is giving England a tool for the shaping of thought, a weapon for the battles of discussion. This will have consequences possibly greater than even Caxton can see at this moment in 1476. The printing press will be an instrument for the propagation of knowledge, thoughts, ideas, ideals and a tool for education on a wider scale. Just consider how this early technology will have an impact on education, literature, philosophy and religion, science and art.

TASKS

Using the headings provided make your list of places to visit and people to meet. Add a commentary on each of the final five that are chosen. Mention those that came close to inclusion.

KEY SKILLS: *Communication*

Producing a travel brochure with illustrations to advertise a visit to one of the people or places you selected would generate evidence for C3.3 and possibly C3.2.

Synoptic case study 2: The challenge of the future

Recently, scientists have made many discoveries in the field of genetic engineering. One of these involves their ability to detect a baby's characteristics from the foetus in the womb. For example, the latest genetic technology will enable a baby's intelligence to be detected. This raises a whole set of issues concerning designer babies and the question of abortion on demand.

For example, consider the following.

Couple A

This couple had a child some three years ago. Recently the child has developed a rare disease of the blood that can only be helped through a bone marrow transplant. The family has been searching for a bone marrow match. The medical authorities have checked all of the family but unfortunately no match was found. Doctors have suggested that if the couple have another child there is a good chance that its bone marrow would be a match. However, they have also pointed out that this second child has a risk of having the same blood disease as the three year old. If they did decide to go ahead and have a second child the doctors would be able to detect problems early in the pregnancy. Should the couple go ahead?

Couple B

This couple was part of a family of seven. They had four boys but their youngest child was the long-awaited girl. Recently the daughter was tragically killed in a motor car accident. The family is desperate for another baby girl to replace their lost daughter and sister. If the parents did become pregnant again the doctors would be able to determine the sex of the child early in the pregnancy.

In both of these cases, difficult decisions have to be made by the prospective parents. The medical authorities can advise them but in the end the decision is theirs.

Relevant areas of study

If you search the General Studies specification you will find statements that are relevant to the issues raised by the two specific cases given above and by genetic engineering in particular. Here are some examples.

Cultural domain (AS)
Beliefs values and moral reasoning
Matters of conscience and public morality
Media and communication
Ways in which the media influence public opinion
Moral issues arising from the activity of the media

Science domain (AS)
Characteristics of the sciences
Genetic engineering and biotechnology
Understanding of scientific methods
Forecasting and reliability
Mathematical reasoning
Sampling and probability

Social domain (AS)
Political systems, processes and goals
The use and value of opinion polls
The nature of scientific objectivity in the social sciences
Distinguishing facts and opinions

Cultural domain (A2)
Religious experience and its alternatives
Central tenets of one religion and how they are translated into day-to-day living

Science domain (A2)
The nature of scientific objectivity
Disease control and health
Moral responsibility
The implications of scientific discoveries and prospective inventions

Social domain (A2)
Ideologies and values
Important current social issues
Explanation and evaluation of human behaviour
Influences on human behaviour
The relationship between law, culture and ethics
The law and ethical dilemmas

You should not expect to be able to write about all of these topics during a synoptic essay. However, you should attempt to include something from each of the cultural, scientific and social domains. This will show that you're able to be synoptic and make connections between the different parts of the subject. Almost certainly you will have more knowledge in one of these areas. Use your strength in one area to start thinking about what the other areas have to offer.

Planning a synoptic essay

The essay could have eight sections and two possible approaches are shown:

	Approach A	Approach B
Stage 1	Interpretation of the question	Interpretation of the question
Stage 2	Clarifying definitions	Clarifying definitions
Stage 3	Describing a plan	Describing a plan
Stage 4	Science domain connections	Case study 1: making connections
Stage 5	Social domain connections	Case study 2: making connections
Stage 6	Cultural domain connections	Case study 3: making connections
Stage 7	Review of what has been said	Review of what has been said
Stage 8	Conclusion	Conclusion

The question

Comment on the news that the latest genetic technology could detect a baby's level of intelligence using the foetus in the womb.

Starting to plan your essay

	Approach A	Approach B
Stage 1	*Interpretation of the question* The question asks you to comment on the ability of the medical profession to detect the level of intelligence. You will need to specify the accuracy of prediction and who has the knowledge.	
Stage 2	*Clarifying definitions* Definitions needed include genetic engineering, intelligence, source of news and stage of pregnancy.	
Stage 3	*Describing a plan* Description of the three paragraphs that are to follow and why you have used this approach. Need to identify common features towards the conclusion.	
Stage 4	*Science domain connections* Knowledge of genetic engineering, reliability of forecasts, moral responsibility of scientists.	*Case study 1: making connections* Case study of couple A.
Stage 5	*Social domain connections* Are these facts or opinions? Social issues raised. Ethical issues, for example, the rights of the baby, the effect on the family.	*Case study 2: making connections* Case study of couple B. *Case study 3: making connections*
Stage 6	*Cultural domain connections* Moral reasoning, public morality. Religious perspectives.	Case study that is contrary to the other two, where intervention saves suffering.
Stage 7	*Review of what has been said* Review of the three main sections. Mention the difficulties coming to a conclusion, the need for further work, the problems of progress.	
Stage 8	*Conclusion* Use the rule of three to state three conclusions. These could be concerns and problems recognized or recommendations to deal with the technology.	

Synoptic case study 3: Do you want to know a secret?

The project closest to my heart is a blueprint for a much more formal and impressive clearing-house for new ideas: An Academy of Invention. It's an idea I have been pressing the government to put their weight behind for the past two years in a campaign that has involved writing hundreds of letters, numerous visits to Parliament and Ministers, and giving evidence to the House of Commons Science and Technology Committee.

The Academy will be a place where inventors can safely take their ideas to establish their merit and have them developed until they are marketable products. Initial funding would come from industry and the government, via the lottery fund, but in the long term the Academy would generate its own income through a share of the profits from inventions which it helps to launch.

The Academy would have to cherry-pick the best ideas. Even academicians wouldn't always make the correct decisions. Hindsight makes sages of us all. In 1933 the J B Morton fictional comic creation, Dr Strabismus of Utrecht, patented a new invention. An illuminated trouser-clip for bicyclists using main roads at night. It was meant to be a silly joke. But what do we find selling well today? Ha, Ha! Luminous trouser-clips for the bicyclist who uses main roads at night.

Inventors are often not very good business people. It comes with the territory. I don't suppose many classical composers or lyric poets, people who work at a similar pitch of intuitive creativity, would be very good at working out detailed business plans and patent applications either. So the prime purpose of the Academy would be to ensure that when people come to sell their products they don't get ripped off. Another aim would be to ensure that ideas conceived in Britain are developed here, to generate jobs and exports that would benefit our economy. Too many inventors have to take their ideas or projects abroad to earn a living. The most extraordinary statistic is that 56% of all Japanese exports since World War II are based on British innovation.

An Academy would also make its voice heard about the syllabus in our schools, which, I believe, needs to give students a stronger grounding in practical skills. The standard of craft, design and technology teaching in our schools has improved considerably in recent years. It's no longer regarded as the preferred subject for the dim and the slow. But even more progress needs to be made. If there is room in the syllabus for 'media studies', 'leisure studies' and 'sports studies', why not courses on invention studies?

A grant of £3 million a year for three years would get the Academy up and running. (That's less than the price of three operas at the going rate.) It is vital that the Academy is run on a strictly commercial basis. It mustn't become a place where extinct volcanoes sit around waiting for their knighthood. So my hope for the Millennium and beyond is that the government will fertilize the nation's innovative talents with funds for an Academy of Invention. Lord Puttnam has been given an annual budget of £10 million as seed money for science and the arts through his National Endowment for Science, Technology and Arts. But his organization straddles so many different interests I don't think his money will stretch as far as it should to promote new inventions. As we go into the twenty-first century our future will depend on how successfully we can generate, protect and exploit new ideas.

Trevor Baylis, *Clock This*, Headline Books, 1999

If you really want to know about the secrets of Trevor Baylis, you will have to read his book. Although he is a passionate believer in the power of education, Mr Baylis is less kindly disposed towards the education system. He 'failed' the 11+ examination and observed that:

> 'The British education system has always relished winnowing out successes from failures, categorizing them, setting them apart and the earlier the better.'

The sentence itself requires reflection and debate. Among many things that Trevor Baylis went on to do was to invent the clockwork radio. In terms of perfecting the technology, it took a long time to get right. Its impact on communication, and its social and economic implications, were massive because Trevor Baylis was a man with a mission. The people of poorer countries needed radios, but electricity was rarely available and the batteries that we take for granted were far too costly. In the end – and it was a long and frustrating process – the inventor succeeded and, in doing so, he provided the inspiration for this synoptic exercise. What may seem abstract and mainly technological will almost always allow a human story to unfold.

Further study suggestions and example questions

Further reading

Cohen, M. (1999) *101 Philosophy Questions*, Routledge, London.

Cohen, N. (1999) *Cruel Britannia*, Verso, London.

Gribbin, J. (1998) *Almost Everyone's Guide to Science*, Weidenfeld and Nicholson, London.

Humphrys, J. (1999) *Devil's Advocate*, Hutchinson, London.

Thomas, A. (1996) *Critical Reasoning*, Routledge, London.

Thomasma, D. and Kushner, T. (1999) *Birth to Death: Science and Bioethics*, Cambridge University Press, Cambridge.

Synoptic questions

The passage from *Clock This* allows for several possible questions which 'make connections' between culture, science and society.

1 Trevor Baylis is a great inventor and his clockwork radio has revolutionized communication across several continents. What is the role of an innovative inventor? Is Trevor Baylis a creative artist, a social engineer or a pioneer in technology?

This question requires you to look at the work of an 'innovative inventor' from different perspectives. Trevor Baylis is just one example and others could easily be used. You will need to explore the concept of an 'innovative inventor' and to analyse, from different perspectives, what he or she may seek to achieve in terms of being creative, in making a contribution to society and as someone who develops something new in technology.

2 Trevor Baylis claims that 'Inventors are often not very good business people. It comes with the territory. I don't suppose many classical composers or lyric poets, people who work at a similar pitch of creativity would be very good at working out detailed business plans and patent applications either.'

What do inventors need to make themselves successful? Give reasons and examples to support your answer.

As the passage indicates, '56% of all Japanese exports since World War II are based on British innovation'. Lots of clever people have not seen their talents fully rewarded. Their good ideas may need to be refined technically, financed, protected, publicized in the media, marketed – to name but a few things. James Dyson's Dual Cyclone vacuum cleaner is now the country's leading model – but he spent years looking for financial support.

3 How far would you agree with the view of Trevor Baylis that we need 'An Academy of Invention'? Why, more than two hundred years after the first industrial revolution, are we still waiting for one to be set up in Britain?

Politically, there hasn't been the will to do it. This may be because it would be expensive and money could easily be wasted on the inventions that are useless. Only a few politicians come from scientific or technological backgrounds. Scientific and technical advance is not always very glamorous – unless it prompts a major medical breakthrough. It gets little media attention. It often lacks prestige and status. The work involved may be seen as 'difficult'. You have to ask 'why'. As the passage says:

> 'If there is room in the syllabus for "media studies", "leisure studies" and "sports studies", why not courses on invention studies?'

Writing a successful essay

When writing an essay you have to remember that entire books may well have been written about the topic or issue on which you are about to write! You will have 35 minutes to consider, plan and write your response.

What is an 'essay'?

The word comes from Latin and means an attempt or try. This suggests, perhaps, that there is no right answer; but clearly some answers are going to score more marks than others. Perhaps a better word for your response is 'exposition', a piece of writing that *exposes* the issue – and your opinions, knowledge and understanding – with clarity.

Where to start

- Analyse the question or task. What does it require?
- Be aware of the command words in the title (see page 192).

Consider the following examples of essay questions.

1 Is there a case for compulsory vaccination against certain diseases? Consider the arguments both for and against compulsory vaccination.

This question requires:

- a definition of vaccination
- an indication of diseases concerned
- a balance of arguments for and against
- a statement of your position
- technical knowledge.

2 Describe three different methods of supplying power for generating electricity. Consider any disadvantages arising from each.

This question requires:

- technical knowledge
- a review of any disadvantages.

It has two parts: (i) description (ii) consideration (analysis and comment). The two parts are likely to need equal attention in this case.

3 How far should censorship extend to some advertisements or advertising campaigns?

This essay requires you to express opinions and be prepared to justify them. A good answer will comment on specific advertisements or campaigns, and give some insight into the role of censorship in a democratic society.

How to proceed

Having analysed the question the next step is to plan the content. This is where you assemble your knowledge and expose your understanding. A plan is vital if your essay is to have structure and clarity.

Look again at question 1.
A possible plan might be:

- *Definitions of:*
  'vaccination'; 'disease'; 'compulsory'.
- *Possible diseases to include:*
  measles; mumps; whooping cough; German measles; polio; diphtheria.
- *Arguments for vaccination:*
  possible eradication of disease; protection of community/individual; guards against birth defects; cost-effective in the long term.
- *Arguments against vaccination:*
  adverse side-effects; religious beliefs; human rights issues; initial cost; administrative problems.

The above plans the content and your judgement finishes your essay.

Another way of planning the content is to use a spider diagram. Consider the following question.

4 What do you understand by the term "poverty"? Consider some of the causes and suggest ways in which they might be tackled.

Here we have planned a six-paragraph essay. Paragraph one consists of your definition and understanding of poverty and five paragraphs (the spider legs) address the issues. A good essay, of course, may well evaluate the likely effectiveness of particular solutions.

So, the notion of introduction–middle–conclusion has to be much more flexible when dealing with the complex issues that arise in General Studies.

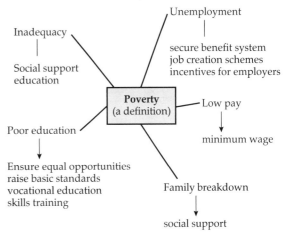

Figure 22 A spider diagram can be used to plan out an essay

Understanding the command words in examination questions

Students are occasionally confused by the command words used by examiners. What *is* the difference between **assess**, **evaluate**, **appraise**, or **analyse**, **consider**, **examine**?

Often the difference is simply a matter of focus. Here are some suggestions to help you get the focus right for some of the more demanding command words.

Analyse

This means to take something apart, to examine it critically.

Q Analyse the effect of instant coverage of news by radio and television on the role of newspapers.

A thorough examination of the changed role of newspapers is required here. What *are* the changes and what is it about instant coverage that has forced these changes? It is not just a question of *listing* the changes.

Assess

If you assess something you decide its worth, value, significance or importance. To give a rationale is not to assess. Consider the question: 'Assess the arguments for and against the banning of country pursuits.' This title does not simply require a list of reasons why certain activities should or should not be banned. In order to gain high marks the significance or relative importance of the reasons given must be considered.

Evaluate

This requires a similar response to those asking you to assess, in that you are being asked to determine value. You are further asked for a judgement following a summing up of an argument.

Appraise

In order to appraise you have to investigate. Again, this command word requires very similar thinking skills to 'assess' and 'evaluate'. You are asked to weigh up evidence and make a judgement. This word is often used in short-answer questions where you are required to respond to resource material.

Comment on

This might seem to be the most straightforward of all command words, but don't underestimate its demands! If you are commenting you are, in effect, giving a commentary. This can involve explaining or giving critical analysis, making personal observation or illustrating a point of view. The question 'Comment on the ways in which funds generated by the British National Lottery have been used' demands more than just a borderline pass response of 'write all you know about the use of funds in the British National Lottery'. You would need to describe how the funds have been used and critically analyse their distribution.

Counter

This often causes problems. To counter an argument you write in opposition to it. Think of it as responding to a speaker in a debate. You take their arguments point by point and show that each is flawed in some way. You then proceed to add further points or evidence of your own to strengthen your case.

Discuss

This is a commonly used command word and again it's easy to underestimate the demands it makes. When you discuss an issue orally, you examine it in detail by debating and disputing. Think of 'discuss' in terms of debating with yourself … on paper!